Pakistan
A Personal History

Imran Khan

BANTAM PRESS

LONDON • TORONTO • SYDNEY • AUCKLAND • JOHANNESBURG

TRANSWORLD PUBLISHERS
61–63 Uxbridge Road, London W5 5SA
A Random House Group Company
www.rbooks.co.uk

First published in Great Britain
in 2011 by Bantam Press
an imprint of Transworld Publishers

This book is a work of non-fiction based on the life, experiences and
recollections of the author.

A CIP catalogue record for this book
is available from the British Library.

ISBN 9780593067741 (hb)
9780593067758 (tpb)

Addresses for Random House Group Ltd companies outside the UK
can be found at: www.randomhouse.co.uk
The Random House Group Ltd Reg. No. 954009

The Random House Group Limited supports the Forest Stewardship Council (FSC®),
the leading international forest-certification organisation. Our books carrying the FSC
label are printed on FSC®-certified paper. FSC is the only forest-certification scheme
endorsed by the leading environmental organisations, including Greenpeace. Our
paper-procurement policy can be found at www.randomhouse.co.uk/environment.

Typeset in 11.5/16pt Sabon by
Falcon Oast Graphic Art Ltd.
Printed and bound in Great Britain by
Clays Limited, Bungay, Suffolk

2 4 6 8 10 9 7 5 3 1

This book is dedicated to Sulaiman, Kasim,
and the youth of Pakistan.

Contents

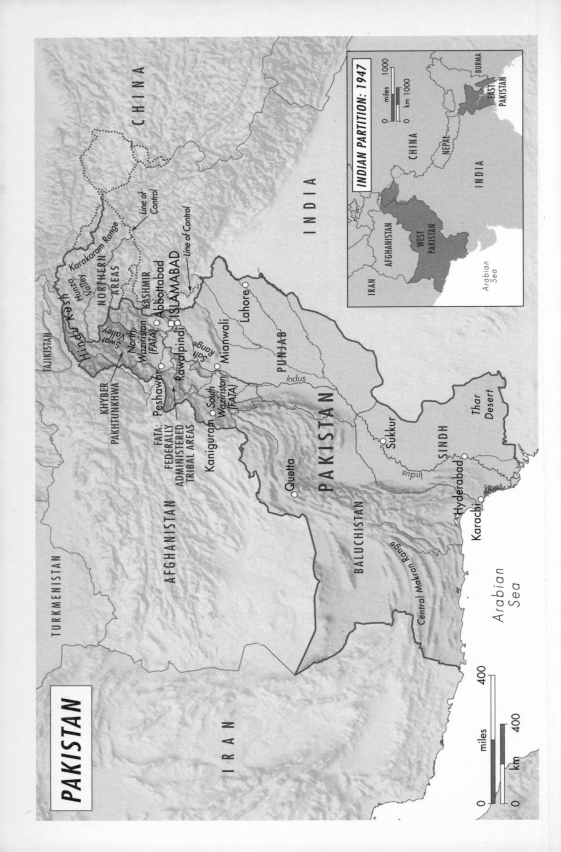

Prologue

A Coalition of the Crooked,
November 2007

BLANK FACES. FACES WITH NO EXPRESSIONS. THAT'S WHAT I remember. About twenty of them had surrounded me and a few were pushing me. I asked them, 'What is it you want? Do you know what you are doing?' I could see some had pistols. Beyond the locked gates of the courtyard, people were shoving and shouting. More crowds of students peered down at me from the windows of the floors that ran round the quadrangle as they tried to see what was happening. I was furious. My political party, Tehreek-e-Insaf ('Movement for Justice'), was allied to this group, as the students that had surrounded me were in the Islamic Jamiat-e-Tuleba (IJT), the students' wing of the Jamaat-e-Islami, Pakistan's oldest and most organized religious party. Both Jamaat-e-Islami and Tehreek-e-Insaf were part of the All Parties Democratic Movement campaigning for an end to General Pervez Musharraf's military dictatorship and the restoration of Pakistan's chief justice. Yet here these students were working for a dictator who had issued orders to arrest me and behaving just like a gang of street thugs.

Although I had heard tales about the IJT, I had not fully realized the kind of people they were. Everyone on the campus of the university is scared of them. Once known for their ideological views and great discipline, they appear to have degenerated into a kind of mafia or fascist group operating inside the university, bearing guns and beating people up. They stifle debate in an educational establishment that has in its time produced two Nobel laureates – the University of the Punjab was established in the late nineteenth century by the British, in the country's second city, Lahore. No government dares tackle them, ordinary students at the university are petrified of them and even the party they belong to, the Jamaat-e-Islami, does not seem to be able to control them. Much later I heard the Jamiat activists had been paid large sums of money to turn on me – allegedly by the government.

I knew the police would probably arrest me when I arrived at the university, so I sneaked in the evening before and spent the night in the rooms of one of the professors. The IJT had expected me to walk through the main gate the following day with my party supporters. Later on I discovered the plan had been to beat us all up. Two things saved me: I surprised them by appearing alone, and from inside the university; and the international media was there with their cameras all lined up. As soon as I appeared, other students in the university gathered around me and hoisted me up on to their shoulders. But then came this group of Jamiat students, about twenty or thirty of them. They began pushing me, but they did not know what to do because they had not expected me to come alone and there were hundreds of them watching this spectacle. They shoved me into a quadrangle and locked the gates. That is when I kept saying, 'What is it you want?' They asked why I had come without their permission and I told them the university did not belong to them. I asked them if they realized their party's policy was to oppose the state of emergency Musharraf had declared and yet here they were supporting it. 'Do you know what you are doing?' I said. There was no response. I saw the head of the IJT standing about twenty yards away and speaking on his mobile. He was looking at me and clearly talking about me. I don't think he knew what to do. Some professors arrived and the Jamiat youths shoved them around too and I could see the professors were scared of them.

At this point I had been eluding arrest for almost two weeks. The country was undergoing yet another period of turmoil and President Musharraf had declared a state of emergency. On the evening of 3 November 2007, I had been giving a talk at the Lahore University of Management Sciences when someone passed me a note saying that the heads of all the political parties opposed to Musharraf were to be put under house arrest, including me. I had already been held under house arrest the previous year when President Bush visited Pakistan. That was aimed at stopping me staging a protest against the US president because of his hypocrisy in supporting Musharraf, a military dictator, while invading Iraq with the justification of installing democracy. So initially I was not too worried. Even under house arrest, I could still manage my political party. I finished my speech, held various meetings and returned some time after midnight to my old family home in Lahore's Zaman Park, where my father and younger sister lived with her family. It was only when the police barged into our house that I began to sense a difference. Normally the police were very polite with me. This time their manner was more aggressive. There was no mention of house arrest, but rather of 'orders' for my 'detention'. I insisted they show me a warrant and while they went off to get it, a journalist called me on my mobile. 'Imran, I'm sitting with the superintendent of police here,' he said. 'All of the other political leaders have been put under house arrest, but you are going to jail. Your orders are for jail.'

With barely minutes to spare I asked my nephew to check outside to see whether there was any possibility of escape. He told me that while the police had surrounded most of the house, they had left unguarded a ten-foot-high wall on the edge of our garden. I slipped out the back and sprinted for the wall, and my nephew helped me climb over into the garden next door. I had spent my childhood in Zaman Park and many of my relatives still lived nearby. While the police came in and searched our family home – even my father's bedroom, despite him being sick at the time – I made for my grandfather's old house and from then on began moving from place to place every other day. Every now and then I surfaced to give a telephone interview to the press to try and get my message out to the people of Pakistan, and specifically to my workers. Then I moved again. Two or three times the police arrived at a house to look for me barely fifteen minutes after I had left. Later, I heard that at least five thousand people had been detained. I was one of the last of the leading opposition politicians who remained free. I had to organize my party as best I could by word of mouth, since we had all switched off our mobile phones and many members had gone underground.

Benazir Bhutto, the daughter of the former president and prime minister of Pakistan who had been executed in 1979 (she herself was prime minister in 1988–90 and again in 1993–96), had recently returned from political exile. She arrived in Lahore to organize a protest march but the police surrounded her house and the plans fizzled out. She was, however, pursued by the international media, and I decided I should take advantage of their presence to give myself up with as much publicity as possible. The best place to do this was the University of the Punjab, the biggest university in the country, where I wanted the students to mobilize against Musharraf's state of emergency. My party, Tehreek-e-Insaf, was already popular amongst the students, mainly because of the stand we had taken against the military dictator. The young people of Pakistan were my main strength, and I had seen over the years how youth across the world had played a vital role in popular campaigns, from the anti-Vietnam War movement of 1960s America to the ousting of Indonesia's President Suharto in the 1990s and, yet to come, the Arab uprisings of 2011. I wanted the students to be politicized, since dictators always try to depoliticize people in order to maintain control. They and the international media would witness my arrest. I would not be taken quietly in the night.

I told the students at the university I had come to give myself up and to take me to the police. They took me outside, pushed me into a van and drove me to the gates where a police inspector was waiting for me. He looked at me over and over again until I asked what was wrong. 'I am so happy to see you,' he said. 'What do you mean?' I asked. He made me wait until we had reached the police station and there he told me. 'Since last night we have been in touch with these guys and my information was that they were going to hand you to me in such a state that I would have had to rush you to hospital. They were going to break your bones; that was the plan.' He had stationed some plain-clothes officers inside the university with instructions to try to save me, but there was little else he could do. It was only then that I realized how narrowly I had escaped.

(He was right to be concerned. A couple of years after my unpleasant experience with the Jamiat youths, they beat up one of the university staff, an environmental science professor called Iftikhar Baloch, after he took a stand against them. I saw him soon after the attack, which almost killed the man and left him with broken bones and covered in bruises.)

My detention was to prove a formative experience; time spent in a Pakistani jail only reinforced my conviction that a lack of the rule of law lay at the heart of our troubled nation's problems. After my conversation with the police inspector, I was taken to another police station and kept there until about midnight when they moved me again, this time to Kot Lakhpat, one of the main jails in Lahore. At first it took some time to register what had happened. It was an A-class cell and I was given a room to myself, so I was able to sleep, and the next day I was allowed to sit outside. The jailers were very sympathetic and brought reports about what was going on outside. They told me that the day after my arrest there had been a huge and unprecedented demonstration at the

University of the Punjab against the Jamiat thugs. The strength of the rally and the students' anger was such that for the first time in thirty years the organization was on the back foot, although it sadly regained its influence later on. I also learned that a mini-revolution had taken place in Zaman Park; my eighty-five-year-old aunt, along with my sisters, gathered all the women of Zaman Park to stage a peaceful demonstration against my detention. It was unprecedented in my very conservative family for the women to come out and demonstrate in public. What happened next was also unheard of in Pakistan politics, where women are always treated with great respect; their peaceful protest was violently disrupted by the police and in front of the national and international media, they were bundled into police vans, and taken to jail before being released later that night. This incident dented Musharraf's 'liberal' credentials.

I was locked in overnight. On the second night, at three in the morning, I was sleeping when the cell door opened suddenly. A policeman was standing there, looking quite hostile. 'Pack your things up,' he said. 'Get ready to leave.' Then I was bundled into the back of a truck, where I would spend a nine-hour journey lying on a wooden bench, freezing with only a single blanket, as the wind and dust of a chilly November night blew in through the open slats. Three policemen were sitting in front, and when we stopped for tea early in the morning, I asked them where we were going. They told me we were going to Dera Ghazi Khan, far to the south-west in the centre of the country. DG Khan is one of the worst jails in Pakistan. If the authorities really want to break you, they'll send you there. It occurred to me that they might torture me as they had two parliamentary colleagues, Saad Rafiq and Javed Hashmi, who had been jailed for years and they had told me what had happened to them. But mostly it was the pettiness of it all that troubled me. It was unnecessary to send me on a nine-hour journey in a truck to a jail in DG Khan when other political leaders were being put under house arrest. I had been in the public eye for thirty-five years and everyone knew I was not a terrorist. Yet I was being arrested under draconian 'anti-terrorism' emergency laws that carried the possible penalty of life imprisonment or death. It felt like a deliberate attempt to humiliate me. And since the jailers and police dealing with me were generally sympathetic and polite, I sensed the orders had come from the top.

If I struggled over just eight days in prison, the suffering of the many thousands who spend years in Pakistan's jails was infinitely worse. And compared to them, I was treated like a king. The jail was dirty and crowded, with ten to fifteen people crammed into each cell. My own cell was in the hospital wing and had a little bed and a filthy bathroom, but I had a room of my own. During the day I was allowed to sit outside, although at sunset I was locked in my room for the night. I could hardly eat in jail since I had no exercise and the food was terrible. After so many years of sport my body was conditioned to expect exercise. The worst of it was that time would not pass. I thought I was going to die of boredom. At dawn, when they woke me up and I heard the commotion of other prisoners being let out of their cells, I would try to linger in bed to make the day shorter. I would think I had been staying hours in bed, look at my watch and realize it was still only eight o'clock. Then I would go and sit outside and in the afternoon they brought me a newspaper to read. I imagined a whole day must have passed only to realize that about an hour to an hour and a half had gone by. But still the day would just drag on.

I am a completely outdoor person; I always have been – even as a boy during the hot summer months in Lahore my mother had trouble making me stay indoors. Since 2005 I have lived in my farmhouse on a hill outside the capital city, Islamabad, a place I call my paradise, recreating the sense of wilderness that I love. I am surrounded by hills and greenery with a panoramic view of Rawal Lake and the foothills of the Himalayas. I grow my own fruit and vegetables and keep chickens, cows and water buffalos. Wild birds and animals surround me too – partridges, porcupines, snakes, lizards, jackals and peacocks. And suddenly I was stuck inside these four walls.

In the courtyard, where I was allowed to sit during the day, there was a little bit of grass but not so much as a tree. The real problem was that I did not know how long I would be in prison. And I could not bear the waste of time. I had set up a hospital in Lahore offering free cancer treatment to the poor. I ran a political party, and I was trying to set up a new university in Mianwali, my father's ancestral home town, over two hundred miles to the north-west of Lahore. Normally twenty-four hours are not enough in the day for me. And here I was removed from life, watching time that did not pass.

Yet jail gave me the chance to hear first-hand about the other prisoners. A young man from Khyber Pakhtunkhwa, the region formerly known as the North-West Frontier, next to the border with Afghanistan, was sent to clean my room. I learned he had been there for six years after being arrested at the age of sixteen. He had not even been tried for the crime for which he was arrested. He had been involved in a family feud and had brandished a gun. That was all. If he had been convicted, the maximum penalty would have been a year. He had been in jail for six years because the family was too poor to afford a lawyer. When his case came up in court, the authorities did not even bother to send him a police van to take him there. According to the deputy inspector of jails, Salimullah Khan, who visited me, this boy's case was not an exception. Sixty per cent of people in Pakistani jails were innocent, he said. Their crime was their poverty. Later, I began avidly reading newspaper stories about prisoners trapped in jail. In Karachi, the vibrant financial city on the Arabian coast, a man was found not guilty after spending nine years locked up; when he was arrested at the age of twenty he had a wife and a year-old baby. It is hard to think about what might have happened to them in that time. In Sindh, the province of which Karachi is the capital, three men were found not guilty after twenty-two years in jail, and in another case a man remained in Lahore's Kot Lakhpat prison for fifteen years because his file had got lost. That was the biggest impact jail had on me. Seeing these people crammed in together horrified me. Some of them had been framed. Often, I heard later, the head jailer made money by charging the relatives if they wanted to see a prisoner. And as was the case with the boy who cleaned my room, the police van meant to take a prisoner to court frequently failed to turn up so they missed their court hearing. And yet many of the biggest criminals in the country were sitting in parliament and some were even given police escorts at taxpayers' expense. The injustice and cruelty of it all stayed with me. The squalid conditions. The inability of the poor to get justice.

I decided to go on a hunger strike on the sixth day to put pressure on Musharraf. But I made the mistake – if it ever happens again I would not do it the same way – of going on a complete hunger strike rather than just having liquids. I am used to fasting at Ramadan – it is excellent discipline, and normally I carry on as usual with the same exercise routine – but then you break your fast at sunset. I had not realized how quickly one weakened with nothing to drink. I had fasted for barely over two days when I discovered I did not have the strength to walk. Having announced the hunger strike, there was no way I was going to back down after two days. Then finally at about eight in the evening, the jailers came and said, 'You are free.' I walked out into what became one of the most turbulent periods of Pakistan's history.

Chapter One

Can I Still Play Cricket in Heaven?
1947–1979

OUTSIDE OF PAKISTAN, I AM MAINLY KNOWN FOR MY 21-YEAR-long cricket career. But in my home country, I am the head of a party that is battling to take on a political elite that has for more than six decades stymied this great country, depriving it of its God-given potential. Ruled alternately by military dictators like President Musharraf, or as a fiefdom by families like the Bhuttos and Sharifs, Pakistan has drifted far from the ideals of its founders. Far from being the Islamic welfare state that was envisaged, Pakistan is a country where politics is a game of loot and plunder and any challenger to the status quo – even somebody with my kind of public profile and popularity – can be suddenly arrested and threatened with violence. Founded as a homeland for Indian Muslims on the principle of the unifying qualities of Islam, it remains a fractured country. Kashmir to the north-east has been, since independence, the subject of a violent dispute between India and Pakistan, the region divided between the two. In the north-west a civil war between the army and militants plagues the Pashtun heartlands of Khyber Pakhtunkhwa and FATA (the Federally Administered Tribal Areas). Baluchistan, a vast, rugged, unexplored and thinly populated province bordering Iran and Afghanistan, simmers with a separatist insurgency. To the south the Arabian Sea washes against the shores of Baluchistan and Sindh, where the provincial capital Karachi is riven with fighting between various ethnic groups, including Pashtun immigrants and the descendants of Muslims who came from the other side of the border at Partition, referred to as Mohajirs or refugees. Meanwhile, Punjab, home to more than half of the country's population, is resented by other provinces for monopolizing Pakistani political power and prosperity.

For me our country's woes began soon after Pakistan was created in 1947, when we lost our great leader Jinnah. Pakistan – which means Land of the Pure – was just five years old when I was born. We had such pride in our country then, such optimism. We were a new nation, wrested out of the dying British Raj as a homeland for Muslims. Gone were the insidious humiliations of colonialism and the fear of being drowned in an overwhelming Hindu majority in an independent India. We were a free people, free to rediscover an Islamic culture that had once towered over the subcontinent. Free, too, to implement the ideals of Islam based on equality, and social and economic justice. A democracy, as Pakistan's founding father Muhammad Ali Jinnah said, not a theocracy. We were to be the shining example in the Muslim world of what Islam could achieve were it allowed to flourish. Such dreams we had. It was only much later that we discovered how hard it would be to fulfil these dreams, even in a brand-new nation like ours, unburdened by the rigidities of history. As the years went by, we built our own tormented history, and drifted further and further away from the ideals that had inspired Pakistan's creation.

Pakistan's roots lay in the final days of the British Raj in India. Before then the territory – roughly defined as the Punjab, the North-West Frontier Province, the coastline on the Arabian sea of Sindh province and Baluchistan – had not been defined as Pakistan but, over the centuries, became first part of one empire and then another. The British, initially through the East India Company and later through the British Army, controlled the area from the early part of the nineteenth century onward. From the 1880s, though, the aim for millions of people throughout the subcontinent who wanted self-determination was the end of British rule. The Indian National Congress, which initially included Muslims, worked to achieve this end. The British did not want to relinquish control but the Second World War weakened Britain economically and politically, and by then the empire on which 'the sun never sets' was in its twilight years.

The Indian National Congress negotiated with the British to bring about the end of their rule over India, and they wanted to see the whole subcontinent remain one country. Here the histories of the two nations starts to diverge; wary of Hindu nationalism, and mindful of the kind of violence that took place at sporadic intervals over the 1920s and 1930s in different cities and provinces in India, the All-India Muslim League took a different view. As part of this league, two men in particular were fundamental in the foundation of Pakistan, Jinnah and Allama Muhammad Iqbal.

Iqbal, who died in 1938, nine years before the creation of Pakistan, is the visionary poet-philosopher considered to be the spiritual founder of Pakistan. In 1930 in an address to the All-India Muslim League, he said, 'I would like to see the Punjab, North-West Frontier Province, Sindh and Baluchistan amalgamated into a single State. Self-government within the British Empire or without the British Empire, the formation of a consolidated North-West Indian Muslim State appears to me to be the final destiny of Muslims, at least of North-West India.' Believing that 'the Indian Muslim is entitled to full and free development on the lines of his own culture and tradition in his own Indian homelands,' Iqbal felt that this was a necessary stage for the Muslim community to develop its collective selfhood, or *khudi*.

Iqbal not only conceived of a self-governing Muslim state, his passionate voice awakened and activated Indian Muslims, motivating them not only to strive to free themselves from the bondage of imperialism and colonialism, but also to challenge other forms of totalitarian control. Believing fervently in human equality and the right of human beings to dignity, justice and freedom, Iqbal empowered the disempowered to stand up and be counted.

When I was older, I found Iqbal's work hugely inspirational. He argued against an unquestioning acceptance of Western democracy as the self-governing model, and instead suggested that by following the rules of Islam a society would tend naturally towards social justice, tolerance, peace and equality. Iqbal's interpretation of Islam differs very widely from the narrow meaning that is sometimes given to it. For Iqbal, Islam is not just the name for certain beliefs and forms of worship. The difference between a Muslim and a non-Muslim is not merely a theological one – it is a difference of a fundamental attitude towards life.

Iqbal considered pride in one's lineage or caste to be one of the major reasons for the downfall of Muslims. In his view, in Islam, based on the principles of 'equality, solidarity and freedom', there was no hierarchy or aristocracy, and the criterion for assessing the merit of human beings was *taqwa* (righteousness). As Prophet Muhammad (Peace Be Upon Him) said: 'The noblest of human beings are those who fear God most.' In other words, those who are humane and just, because when you fear God you believe you are accountable to Him and must act accordingly.

To Iqbal the culture of Islam did not consist of the actual cultural practices of Muslims. It was an ideal value-system, based upon the ethical principles enshrined in the Quran. He believed that Islam provided the guidance needed by human beings to realize their God-given potential to the fullest. In his philosophy of khudi, Iqbal presented his blueprint for action that would lead to intellectually sound, ethically based and spiritually grounded development of individuals and communities. Iqbal and others, such as Sir Sayyid Ahmad Khan (1817–1898), who urged Muslims to obtain a Western education and established the Aligarh University for this purpose, argued that this vision of an ideal society could never be achieved as long as Muslims remained in a minority in a Hindu-dominated India.

It was not only that India, with its caste system and social inequalities, was the antithesis of everything they wanted. It was also that such a bold experiment of recreating the ideals of Islam could never be achieved in a country where Muslims were in the minority. At the time, much of the Islamic world was under European colonial rule, and realizing the promise of Islam required a country – or at least a state within India where Muslims would have the opportunity to live according to the highest ethical ideals and best practices of their faith.

When Iqbal died in 1938 – my father was one of the many who attended his funeral – it was left to the lawyer-politician Muhammad Ali Jinnah to create that country.

Iqbal was an idealist but he offered concrete guidance to Muslims about how to live a life grounded in the integrated vision of the Quran. Jinnah also combined idealism with pragmatism. 'Somewhat formal and fastidious, and a little aloof and imperious of manner, [his] calm hauteur masks a naïve and eager humanity, an intuition quick and tender, a humour gay and winning; the obvious sanity and serenity of his worldly wisdom disguise a shy and splendid idealism,' wrote Sarojini Naidu, the first woman to become president of the Congress Party. Jinnah had originally been a member of the Indian Congress Party and an ambassador of Hindu–Muslim understanding, committed to a united India. Yet he had fallen out with Mohandas Gandhi; when the Islamic Caliphate finally collapsed in Turkey after the First World War, it was Gandhi who led the protests for its restoration, seeing in this a way of challenging the British. Jinnah opposed the movement. He also disliked Congress leader Jawaharlal Nehru, who he felt had used his closeness to Britain's Viceroy of India, Louis Mountbatten, to outmanoeuvre India's

Muslims in their fight for political power. Mountbatten in turn had no patience for the legal constitutional niceties put forward by Jinnah to seek special electorates to safeguard the interests of the Muslims. Mountbatten's wife, Edwina, was so close to Nehru that many Pakistanis afterwards believed they had had an affair, which turned British policy in favour of the Hindus.

Muhammad Ali Jinnah, Jawaharlal Nehru, Mohandas Gandhi and Congress member Maulana Abul Kalam Azad, a Muslim leader of the Indian National Congress who later became education minister in India's government, were four giants of the independence movement – even if they had their own idea of what freedom meant for the people of India. Even Gandhi and Jinnah, despite their differences, held views in common; both believed that their new countries were not secular ones but ones in which religion would play an important role. Gandhi said, 'Those who say religion has nothing to do with politics do not know what religion is,' as he thought that politics without religion would be immoral; while Jinnah, some years later in a speech to the State Bank of Pakistan in 1948, reiterated that 'We must . . . present to the world an economic system based on the true Islamic concept of equality of manhood and social justice. We will thereby be fulfilling our mission as Muslims.' Both Jinnah and Gandhi believed that it was the compassion preached by every religion that could become a counterweight to materialism.

Anti-British unity fractured after the Khilafat movement, and from the late 1920s political battles within the Congress led to unrealistic demands being made of the Muslim organizations. This intransigence 'meant that Hindu revivalists were left with the greater part of the blame . . . for the failure to reach some form of Hindu–Muslim agreement,' observed Professor Francis Robinson. Jinnah no longer believed Muslims would be safe in a united India.

At a meeting of the Muslim League in Lahore in March 1940, Jinnah added his voice to a call for the creation of two states, one for Hindus, the other for Muslims: 'It is extremely difficult to appreciate why our Hindu friends fail to understand the real nature of Islam and Hinduism. They are not religions in the strict sense of the word, but are, in fact, different and distinct social orders, and it is a dream that the Hindus and Muslims can ever evolve a common nationality . . .' he declared. 'The Hindus and Muslims belong to two different religious philosophies, social customs, littérateurs. They neither intermarry nor interdine together and, indeed, they belong to two different civilizations which are based mainly on conflicting ideas and conceptions. Their aspect on life and of life are different. It is quite clear that Hindus and Mussalmans derive their inspiration from different sources of history. They have different epics, different heroes, and different episodes. Very often the hero of one is a foe of the other and, likewise, their victories and defeats overlap. To yoke together two such nations under a single state, one as a numerical minority and the other as a majority, must lead to growing discontent and final destruction of any fabric that may be so built for the government of such a state.' At this time, democracy was still evolving in the world and people did not believe that it could accommodate different religions and ethnic groups.

In what is known as the Lahore Resolution, the meeting

rejected the concept of a united India on the grounds of growing inter-communal violence, and demanded 'that the areas in which the Muslims are numerically in majority as in the North-Western and Eastern zones of India should be grouped to constitute independent states in which the constituent units shall be autonomous and sovereign'. Seven years later, Pakistan was born, although it was, as Jinnah complained, a 'moth-eaten state' with far less territory than its supporters had envisaged. It was created in two wings, West and East Pakistan, separated by 1,000 miles of Indian territory. The great provinces of Punjab and Bengal had been split apart, and at least one million people died in the tide of migration as Muslims moved into Pakistan, and Hindus and Sikhs fled to India. I had an uncle in the Pakistani army who was protecting the Punjab border crossing at the time. He always said that the bloodshed he saw during those six weeks was worse than anything he had seen in four years of fighting against the Japanese on the Burmese Front in the Second World War. He was appalled by the butchery, from which not even women or children were spared. Estimates of the numbers who died range from 200,000 to over one million. More than 12 million were made homeless by the act of Partition and had to travel long distances to settle in new parts of the country, and vast refugee camps sprang up as a result. Families and communities were devastated as those widowed and orphaned in the slaughter had to take what was left of their belongings on a voyage to a new part of the country, where they would be unknown and – often – unwanted. Margaret Bourke-White, the American photographer and the first female war correspondent, called Partition a 'massive exercise in human misery'.

The experience for individuals, in the accounts I heard and read, was heartbreaking. A sixteen-year-old boy joined the Pakistani army and was based on the border: 'There were atrocities committed by all sides – Hindus, Sikhs and Muslims. I saw people arriving on the trains that had been mutilated, women who had been raped and children who had been traumatized. I remember thinking at the time: "Is this what freedom means?" I had three uncles who lived in Simla at the time. Amid the chaos, we had lost contact with them. We never found them.' Amid the horror there were often stories of Muslims concealed from their would-be attackers by their Hindu neighbours, or the same tale but told by Hindu survivors. One such, from Jhang in west Punjab, remembered 'Mr Qureshi' who helped several Hindu families reach the border, only to be murdered as a 'non-believer' by his fellow-Muslims for having saved them.

The madness that took place was exactly that – a madness. No one anticipated or dreamt that such things would happen, and certainly no one expected the violence to reach such heights. Was it a reaction to the end of British rule, a release of pent-up frustrations after the decades of humiliation? It suited the British for there to be division between the peoples of India, and they actively fostered this, as an incoming viceroy, the Earl of Elgin, was informed in 1861: 'We have maintained our power in India by playing off one party against the other, and we must continue to do so.' The haste with which the plan for Partition was implemented certainly contributed towards the hostile atmosphere that created such mayhem, and the British were very much responsible for setting this timetable.

However, the Muslim political leaders, virtually against all odds and in the face of intense opposition from India's dominant Congress Party, had achieved the impossible. They had created a new country. Though we were in dire straits in the early years, the revolutionary zeal that gave birth to Pakistan carried us through.

Democracy, though, never had an opportunity to flourish in Pakistan as Jinnah died in September 1948, leaving us rudderless. In an era dominated by the great superpowers of the USA and the Soviet Union, Pakistan sided with the US, but even this was to prove troublesome. Our first prime minister, Liaquat Ali Khan, died in 1951, assassinated in Rawalpindi (in the same park where many years later, in 2007, former prime minister Benazir Bhutto would also be killed). He was killed by an Afghan opposed to the settlement that had left Kashmir divided, a man who felt Pakistan should be fighting to take it back. Many at the time saw more sinister signs in his murder, amid rumours of American pressure on Pakistan in relation to the access to Soviet airspace Pakistan could provide. The relationship Pakistan has had with America as a nation, although not perhaps with its government, since then has never been a satisfactory one, and after 9/11 it only worsened – but more of that later.

While India spent the early years of its independence with the stability provided by its first prime minister, Jawaharlal Nehru – who remained in office until his death in 1964 – we began a slow slide into alternating military and civilian rule which never allowed the political institutions to mature. We had other problems too, in part because of the division between the Pakistani elite and the masses. The idea of

Pakistan had been conceived within a united India, and found its major intellectual wellspring in what is today the northern Indian province of Uttar Pradesh; the epicentre of the Pakistan movement was in areas that did not eventually become part of Pakistan. Later various ethnic groups, from the Bengalis of East Pakistan, to the Baluch in the deserts running into Iran, to the Pashtun in the tribal areas bordering Afghanistan, would find reasons to rebel against the state, often with disastrous consequences. Since Pakistan, and especially its army, was dominated by Punjabis, these different ethnic groups felt they were denied both their economic and democratic rights, and sooner or later all took up arms against the state. We also began our life as a country at war, fighting India over the territory of Kashmir in 1947–1948, and the festering dispute since then has helped give the army (and by default the majority Punjab element within it) a disproportionately powerful role in Pakistan. Yet in the optimism and fervour of those early years, I believe we might have overcome all those difficulties had we been able to find a political system capable of implementing the egalitarian, democratic and ethical ideals of Islam that had inspired the creation of Pakistan.

Instead, the British-trained bureaucrats had a low opinion of democracy – at least as far as Pakistan was concerned. They had been educated in a system that had taught them to look upon the masses with contempt and, copying the former colonial rulers, had inherited a mindset that the natives were not to be trusted. Without leaders with the vision of Iqbal, or the stature of Jinnah, or for that matter of Nehru, whose long tenure helped bed down Indian democracy, we were condemned to slide back into the kind of discreet authoritarian rule which marked the British Raj. At the first opportunity, the military-civilian bureaucracy stalled the democratic process. Pakistan did not come up with a full constitution until 1956, because the West Pakistan ruling elite did not want to give the Bengalis an equal share in power. Given that the population of East Pakistan was larger than that of West Pakistan, to deprive the latter of their right to an equal share, experiments like the 'one unit system' (where the whole of West Pakistan was treated as one province) were introduced. This helped sow the seeds of Bengali resentment, and eventually led to the break-up of the country.

The 1956 constitution was abrogated by the commander-in-chief of the army, General Ayub Khan, who took over the country in 1958 and announced a presidential form of government. He remained in power for ten years before he was forced to resign amid popular unrest and was replaced by another military man, General Yahya Khan. Under Ayub Khan, Pakistan developed and changed – he introduced the Muslim Family Laws, which modernized some aspects of laws regarding marriage – but his efforts in agriculture and industry benefited the few, not the many. More importantly, he did not believe in democracy, so politically the country stagnated. Discontent in East Pakistan began to grow as the Bengali people, politically and economically excluded, had insignificant representation within the ruling elite. The creation of Bangladesh in 1971 was a direct consequence of this prolonged military rule, along with the reluctance of the ruling classes of West Pakistan to treat East Pakistan as an equal. Paradoxically, economically the country passed through a golden period. Our growth rate was the highest in our history, though the majority of the population was excluded from the fruits of this economic boom. Administratively the country was well run – along with contempt for the natives, the British had also bequeathed us a reasonably efficient bureaucracy. From my vantage point as a child in Lahore, and indeed as I have been told later by my parents, the optimism which had accompanied the birth of Pakistan survived and even flourished in this early period of military rule. It helped of course that we were living in Punjab, the most powerful province in Pakistan, where we had little reason to suspect the many dangerous undercurrents building up in our country.

Pakistan was five years old when I was born. As a child in a comfortably off family in Lahore, I felt only the quiet optimism of a country hopeful for its future. It was an idyllic childhood, with the freedom of plenty of space in which to play and the security provided by the Pakistani extended-family system. In Zaman Park where I grew up we were surrounded by ploughed fields and open spaces; there were few houses and everyone who lived there was family, so it was more like being on a farm. The first house in Zaman Park had been built by my maternal grandfather's brother – whose name was Ahmad Zaman. At Partition in 1947 my grandfather's family also moved there. In the hot summer afternoons I would go out with my air gun to shoot pigeons or to swim in the canal, and in the evenings play cricket with my cousins. There was no such thing as organizing play dates. I would be out till dark – my mother did not worry, she always knew I was with family. For fresh milk every house had a cow or a water buffalo.

Today, Zaman Park is in the centre of Lahore, so fast has the city spread in every direction. All that is left of those green and open fields of my childhood is a small park. There are so many houses that people do not know each other as they once did. Although boys still swim in the canal, it is now dirty and polluted. Lahore's water, which used to be delicious, has become so contaminated it has to be boiled before drinking. I used to go to a school friend's farm that was barely ten miles out of Lahore and there at the age of fourteen I used a shotgun for the first time and bagged fourteen partridges. It was the most thrilling thing I had ever done. My friend's farm is now part of a suburb of Lahore and has been transformed from a place of wildlife and green fields into a concrete jungle. Today in the entire province of Punjab there are probably only a handful of reserved areas where one gun can shoot fourteen partridges.

My mother would make us children go to see our maternal grandmother with our cousins every day for half an hour. These evenings with her were most enjoyable. She would know everything that was going on in our lives. In fact she would get involved in all our problems and we would tell her things that even our parents would not know. The love that my grandmother received from all her children and grandchildren must have been the reason why all her mental faculties were fully intact when she died at the age of a hundred. She might have lived longer, but when my mother died in 1985 she simply could not get over the loss, my mother being her youngest child. It almost seemed as if she decided it was time for her to go. She refused to get out of bed and three months after my mother's death she passed away.

In Pakistan, family is everything. Islam strengthens the family system by making the role of the mother sacred. In the words of the holy Prophet (PBUH), 'Paradise lies under the feet of the mother.' And the greatest influence on my life was my mother. There were five of us and I was the only son. She was a complete mother, happy to sacrifice all her pleasures for her family. I remember I would hide injuries from her just so as not to pain her. Once when I was eight years old my cousins and I were raiding someone's mulberry garden. Suddenly the gardener came. While trying to jump from the tree, I slipped and fell on a branch. The sharp stick pierced a couple of inches in my thigh, almost rupturing my main artery. When I was taken home I refused to show the wound to my mother because I could not bear to see her suffer. So great was my love for her that I hated to do anything that would annoy her. This is how love imposes discipline. She would make me do my homework every day but I was so single-minded about sport that I would be uninterested in studies. It was only her efforts that kept me going. However, apart from my homework my mother would never push me to do anything if I didn't want to do it.

As its name suggests, there is a park in the middle of Zaman Park, where all us cousins – ranging from children to adults in their twenties – would play cricket and hockey. Matches would be played with such aggression that one year visiting hockey teams refused to play us. My passion for cricket, along with partridge shooting, developed thanks to my uncles and cousins. My mother's family was passionate about cricket. I was inspired to become a test cricketer at the age of nine, when I saw my older cousin Javed Burki score a century against England at what is now the Gadaffi stadium in Lahore. I used to treat my aunts' and uncles' houses as my own, as all social life revolved around the family, with my grandfather's and his brother's houses as the focal points. At family dinners everyone would be there, from babies to the oldest members of the family. The rules of etiquette were clearly defined. Age was to be respected. The older the family member, the more respect they were accorded. When the elders spoke, all the younger members listened attentively. In turn, the elders took personal responsibility for all the children. Hence a member of the younger generation could be disciplined by any elder, not just their parents. Any rudeness to an elder meant disapproval from all the senior members of the family. Unfortunately, amongst the westernized elite in Pakistan the respect for age is diminishing. Some, who are uncritically adopting Western culture, almost consider a lack of respect for age a sign of progress. (I remember how odd I found it when my tutor at Oxford asked me to call him by his first name. It was even more awkward for me when friends' parents would also insist that I did the same.)

Our value system was also moulded by the attitudes of the elders. The younger members would carefully observe what was approved and what was condemned by the seniors. It was never the fear of being punished that made all of us follow family etiquette, but the fear of everyone's disapproval. Moral standards were high because immorality would have meant being ostracized. The greatest fear was to give a bad name to the family. Everything depended upon the reputation of a family, from arranged marriages to social acceptability. Any slight by an outsider on the character of a family member would mean an immediate closing of ranks by a united family front. It also put immense responsibility on family members to conform to certain moral and ethical standards. When I became a successful test cricketer and gave interviews to the press, I would be extremely conscious of what I was saying as I constantly worried about how my extended family would react to my comments.

Like most Muslim children, I grew up with religion. My mother used to tell us bedtime stories, each one with a moral message – about Moses and the arrogant Pharaoh, Joseph and his treacherous brothers, and of course about the life of the Prophet Muhammad (PBUH). We were also taught about Jesus, considered in Islam to be a messenger of God like Muhammad (PBUH). Muslims believe that God had previously revealed His message for mankind to the Prophets of the Jews and Christians but that Muhammad (PBUH) perfected the religion first revealed to Abraham. Muhammad (PBUH) is seen as the 'seal of the prophecy' – the last in the series of Prophets God sent to the world. Islam recognizes the teachings of the Jewish Torah and the Christian Bible and while it teaches that Jews and Christians have in some areas strayed from the true path, it acknowledges them as 'People of the Book'. Every night before going to sleep my mother would make us say our prayers, and tell me stories about the Prophet (PBUH). There was one particular story my mother would tell me: an old Meccan came before the Prophet (PBUH), and said to him, The only reason I want to become a Muslim is because all my clan has converted to Islam, but I am too old to change my habits. Tell me one thing I can do so that I can become a Muslim but keep my habits. The Prophet (PBUH) replied, Tell the truth, that is the one thing you need to be a Muslim. This story appealed to me as a boy, because I too found the rituals to be cumbersome. Besides, I could never lie to my mother, as she would always catch me out simply by looking at my face.

My mother also told me how her father, Ahmad Hasan Khan, modelled himself on the Prophet (PBUH), and would tell me stories about how, whatever he did, he would always tell us 'This is what the Prophet (PBUH) did' – even to the point of liking honey and dates.

The concept of heaven and hell was made clear to me ever since I can remember. The only problem was that I could not understand heaven. My poor mother frequently had to answer questions like – would I be able to play cricket in heaven? And would I be able to shoot?

When I was seven years old a *maulvi* (Islamic scholar) came to teach me and my sisters the Quran in Arabic. In school we had a religious knowledge class and our daily assembly started with a verse of the Quran. Every Friday I went with my father to the mosque. On Eids, the two biggest festivals of the Muslim calendar, all the males of Zaman Park, young and old, would go to the shrine of the great sixteenth-century Sufi saint Mian Mir Sahib. Mian Mir is also a legendary figure for Sikhs, who come to pray at his shrine in Lahore. Our family graveyard is outside the shrine – so after Eid prayers we would go to our relatives' graves and pray for their departed souls. Such shrines are common in the subcontinent, where Islam was spread from the ninth century onwards in large part through the Sufis. Their egalitarian message and doctrine of love, peace and compassion appealed to the poor and dis-possessed. The Sufis' tolerance of other religions and cultures meant that as they made their way through what became the Islamic world the religion they spread blended with local customs to become a kind of populist Islam. Their followers made shrines of their graves, which became places of pilgrimage. Rich and poor alike still flock to these shrines to pray and make offerings. Once a year, usually on the anniversary of the saint's death, there is an *urs* (a festival), when prayers are accompanied by devotional dancing and singing and the distribution of food. This is the kind of Islam that the austere Wahhabi branch, which has influenced the Taliban, opposes.

My parents were both easy-going Muslims who always taught us that Allah was 'the most beneficent and the most merciful'. We were never forced to read our prayers or fast. At Ramadan, the month when Muslims fast from sunrise to sunset, it was we children who would choose to compete with each other to keep our fasts. I kept my first fast around the age of nine and was rewarded with presents from my father and mother. If there was anything said against Islam, both my parents would defend it vigorously.

My mother's extended family was originally from the Burki Pashtun tribe in Kaniguram, the biggest town in South Waziristan, which rests in a fertile valley close to the Afghan border in the tribal areas. She instilled in me a pride that the Pashtuns had never been subjugated and had constantly fought the British. Her family had ended up living in twelve fortresses, known as *basti Pathan*, near the town of Jalandhar (where she took much pride in saying my grandfather had hosted Jinnah), south-east of Amritsar, only forty miles or so away from Lahore but in what became India. The whole family had emigrated to Lahore at Partition, although none of them had been killed. When they moved out in a convoy the Sikh gangs who were massacring the Muslims in Punjab believed – wrongly – that they were armed, and left them alone.

My father's family were also Pashtuns (also known as Pathans), but from the Niazi tribe, which had come to India with invading Afghan tribes around the fifteenth century. Much of his family still lived in Mianwali (a town on the river Indus on the border with Khyber Pakhtunkhwa, formerly known as the North-West Frontier) and family ties are still very strong there. In time amongst the Burkis (my mother's tribe), the family system will begin to weaken, and my children will only know their first cousins, but in Mianwali even third cousins know each other – I frequently meet Niazis who will tell me how they are related to me through my great-grandfather. Village communities have stronger family systems than urban ones.

In a place like Mianwali people often operate as part of a family group of maybe a hundred people. There is a network of siblings and first, second and third cousins. Everything is shared – salaries, responsibilities, friendships, enemies, hardships and successes. When people from rural areas go to look for jobs in the cities, the first people they contact are their relatives. If there are none, then they seek out people from their village or tribe. Millions of people have been displaced by fighting or floods in recent years, but you do not see hordes of hungry, homeless people sleeping on the streets of Pakistani cities. Many have been absorbed by the family and tribal network – people with little have taken in, fed, clothed and housed people with still less than them. All this of course helps free the country's rulers and elite from bearing the burden of so many displaced people, let alone the responsibility of paying taxes and implementing any kind of effective welfare system. As I have so often observed in Pakistan, the poor have taken the blow for the rich.

Growing up in Lahore, I became aware of two strong prejudices. One was against colonialism. This, according to my mother and father, was the ultimate humiliation for a people. At bedtime, my mother would tell me stories of resistance to the British, about heroes like Tipu Sultan, the 'Tiger of Mysore', who died defending his city when he was attacked by three armies, the British, the Nizam of Hyderabad's and the Marathas', in 1805. At the same time, she would contemptuously relate the story of the surrender of the last Mughal emperor, Bahadur Shah Zafa, who died in 1862 in captivity in Burma. She would quote the Tipu Sultan's remark, 'The day of a lion is better than a thousand of a jackal.'

The general thinking in the Indian subcontinent is that the greatest damage inflicted by colonialism was material. There is no doubt the subcontinent did suffer in such a way. In the 1700s the GDP of India was almost 25 per cent of the world's economy. By the time the British left it was around 2 per cent. The British lawyer Cornelius Walford estimated in 1879 that there had been thirty-four famines in the previous century or so of British rule – but only seventeen in the preceding two thousand years. M. J. Akbar writes, 'The Mughal response to famine had been good governance: embargo on food export, anti-speculation regulation, tax relief and free kitchens. If any merchant short-changed a peasant during a famine, the punishment was an equivalent weight in flesh from his body. That kept hoarding down.' Millions died in these catastrophes. A materialist lobby feels that British rule gave India a strong administrative system along with an infrastructure of roads and railways. Up to a point this is true as well. In my opinion the greatest damage done to the people of the Indian sub-continent was in the humiliation of slavery and the consequent loss of self-esteem. The inferiority complex that is ingrained in a conquered nation results in its imitation of some of the worst aspects of the conquerors, while at the same time neglecting its own great traditions. It destroys originality as the occupied people strive only to imitate the occupiers. Furthermore, this slavish mimicry wrecks any sense of leadership in the elite – the people with the most expensive education in the country. One of Iqbal's great qualities was that he provided such new and original thought, despite having lived his entire life under colonial rule. In a well-known verse he told his son:

> My way is not one of being wealthy but of *faqiri*
> [spiritual poverty]
> Your *khudi* [self-hood] do not sell, in poverty make
> a name

The legacy of colonialism led to our other prejudice, against India. We as a nation felt we had been cheated out of Kashmir by the pro-Indian last Viceroy of India, Lord Louis Mountbatten. Hatred against our neighbour, in Punjab especially, reached its height in the 1950s and 1960s since so many Muslims had migrated from East Punjab at Partition in

1947 and hardly a family had not lost loved ones in the bloody massacres during the border crossing. It was only later, when I toured India playing cricket, that I realized how much we have in common and lost this prejudice.

Islam, we were told, was tolerant, and it had spread in the subcontinent not by the force of arms but by the great Sufi saints, such as Khwaja Muinuddin Chishti (known as 'Gharib Nawaz', the benefactor of the poor, who lived in north India in the late twelfth and early thirteenth centuries), who won people over with their humanitarian message. Sufis were held in such esteem that, in 1303, when a Mongol army under Targhi laid seige to Delhi, Sultan Alauddin Khilji appealed to the great Sufi saint Nazam Uddin Auliya for help. Since both my parents had Hindu and Sikh friends from school and college before independence, we were never taught to hate people from other religions. There was no militant fundamentalism in those days and those few who could be classified as religious bigots were not taken seriously. We were told, however, that Islam was the superior religion since the Quran had been dictated to the Prophet (PBUH) by God himself, whereas the other holy books had been written by man and so human faults had slipped in. Muhammad (PBUH) was unlettered. He therefore had to ask other people to write down the messages he had received from God. Apart from being a book of wisdom, the Quran is still considered the greatest work of Arabic literature and the beauty of its words has converted many, including the great caliph Umar. One of the Meccans most opposed to the new religion being preached by Muhammad (PBUH), Umar was at the forefront of plans to assassinate the Prophet (PBUH). But according to Muslim tradition, when he heard his sister recite from the Book his heart softened, he wept and Islam entered into him. He went on to become one of Muhammad's (PBUH) main companions, inheriting leadership of the Muslims after his death. The only time I truly understood what the caliph might have experienced was when I took my sons once to the Faisal Mosque in Islamabad for Friday prayers. A visiting imam from Egypt was delivering the *khutba*, the sermon. Often you sit there during the sermon and become lost in your own thoughts because you cannot understand the Arabic. But when the imam started reciting I was immediately struck by the sound that gently filled the whole mosque. Looking around I saw that as his voice resounded through the building it was having the same effect on other worshippers. It was like listening to a classical symphony. It gave me goose bumps. I have never heard anything like it before or since, not even in the two great mosques of the holy cities of Mecca or Medina.

Islam is not just a religion to be practised privately by individuals, but a way of life. The Quran lays out clear rules for how a society should be governed, and guidance on how people should behave. I was taught it was also a forgiving religion that laid special emphasis on justice and compassion.

There were many challenges, most of all the incendiary issue of Kashmir. In 1965, when I was just thirteen, war broke out for the second time since independence. I will never forget this period; late one evening we started hearing the sound of bombardment, and the windows began to shake. From our rooftop we caught sight of the flashes of explosions along the border. I remember the anxious faces of my parents as the bombardment continued all night. The Indian army was advancing towards Lahore. There were rumours that Indian paratroopers might land in the city, and patriotic fever gripped the country. The elders of Zaman Park were called to my uncle's house for a kind of council of war. It was decided that my older cousins should group together in a civil defence force to defend Zaman Park. I was itching to be part of this force and, armed with the .22 rifle that my father had just given me for my birthday, I marched out to join them, only to be sent back and told I was too young. I cursed myself for not being old enough to join in. Along with my mother and sisters, I was sent away from the city for my safety. As we approached Pindi, I remember seeing open areas outside the city swarming with warriors from the tribal areas volunteering to assist the army. Later I found out that my overzealous cousins almost ambushed, shot and killed two innocent people, mistaking them for Indian paratroopers. Everyone in the country was united in a desire to defeat the enemy. I don't think Pakistan had ever witnessed such unity. The nearest thing to it was perhaps when we won the World Cup in 1992.

As I grew up I developed a passion not only for my country but also for the Pakistani countryside. Every summer I would go with my parents and sisters to the hill stations to escape the oppressive heat of Punjab. I can still remember the thrill I felt as the car slowly ascended the mountain road and the air cooled. Only those who have experienced the intense heat of the Punjab summer can understand such relief. There was no air conditioning in those days. We had picnics and walks in the forest, saw monkeys, jackals, porcupines and a huge variety of birds. Occasionally we even saw the tracks of a leopard. Once, when I was about five years old, during a trip to the hill station Doonga Gali, over two hundred miles to the north-west of Lahore, a leopard killed a donkey right outside our rest house in the middle of the night. I can still recall how fascinated I was by the poor donkey's partially eaten corpse. In the winter I went partridge shooting with my uncle and male cousins in the Salt Range, a low mountain range about two and a half hours' drive west of Lahore. Some of my best childhood memories are of these trips. We stayed in colonial rest houses in the wilderness, ate sumptuous picnic lunches and returned in the evening to relax around a log fire. The Salt Range used to be teeming with wildlife: wolves, leopards, hyenas, jackals, foxes, deer and wild sheep. There are fewer animals now but the Salt Range remains my favourite place for shooting partridge because of its beautiful weather in the winter and hilly terrain. My mother also loved wildlife and the mountains and she fuelled my passion by telling me stories from her childhood. Some were set in the Indian hill stations of Simla, the summer capital of the British Raj, and the beautiful Himalayan station of Dalhousie where she would holiday with her parents. Like most small boys, I was intrigued by the more grisly tales. I particularly liked the one about how her dog was taken by a leopard while her father was posted at Skaser in the Salt Range. I also loved the family legend on my father's side about how my great uncle from Mianwali, a policeman, had fought with a leopard that had been terrorizing the local villagers and killed it with the bayonet of his gun, then spent six months in hospital from the mauling he received. He was given the highest award the police could bestow.

The 1965 war over Kashmir ended in seventeen days, but it left the military dictator President Ayub Khan in a vulnerable state, allowing room for democratic developments as his grip on power slipped, leading to the rise of a new political party – the Pakistan People's Party (PPP), under its leader Zulfikar Ali Bhutto. Bhutto had studied at university in California and Oxford before he became a lawyer in London, and he represented Pakistan at the United Nations before being appointed the country's foreign minister in 1962 when he was only thirty-four. After the war he fell out with the president and left government to form the PPP. Bhutto, like so many who come to power in Pakistan, was seen at first as someone who could lead us back to democracy – but later was to prove the opposite.

Here was a man who understood history, one with an exceptional mind, highly educated and charismatic – Bhutto could have changed Pakistan completely. He was a true Pakistani nationalist, he formed the first national grass-roots political party in Pakistan. However, he had a fatal flaw in his character that undermined all that he could have achieved – his feudal mindset couldn't tolerate dissent, and as a result his government became known for its brutality in victimizing opponents.

But his ideas, which he expressed in his 1967 book *The Myth of Independence*, carried great weight – and still do. It is a great shame that he himself could not live up to all of his words. He called the story of all the civilizations of the world, from ancient Egypt to the British and French empires, the story of 'greed urging domination and colliding with the struggle for equality'. And he noted that 'Domination has been justified as "the survival of the fittest"; it has been given the name of the White Man's Burden . . . today that ancient struggle has been epitomized in the creed of democracy against dictatorship.' And most presciently he remarked that

'Twenty years of independence have revealed to the people of Pakistan and India the sharp difference that really exists between independence and sovereign equality. This was the beginning of neo-colonialism. It no longer became necessary to control the destinies of smaller countries by any jurisdiction over their territories.'

(The British had developed neo-colonialism in India in the previous century, in the Princely States – of which there were well over five hundred – where they didn't have to rule directly as they had puppet rulers to do their bidding. Today in Pakistan, with drone attacks and raids in our cities, our sovereignty is compromised by those who are puppets of the US and have followed US diktats against the interests of the people of Pakistan. It is this aspect of neo-colonialism that is breeding extremism in Pakistan today.)

Back then I was still young, a teenager, and in the late 1960s I trekked in the Karakoram, the mountain range spanning the borders between Pakistan, India and China. Some of my favourite holidays have been spent there. It is one of the best places for trekking in the world, with the greatest number of peaks over 24,000 feet (7,300 metres) including K2, the second-highest mountain on earth. It really is the roof of the world; I have never seen such natural beauty anywhere in the world as in the Domel valley at 9,000 feet, where the army holds its skiing competitions in the winter. The valley floor was covered in red and white flowers and crossed by a crystal-clear stream. It seemed to be the picture of paradise and every morning I was there I had to tell myself I wasn't dreaming. The people in this area of Pakistan were warm and friendly, untainted by tourism.

On one trip one of our two jeeps broke down on the Karakoram Highway. A young man passing by offered to take us to his village for the night. We zigzagged up a dirt track for about forty minutes before ending up in a tiny village on the edge of an emerald-coloured lake and surrounded by thick pine forest. The villagers served us delicious food, including the best mushrooms I have ever tasted. There was a full moon and we sat all night by the lake listening to the wind blowing through the pines. Pakistan's Northern Areas are almost twice the size of Switzerland. Who knows how many such idyllic places still exist there? We came across similar hospitality in Hunza, a stunningly beautiful valley supposedly the inspiration behind the mythical land of Shangri-La; when I first went there in 1967 locals untouched by materialism greeted us with apricots and peaches, inviting us to stay in their houses. Amongst the endangered species to be found in the Karakoram is the secretive snow leopard with its distinctive grey-green eyes and I remember seeing snow leopard cubs, found by a shepherd and presented as a gift for the Mir of Nagar, the ruler of what was until 1974 still a princely state located in the north of Gilgit-Baltistan, the most northerly point of Pakistan.

Hunza used to be so remote it could only be reached via a terrifying journey up hairpin bends overlooking thousand-foot drops in old Willys Second World War jeeps. Every so often if you dared to look down you would see the wreckage of a jeep that hadn't made it. Then came the Karakoram Highway, sometimes known as the ninth wonder of the world because of its elevation, the highest in the world for a paved road, and because of the sheer difficulty of building it. It took the Pakistanis and the Chinese twenty years to finish and cost the lives of almost nine hundred construction workers. The Karakoram is still by far the most beautiful mountain wilderness in the world and the people are still friendly but 'progress' has taken its toll. Population explosion, massive deforestation by the timber mafia and package tours are quietly threatening this paradise. Sadly, the modern world has brought unwelcome changes to many parts of Pakistan.

Among those changes is the rapid increase in the population, which has grown from 40 million in 1947 to 180 million by 2011. The beauty and wilderness of our country is fast disappearing, but it was already evident in the 1950s and 1960s that this is only one of the problems that would bedevil Pakistan. These problems began in the very fabric of the state itself, born out of our slavish adherence to the traditions and institutions of the departing British. Far from shaking off colonialism, our ruling elite slipped into its shoes. The more a Pakistani aped the British, the higher up the social ladder he was considered to be. In the Gymkhana and the Punjab Club in Lahore, Pakistanis pretended to be English. Everyone spoke English including the waiters; the men dressed in suits; we, the members' children, watched English films while the grown-ups danced to Western music on a Saturday night. Indeed some Pakistanis even spoke Urdu with an English accent and ate curry and chapattis with a fork rather than with their hands. While a native had to struggle to get membership of these clubs, any European could simply walk in – the waiters would not dare question whether he was a member or not. The Sind Club in Karachi, the ultimate refuge of the self-loathing brown sahib, did not allow itself to be contaminated with any native Pakistani symbols. Established by the British in 1871, it resisted even Pakistani national dress, banning it until 1974.

The small westernized elite, comprised mainly of civilian bureaucrats and military men, also inherited the colonial contempt for the natives. Far from trying to implement Iqbal's vision, they took advantage of a colonial system meant to control the people. All the colonial institutions were left intact and as a result the only change for ordinary Pakistanis was that they had a new set of rulers, the brown sahib instead of the *gora* (white) sahib. Often these people were even more arrogant in dealing with the masses than the colonialists, just as slave foremen were sometimes more brutal to the slaves than their masters were. (A practice that continues to this day, as we'll see in Chapter Eight, with the way Pakistani security forces acted in their treatment of Afghans.) Almost all the bureaucrats came from the elite English-language schools built by the British and modelled on their own public schools.

When my father returned after doing his postgraduate degree at Imperial College London in 1948, he was only the second person from his home town to have become an 'England returned', and almost the entire town came to greet him at the railway station. An 'England returned' would find his social status rise dramatically and he could have his marriage arranged to a girl well above the status of his family. Then, as even now, marriage advertisements in India often state a preference for a girl with fair or 'wheatish' complexion. Centuries of invasions from the north-west meant that the ruling classes were often fairer than those ruled, leaving an ingrained colour consciousness on the Indian psyche. An 'England returned' would automatically become a VIP in

Zaman Park. When any of my older cousins came back after studying at an English university, we would bombard him with questions about life there. That knowledge alone gave them status.

During their time in India, the British had embedded an inferiority complex amongst the natives with great care. Waiters and attendants were made to wear the clothes of Mughal army officers and the Mughal aristocracy, while the officers of the symbols of British power, the army, the police and the civil service, wore the dress of the colonials. The Mughal Empire, which covered most of the subcontinent from mid-way through the sixteenth century, had begun its decline in the early 1700s. But when the British East India Company started to establish its power in the subcontinent halfway through the sixteenth century, the Mughal court still held sway culturally and politically over much of northern India, whose inhabitants – whether Hindu or Muslim – regarded its splendour and culture with awe and its emperor as the embodiment of political and religious power. For half a century many of the early colonialists aped the customs of the court. They spoke Farsi, wore the clothing of the Mughal aristocracy, gave up beef and pork and married local women, sometimes even taking several wives. The British historian William Dalrymple has done much to chronicle the change in attitudes as, between the mid-eighteenth and the mid-nineteenth century, the British took on and defeated all their military rivals in South Asia. With the French, the Siraj ud-Daula of Bengal, Tipu Sultan of Mysore, the Marathas and the Sikhs all vanquished, the British became more confident of their grip over the region, and imperial arrogance set in.

Evangelical Christianity also played a major part in breeding a culture of British superiority and a determination to unseat the Mughal emperor and humiliate the once-great dynasty. As Dalrymple writes in *The Last Mughal*: 'No longer were Indians seen as inheritors of a body of sublime and ancient wisdom as eighteenth-century luminaries such as Sir William Jones and Warren Hastings had once believed; but instead merely "poor benighted heathen", or even "licentious pagans", who, it was hoped, were eagerly awaiting conversion.'

India had a decentralized system of education before the arrival of the British. Each village had its own schools supported by revenues generated locally, while colleges and *madrassas* (religious schools) of higher education were run by educational trusts, or *waqf* boards. (*Waqf* is an Islamic term for an endowment for a charitable purpose.) When Bengal was conquered by the East India Company in 1757, it was discovered that 34 per cent of the land generated no taxes because it was owned by various trusts, giving free education and healthcare. According to a survey by G. W. Leitner in 1850, some of these madrassas were of an extremely high standard – as good as Oxford and Cambridge. Thanks to the properties owned by the trusts, they could afford to pay handsome salaries to attract high-quality teachers. Leitner also surveyed the Hoshiarpur district in East Punjab and found there was 84 per cent literacy in the area – when the British left India it was down to 9 per cent. The British abolished the trusts, confiscated the *waqf* land endowments, centralized the education system and set up elite English-language schools. These were meant to create a class of Indians who, in the words of the nineteenth-century administrator Lord Thomas Macaulay, would be 'Indian in blood and colour but English in taste, in opinions, in morals, in intellect . . . to render them by degrees fit vehicles for conveying knowledge to the great mass of the population.' Behind their backs, the British used to contemptuously call these brown sahibs baboons, later *'babus'* – the Hindi word for 'father', only not so in this context.

The impact of the British-implemented education system ran far deeper than the use of English and a love of cricket. Rather it had been used by the British for a century to subjugate the local culture and create a ruling native elite. The British were too few to dominate India themselves and relied on the acquiescence of a layer of natives to enforce their rule – a form of collaboration which was one of the most humiliating aspects of colonialism. I went to a school very much in the English mode, Aitchison College, the nearest Pakistan had to Eton. Like the majority of my schoolmates, I considered myself superior to those students who went to the government-run Urdu-medium schools. In the English-medium schools not only were all the subjects taught in English, but everyone was required to speak in English. Boys caught speaking in Urdu during school hours were fined, despite it being the official language of Pakistan.

Our Muslim society with its traditions and rituals was left behind with our families, and felt disconcertingly old-fashioned. The message of our education was that you had to copy the ways of the superior colonialists to make progress in life. We were to be transformed into cheap imitations of English public school boys. Our role models naturally became Western, whether they were sportsmen, movie idols or pop stars. Besides, we could not help but notice that the older generation was deeply impressed by the colonials and their culture no matter how much they disliked them. It was only much later that I realized how much our education dislocated our sense of ourselves as a nation. At the time, I thought more about playing cricket on Aitchison's beautiful sports fields. Today our English-language schools produce 'Desi Americans' – young kids who, though they have never been out of Pakistan, have not only perfected the American twang but all the mannerisms (including the tilt of a baseball cap) just by watching Hollywood films. While my generation's land of milk and honey was England, today's youth from the English-language schools want to get to the United States and live the American dream.

When Pakistan became independent we should have rid ourselves of these English-medium schools. In other post-colonial countries such as Singapore, India and Malaysia they set up one core syllabus for the whole country. In Pakistan the governments allowed this unjust system to perpetuate and English-medium schools still import the British syllabus for students studying GCSEs and A-levels. Students educated in these schools had a huge advantage over the children of the masses since all the best jobs, especially in the prestigious civil service, went to those who spoke good English. And these brown sahibs in the ruling elite were conditioned to despise their own culture, and developed a self-loathing that stemmed from an ingrained inferiority complex. To show that one was educated, a stranger would immediately throw English words into the conversation to establish his credentials. At Aitchison, the more anglicized a boy was, the more he was admired. We were impressed by English history, English films, English teachers, English sports, English novels and English clothes. We laughed at someone who could not speak English properly but it was quite cool to speak Urdu with lots of English mixed in. We wore Western clothes and would feel awkward in *shalwar kameez* except on 'ethnic' occasions like Eid.

When I joined the Lahore cricket team at the age of sixteen, I found that because I came from an English-medium school I could barely communicate with the majority of the team as they had been to Urdu-medium schools. Most of the boys would gang up and make fun of me. I felt like an outsider, with this huge educational and cultural gap between us, wider even than that found in the British class system. Their jokes, their humour, the films they liked, their views of the world were all different to mine. It was then that I began to realize how much resentment there was amongst those from Urdu schools towards those from the English ones. I also realized why, despite having the best sports facilities at Aitchison, its boys could never compete with those from poor schools. The latter were much tougher and had a far greater hunger to succeed. Similarly in hockey and squash (other sports that Pakistan has excelled in internationally), all the stars came from the Urdu schools. However, I discovered that they were quick to learn that the way up the social ladder was to acquire Western mannerisms. So most of the cricketers loved shopping for English clothes and learning the English language, preferably with an English accent. Some of the cricketers only started drinking alcohol (which was banned in 1977) because it was a Western, and hence upper-class, thing to do.

National dress was another marker of cultural identity sabotaged by colonialism. When I was a boy I remember one of my uncles asking a cousin of mine, who was wearing shalwar kameez, why he was dressed like a servant. Another time I overheard a friend of my mother talking about someone being an upstart because he had only recently started wearing Western clothes. It was decades later, in the summer of 1988 when I was trekking with a couple of English friends in the Karakoram, that I became conscious of being dressed as a foreigner, while all the locals were in Pakistani clothes. It suddenly dawned upon me – here I was, a national icon, a role model who drew crowds wherever I went – and yet I was dressed like an outsider. Years later I was embarrassed by the Pashtun tribesmen on my first visit to Waziristan who resolutely insisted on speaking to me in Pashto despite the fact I did not speak much of their language. They made a point of it to emphasize their pride in their culture; it is only in the tribal area of Pakistan, where people are fiercely proud of the fact that they have never been conquered, that they feel no need to borrow from anybody else's culture. Colonialism only works if the colonizers are convinced of their superiority and the colonized of their inferiority.

In contrast, the legacy of British colonialism is still strong amongst older or retired army officers and bureaucrats, the Pakistani military and bureaucracy being originally colonial constructs. There is an ingrained inferiority complex. I remember a serving lieutenant-general saying to me: 'But, Imran, my dear chap, why do you insist on wearing shalwar kameez when you look so good in a suit?' I am sure a lot of people who wear Western clothes in Pakistan would like to wear shalwar kameez, especially in the heat of the summer, but they just do not have the confidence. When I had an office in the cancer hospital I founded in memory of my mother, in the early 1990s, I ran the marketing department there. I noticed that most of the regular donors were from the trader class, who wore shalwar kameez, and decided the hospital marketing team should also wear Pakistani dress. A couple of months later a member of the team asked permission to revert to Western suits as he felt that the traders and other people generally did not give him the same respect if he wore Pakistani clothes. He also felt he had less confidence wearing our national clothes when he visited businessmen's offices. This complex worsened and since Musharraf's regime in the early part of the twenty-first century and its superficial drive for westernization, even political candidates in Pakistan, particularly in Sindh and Punjab, also felt the pressure to wear Western dress. Many candidates have their publicity photographs taken in jacket and tie because they feel Western suits make them appear more sophisticated and more educated to the voters.

Retaining the language or dress of occupiers or colonizers has not been that unusual throughout history. For instance, after Sicily won independence from the Arabs in the eleventh century, Arabic remained the language of the island's courts for another fifty years. Yet in Pakistan, the cultural affinities of the English-speaking elite also distanced us from our culture and religion. While no one ever considered becoming a Christian, it was natural that most of us started considering Islam to be backward – just like our culture. After all, the masses were religious but poor. If any student prayed or talked about religion or had a beard he was ridiculed as a traditional Islamic cleric or scholar, a maulvi. Our Western education also laid emphasis on science, which based everything on the premise that what could not be proved, did not exist. This clashed straight away with religion, which wanted us to believe in the unseen. Moreover, since in the 1960s the youth in the West were in rebellion against the older generation and against religion, we too became affected by those attitudes.

By the time I finished school, I still went for Friday and Eid prayers with my father and fasted during Ramadan, yet for me – and indeed for most of my friends – God was confined to the mosque. Our young impressionable minds were convinced by English and American films that Western culture was superior, along with its vastly superior technology. Had we had better understanding of our cultural heritage, or our religion and its history, it might have helped us to resist the lure of the West. Nor could our preachers counter this great onslaught of colonial culture for they had no Western education and could not communicate with us in the language in which we had been taught. Our cultural separation from them reinforced in our minds the idea that Islam was backward – I can remember students laughing at preachers with poor English.

Even nowadays, as the ruling elite despairs of the many young men who have turned to fundamentalist Islam, few grasp how much this great educational divide exacerbates our troubles. While they quite rightly talk about reforming the madrassas, which have sprung up in their thousands and often offer many poor families their only access to education, they rarely look at the problem from the point of view of the masses, who have little reason to feel an affinity with an elite who remain the inheritors of colonialism, representatives of an alien foreign culture. They have nothing in common with these people and see them as a kind of Trojan horse for the West trying to destroy our culture. It is through developing world elites that a more potent and permanent invasion is taking place in many countries. Physical colonialism has been replaced by cultural colonialism. The writer Titus Burckhardt describes this kind of dislocation in his book *Fez, City of Islam*. Burckhardt spent time in the Moroccan city in the 1930s; when he revisited it twenty-five years later, he observed:

> At the time I first knew it, men who had spent their youth in an unaltered traditional world were still the heads of families. For many of them the spirit that had once created the Mosque of Cordova and the Alhambra was nearer and more real than all the innovations that European rule had brought with it. Since then however a new generation had arisen, one which from its earliest childhood must have been blinded by the glare of European might and which, in large measure, had attended European schools and henceforth bore within it the sting of an almost insuperable contradiction. For how could there be any reconciliation between the inherited traditional life which, despite all its frugalities, carried with it the treasure of an eternal meaning and the modern European world which, as it so palpably demonstrates, is a force oriented entirely to this world, towards possessions and enjoyments, and in every way contemptuous of the sacred? These splendid men of the now dying generation, whom I had once known had indeed been conquered outwardly, but inwardly they remained free; the younger generation, on the other hand, had

gained an outward victory when Morocco gained independence some years ago and now ran the grave risk of succumbing inwardly.

The jolt came in 1971. In the elections of 1970, the Awami League of East Pakistan (the party demanding autonomy there) had won a majority in parliament. Yet Zulfikar Ali Bhutto, the leader of the Pakistan People's Party (PPP) which had won in West Pakistan, conniving with the military dictator General Yahya, deprived the Awami League of East Pakistan of the chance to form a government. The people of East Pakistan rebelled against what they saw as their disenfranchisement by the more powerful West Pakistan. Yahya Khan, the president and army commander-in-chief, sent in the army to suppress the dissent – the same army that had held the first free elections on an adult franchise in the first place. As the troops descended on East Pakistan, Bhutto returned to Karachi from Dhaka triumphantly proclaiming that Pakistan had been saved. But the result was a terrible war in which thousands of civilians died and millions of refugees poured into India's West Bengal. I was with the West Pakistani Under-19 cricket team on the last flight out of East Pakistan before the army went in. As we played the East Pakistan team we could feel the hostility towards us, not just from the crowds in Dhaka stadium but from our sporting opponents too. The captain of the East Pakistan team, Ashraful Haque, who later became a friend of mine, told me at dinner that evening about the great antagonism felt towards West Pakistan. He told me that many like him would want to be part of Pakistan were they to be given their due rights but as things stood there was a strong movement for independence. I was shocked to hear this because we had no idea about the feelings of the people of East Pakistan, thanks to total media censorship in West Pakistan. However, it had never occurred to me or many others that there was any chance of the country breaking apart. West Pakistan made a series of blunders which allowed India to subsequently exploit the situation. India, then led by Nehru's daughter Indira Gandhi, invaded East Pakistan in support of the Bengali insurgency. Unlike the 1965 war with India, this time we were quickly defeated. Our army signed a humiliating surrender in Dhaka and the Indians took 90,000 prisoners of war. Our country was split in two and East Pakistan became the newly created Bangladesh. Indira Gandhi had achieved far more than her father had ever done in destroying Jinnah's idea of Pakistan. It was meant to be a homeland for the Muslims of the subcontinent; now after a bitter civil war and a crushing defeat, which still haunts our army, it had become a homeland only for West Pakistanis.

A few years later, in 1974, I met up with Ashraful Haque again, and I was shocked at the number of Bengali civilians he told me had been killed in the military action. The figures listed by both sides are hard to verify but it is possible that hundreds of thousands of civilians died in the civil war that lasted several months, and millions more fled into India seeking safety. I had previously argued with English and Indian contemporaries that this was all propaganda against the Pakistani army and Pakistan. After hearing Haque's side of the story, I vowed I would never again accept our government's propaganda at face value or ever back a military operation against our own people.

My career in cricket had just started – I played my first international match for Pakistan in England in the summer of 1971 – and away from the censored newspapers and the government TV channel, I was exposed to the international media. Seeing our surrender was only made worse when the massacres attributed to us were shown. The shock was greater because the government, and the military, kept telling the people that they would 'fight to the end'. Only twenty-four hours before the surrender, General Niazi from my tribe, the commander of the forces in East Pakistan, had defiantly given an interview on the BBC where he declared the army would fight to the last man. The surrender caused mass depression and a loss of faith in our country. Like everyone else in Pakistan, I had believed the propaganda of our state television, who had labelled the Bengali fighters as terrorists, militants, insurgents or Indian-backed fighters – the same terminology that is used today about those fighting in Pakistan's tribal areas and Baluchistan. Then, as now, we fought the symptoms rather than addressing the root cause of the violence – our failure to address the legitimate aspirations of Pakistan's many ethnic groups. I also had the opportunity to see for myself how my country was perceived abroad. I had a rude awakening, for, without the protection of my family, I suddenly felt lonely and insecure. For the first time, I had to make an effort with people and found it quite difficult. After the tour I stayed back to finish my education at the Royal Grammar School in Worcester. I found it almost impossible to make friends with the British. My friendships with my cousins and a few school friends were informal and deep; we would drop in at each other's houses at all hours, and, since we had grown up together, our bonds were strong and could withstand fighting and jealousy. Now I was faced with a situation where I did not know anyone, nor did I understand British culture, which was very different to the joint family system in which I had grown up. The friendships that I had in England were never as meaningful as those I had in Pakistan – until much later.

Following the completion of my A-levels in 1972 I began my studies at Oxford. It was a huge culture shock. The youth rebellion was in full swing and the English culture we knew through our English schoolmasters, books, stories and anecdotes of my parents' generation had disappeared under a blitz of sex, drugs and rock and roll. Traditional British values – which stemmed from the Victorians' ideas on morality and had so impressed the older generation in Pakistan – were being rapidly discarded in Britain itself, dismissed as hypocritical. Films and pop stars were advocating free sex, drugs and bad manners; it was fashionable to swear and prudishness was dismissed as boring. The biggest attack was on religion and on God. In Pakistan, the English-speaking elite considered the mullah backward, but even they never dared publicly attack him. Most of them would follow Islamic rituals and considered themselves religious. However, in Britain, religion became a source of ridicule, lampooned in *Monty Python's Flying Circus* and in the film *The Life of Brian* in the 1970s, as well as in television skits by Benny Hill portraying priests and nuns as sexual perverts. Our role models were Mick Jagger and David Bowie, while our intellectual thinking was defined by the then popular Marxist rejection of religion. From Darwin's theory of evolution to

Nietzsche proclaiming the death of God, we were encouraged to believe religion belonged to a 'pre-logical' stage of human development. Freud thought God was an illusion created by man to fulfil his own needs; Jung termed religion an alternative to neurosis. If there was any spirituality at university, it was that of the hippies. The only problem was it was usually drug-induced and included free sex.

What little belief I had in God took a real beating in this atmosphere. At best I clung to my Muslim identity, though this had little to do with submitting to the tenets of Islam. I never drank alcohol, but that was because my boyhood hero and first cousin, Majid Khan, later to be captain of the national cricket team, was a teetotaller and I wanted to emulate him. The best way to describe my faith was 'no acceptance, no rejection'. My Islam was reduced to rituals like attending mosque and that too only when I was in Lahore. Similarly fasting was also something I did if at the time I happened to be home. If there was a God, then he had nothing to do with my life outside the mosque. My mother, who by this time had become deeply spiritual, was alarmed at my lack of faith and would constantly ask me to read the Quran in the hope that it would guide me. Out of love for her, several times I tried to read it and each time gave up. It was only much later that I discovered why it made no sense to me.

My first winter at Oxford made me miserable. The bleak cold and wet, dull days really made me miss home and the weather in Lahore. There is no climate in the world better than the winter of Punjab – warm, sunny days and cold nights just right for sitting by a log fire. I would never tell my mother I was unhappy, but nevertheless, in one of my letters she must have sensed I was homesick. Immediately she wrote, asking me to come back. She told me I could always return to England at some other time to resume my studies and if I did not want to study any more it did not matter anyway. It was this love and support that made me grow up with such a complete sense of security. Her total belief in me gave me self-esteem, a vital characteristic for success. This was in sharp contrast to the British students, who were under great pressure to find jobs after university. Most of them had already moved out of their parents' homes. For me, as for any Pakistani, the concept of moving out was completely alien. It was unthinkable for the eldest or only son to ever leave his parents' house, as his parents were his responsibility for the rest of their lives. Perhaps it is no surprise that my best friend at Oxford was an Indian, Vikram Mehta, who came from a similar family structure to mine, and had like me been to a private, English-language school. At that time, Benazir Bhutto, the daughter of Zulfikar Ali Bhutto, Vikram and I became good friends; not only because we were from similar subcontinental backgrounds, but because we were taking the same subjects – politics and economics. Vikram and I would visit Benazir's lodgings in Lady Margaret Hall every Sunday, when she would have an open house serving cheese and snacks all afternoon as part of her lobbying to become president of the Oxford Union. Vikram and I had little interest in the union, but we would show support for Benazir. A friend of mine who played cricket for Oxford, Dave Fursdon, I discovered was the flatmate of one Tony Blair, who later became Britain's prime minister.

After leaving university, I would spend the winter in

Pakistan and the summer playing professional cricket in England. In Pakistan I kept meeting people with a strong faith in God. The common people led their lives with God. Even though they did not always obey God's commands all the time, he featured prominently in their lives. They would sin but they would know they were doing wrong and beg for forgiveness. Often, they had a fatalistic attitude to life whereby they accepted any disaster as the will of God. I considered this to fit in with Marx's idea of the 'opium of the masses'. In contrast to the ubiquity of religion and mysticism in Pakistan, the only spiritual people I remember meeting in England were Andrew Wingfield-Digby, a theology student who played with me at Oxford and was later to become a vicar, and, some years later, the English wicketkeeper Alan Knott.

(There was one incident involving Knott that struck me in particular, when we were part of a world eleven playing in Kerry Packer's world series in Australia in 1978. The team was discussing what to do with the prize money – whether to divide it up amongst the twelve of us who were sitting there or to also share it with the six others who were not present because they were playing elsewhere but were part of the squad of eighteen. We all decided that we should exclude the six, justifying it to ourselves on the grounds that only those who had performed should be rewarded. Knott was shocked by our greed and immediately condemned us, saying we were being unfair to the others. Such was his moral authority that we all felt embarrassed and meekly consented to sharing the prize money with the entire squad.)

While I was adjusting to life in England, my country too was changing. Despite his own contribution to the disaster in

East Pakistan, Bhutto became president in 1971, and used all of his abundant charisma to restore some of our battered national pride. For the first time in our country's history, he told the masses that they mattered. Unlike the civilian and military elite, with their English coldness, he was a popular and populist leader. As a young Pakistani at the time I could not help but be proud when he made his famous speech over Kashmir to the UN Security Council in 1965, threatening to 'wage war for a thousand years', before storming out. His standing up to the West like that just as the country was emerging from colonialism boosted our self-esteem. Yet Bhutto's great intellect and charisma could not translate into success for Pakistan. His misdirected nationalization choked the economy and the feudal mindset that tolerated neither criticism nor opposition further damaged Pakistan's democracy. But perhaps the greatest disaster of Bhutto's years was the nationalization of the school system in 1972, an act which led to the departure of many qualified teachers without adequate teacher-training programmes being put in place beforehand. From then onwards our state school structure declined and generations of Pakistanis have suffered because of his policy.

In the end it was apparent that Bhutto was just using the Pakistan People's Party (PPP) to further his personal ambitions, his promise of power to the people forgotten. Opposition to him grew, and in 1977 he was accused by political opponents of rigging the elections in the PPP's favour. Protests against the results of the elections were brutally crushed and in a last attempt to regain ground and shore up support amongst the Islamic parties Bhutto banned alcohol, nightclubs and gambling. As protests escalated into riots, the army were called out to control the streets. Martial law was declared and the country was to remain under it for eleven years. General Zia ul-Haq overthrew Bhutto, appointed himself president in 1978, and the following year had Bhutto hanged in a jail in Rawalpindi. I was playing cricket in Sri Lanka when I heard the news and felt an incredible sense of sadness. Even though I knew he had done wrong, I did not expect him to be executed. More upheaval was to come. The year 1979 was to prove a turning point for our country. In neighbouring Iran, the Shah's westernized regime was swept aside by Imam Khomeini's Islamic revolution. Later that year, the Soviet Union invaded Afghanistan and Pakistan became a frontline state in the Cold War.

Chapter Two

Revolution, 1979–1987

To tell the truth, I had no interest in politics in the 1970s or much of the 1980s. From the time I had left university in 1975 until 1983, I had been so single-mindedly and obsessively involved in international cricket that I had no time to think about much else. Anyone who has played professional sport would understand how it completely takes over one's life. One lives and breathes the sport, so intense is the competition and hence the focus. Over the years, I came to the conclusion that 'genius' is being obsessed with what you are doing. So I was too absorbed to worry about the consequences of Zia's military regime, his slow reversal of Bhutto's nationalization programme, or the turmoil in neighbouring Iran and Afghanistan. Life continued as normal for most people – the only ones who really felt Zia's rule were his opponents. As the captain of the Pakistan cricket team I had a good relationship with Zia. He used to call me personally when we won matches and when, in 1987, he asked me on live television to come back out of retirement for the sake of the country, I agreed. Only after his regime ended did I realize his devastating legacy and that, like so many of Pakistan's leaders, he was motivated purely by his desire to stay in power and was oblivious to the country's decline, or the long-term consequences of his policies.

Amidst the steady erosion of the country's political and social fabric, the Pakistani people drew solace from its success in cricket. During the 1970s and 1980s our team started growing in strength to the point that we could match our former colonial masters. For teams like Pakistan, India and the West Indies, a battle to right colonial wrongs and assert our equality was played out on the cricket field every time we took on England. My friends, and two of my greatest opponents on the cricket field, Sir Vivian Richards from the West Indies and Sunil Gavaskar from India, were both examples of sportsmen who wanted to assert their equality on the cricket field against their former colonial masters. I know that the motivation of the great teams produced by the West Indies in the 1970s and 1980s was to beat the English. For Viv in particular, it was about self-esteem and self-respect, the two things that colonialism deprives the colonized of.

Sport was not the only way to demonstrate post-colonial independence. I little realized how far the Islamic Revolution in Iran in 1979 would transform the Muslim world. However, it was a watershed moment in the way the West would view the Muslim world. When the Soviet Union invaded Afghanistan later that year, putting Pakistan in the frontline of the Cold War, few of us fully grasped the extent to which that too would affect Muslim thinking – in the world in general and Pakistan in particular. I had visited Iran in 1974 when I went to stay with a school friend from my time at the Royal Grammar School, Worcester in England. Seeing the economic and cultural divide of Iranian society and women in miniskirts in the bazaars of Tehran surprised me. In today's Lahore and Karachi I have seen a similar disparity – rich women going to glitzy parties in Western clothes, chauffeured by men with entirely different customs and values. But at the time I had never seen people behave in such a westernized way in a Muslim country and was shocked by their disregard for the cultural mores of the masses. I remember the look on the faces of the stallholders in the bazaars as these women in short skirts sashayed past. The Iranian Islamic Revolution a few years later was to draw heavily on the support of the bazaaris, who formed the backbone of a traditional, devout middle-class in Iran that felt threatened by the Shah's attempts to impose an alien culture upon them and enraged by his role as a puppet of the West. In Pakistan, however westernized people like me were, when we visited our ancestral villages or went into rural areas – or even the old city of Lahore – we had to respect local customs and sensitivities. The women in our family would wear the *chador* (a cloth covering the head and shoulders, leaving only the face exposed), or the *burka* (a long garment covering the whole body). Even in Lahore my mother always covered her hair when she went shopping in the bazaar. To this day most women in Pakistan wear the traditional shalwar kameez with *dupatta* (headscarf). Only very recently have younger urban women started to wear jeans.

The Iranian Revolution was a reaction in part to rapid west-ernization and secularization campaigns in Iran by Reza Shah (the ruler of Iran from 1925 until he was forced to abdicate by the Allied powers in 1941) and then his son Muhammad Reza Shah Pahlavi. The latter was a brutal autocrat seen to be beholden to the United States after he was restored to power following a 1953 CIA-backed coup to overthrow nationalist prime minister Mohammed Mossadegh. Mossadegh had had the temerity to stand up for the rights of the Iranian people and seize the country's oil production, which had hitherto been controlled by the British government's Anglo-Iranian Oil Company. Muhammad Reza Shah's sweeping social and economic changes alienated the poor, the religious and the traditional merchant class who grew resentful of an elite enriched by the 1970s oil boom. Meanwhile, there was a growing class of rural poor who had moved to the cities in the hope of benefiting from the petrodollar-fuelled economic growth but found themselves unemployed, consigned to the slums and increasingly under pressure from inflation as the economy overheated.

The revolution led by Khomeini promised to return power to the people and restore religious purity to Iran. The events of 1979 in Tehran and the establishment of an Islamic state highlighted to the world the revolutionary potential of Islam and its power to threaten the established order in the Muslim world. The overthrow of a tyrant was welcomed jubilantly by ordinary people in Islamic countries, most of whom were also suffering under the anti-democratic rule of leaders they viewed as Western stooges disconnected from the economic realities and religious faith of their people. As with the Middle East revolts in 2011, a sense of euphoria rippled across the region. The broad base and strength of a movement that had toppled such a powerful US-backed regime was also inspiring to people long resentful of colonial interference and Western hegemony. And it had been achieved through relatively peaceful means, with mass demonstrations and strikes.

In Pakistan there was tremendous excitement, and I could sense this when I returned from playing cricket in England in the summer months. Since independence we had already been governed by four different constitutions. We had run through parliamentary democracy, Ayub Khan's 'presidential democracy', which was effectively a military dictatorship, economic liberalization and martial law. Yet here was Khomeini standing up to the West with a new system that was both Islamic and anti-imperialist. The political Islam of the Iranian Revolution filled the void left by the failure of Arab nationalism in the Muslim world. Socialism had been discredited and communism had never really taken off in a culture where religious faith is such an intrinsic part of life. As the Iranian slogan went: 'Neither East nor West'; Khomeini had forged a new path that owed little to either the Western powers or communist Russia. And he explicitly presented his ideology as an exportable political solution to the entire Islamic world.

Consequently, the West was terrified the Muslim world had reached a new turning point. At stake were Western puppet regimes in oil-producing countries like Saudi Arabia – whose royal family Khomeini openly criticized. In the same way that the West turned a blind eye to corrupt regimes that claimed to safeguard the free world from the evils of communism, from then on, autocratic rulers could manipulate Western fears in order to clamp down on any political opposition in the name of fighting Islamic fundamentalism. (The 9/11 attacks on the

United States further reinforced this tendency.) It was also at this point that the West started sending NGOs into Muslim countries to encourage secularization – often in the name of liberating our women or promoting human rights. Whenever there is unrest in an Islamic country, the old fears about 'Iranization' or 'Islamization' of the country in question are raised by the West. Only recently, in early 2011, this happened when the people of Egypt and Tunisia toppled their dictators. Other countries, too, faced internal dissent but dealt harshly with it; however, in Yemen and Bahrain, the actions that in Libya would lead to NATO intervention were allowed to continue as the regimes were deemed pro-Western.

Zia, keen to legitimize his unconstitutional takeover of Pakistan, felt the mood created by the Iranian Revolution and responded accordingly. His predecessor, the Oxford- and Berkeley-educated Zulfikar Ali Bhutto, had used religion to counter his Western secular image by pandering to the religious parties. Bhutto's 1973 constitution confirmed Pakistan's identity as an Islamic Republic, the teaching of Islam was made compulsory in schools and a Council of Islamic Ideology was set up to advise on Islamic legislation. He had declared the Ahmedi sect non-Muslims. His critics, though, only hardened their demands, campaigning for the introduction of more Islamic laws. Zia cashed in on the opposition to Bhutto from the religious parties, which equated secularism with anti-Islamism. He was prepared to go much further than Bhutto, pledging on coming to power in 1977 to make Pakistan an Islamic state. His version of the *Nizam-e-Mustapha* (the System of the Prophet) aimed to overhaul penal codes inherited from the British by bringing them into line with Sharia law. Emboldened by events in Iran, from 1979 he introduced still more reforms, 'Islamizing' the economy and education system. He tried to introduce interest-free banking, imposed the automatic deduction of *zakat* (a proportion of one's wealth which every Muslim has to contribute annually) from bank accounts and invested in madrassas. The Hudood Ordinance imposed strict punishments for crimes, including adultery, and its abuse by a corrupt police and judicial system undermined the legal status of women, especially in the lower strata of society. Zia revamped so many laws, but failed to introduce true Islamic social justice; in fact his regime actually promoted inequality and corruption. His political use of Islam was aimed more at capturing the mood of the time.

Zia also enforced Islamic rituals and promoted traditional dress codes in a bid to 'Islamize' the country; many years later Musharraf attempted to overhaul Pakistan and turn it into a modern, liberal secular state by encouraging the use of English and Western dress, which he thought would westernize Pakistan. Zia's 'Islamization' and Musharraf's 'Enlightened Moderation' failed in their aims, as in such situations people follow the latest diktats, but inwardly carry on as before. Both Zia and Musharraf failed to understand that imposing outward observances will neither instil a sense of religious faith nor propel a country into the twenty-first century.

General Zia's 'Islamization' programme received another boost with the Soviet invasion of Afghanistan. Practically overnight he became a key Cold War ally of the Americans, who now forgot their qualms about backing a military dictator (perhaps this was the origin of the saying that you need the support of the three As to lead Pakistan – Allah, the army and America). It was another example of the US's ability to pick and choose when to object to evil despots, or not, while lecturing the developing world on the universal importance of democracy and human rights. Fearful that the Soviets might push through Afghanistan to reach the Arabian Sea in the Gulf and choke off vital oil supplies, the CIA, Saudi Arabia and other Gulf states – through Pakistan's Inter-Services Intelligence, the ISI – funded, trained and armed thousands of militants to fight them. Many of these jihadis stayed on in Pakistan after the war, unwanted by their own governments. (Having created these foot soldiers to do jihad against communism, the United States and its allies hunted them down as al-Qaeda members and jihadis a decade after the Soviet withdrawal.) At the time, there was a general feeling in Pakistan that the war against the Soviet occupiers was a just war and people made tremendous sacrifices. With my journalist friend Haroon Rashid, I met so many young men in Peshawar who had done time in Afghanistan; 'guerrillas' they might be called now, but they were heroes fighting against occupation, a romantic cause that drew idealists from across the Muslim world in the way the Republicans in the Spanish Civil War had attracted thousands of non-Spanish volunteers in the 1930s. They became rapidly disillusioned with the way the groups changed at the end of the war. However, unlike Musharraf after 9/11, Zia never allowed the CIA to spread its network within Pakistan. It was the ISI who trained the militant groups, funded by the CIA.

Jihad is a vital concept in Islam; indeed it is the most important concept in terms of an Islamic society. Jihad is about standing up to injustice and it keeps a society alive and vibrant. In Islam, there are three types of jihad: the first is the individual struggle to purify one's soul of evil influences, the second is to strive for justice through non-violent means and the third is the use of physical force in defence of Muslims against oppression or foreign occupation. A Muslim must stand up for justice, for any human being's rights, regardless of their religion. When a society does not stand for justice, it dies. Two million people marched against the Iraq war, because they felt it was unjust; were they Muslims, they would have called this protest jihad. After all, the Quran repeatedly points out that 'God loves not aggressors'. And if everyone in a society stands up for justice, then their rulers have to listen. In the 1980s the concept of jihad became glamorous because of the fight against the Soviets; now it is a word associated with terrorism. There remains nothing wrong with the concept of jihad, a struggle for 'doing the good and forbidding the evil'; but like all noble concepts it can be misused. For many men drawn to Afghanistan, this was a clear-cut case of helping the Afghans fighting foreign occupation. The tribal areas on the border with Afghanistan faced for the first time in their history an influx of foreign fighters, gathered from the Muslim world to fight the Russians. Thousands of Saudis, Yemenis, Egyptians, Algerians, Tunisians and Iraqis flocked to Afghanistan, often passing through Pakistan, trained by the ISI and funded by the CIA. A Saudi billionaire who had sacrificed a life of luxury to fight for the Afghan people was one who drew particular admiration. He was Osama bin Laden; my friend the lawyer Akram Sheikh remembers seeing him at a reception at the American embassy in Islamabad in 1987.

I went to a fundraising ball for the mujahideen in 1983 at

the Café Royal, a bastion of London's wealthy elite once frequented by Winston Churchill and Oscar Wilde. It was a very fashionable cause to support, with campaigners in the UK including Lord Cranborne, an old Etonian Conservative MP, and in the United States, Joanne Herring, the Texan socialite portrayed in the book and film *Charlie Wilson's War*. The legendary Pashtun pride, courage and lack of self-pity inspired their backers. In 1985, Ronald Reagan famously introduced members of the mujahideen as 'the moral equivalent of America's founding fathers' during their visit to the White House. Amongst them was Gulbuddin Hekmatyar, leader of the Hezb-e-Islami political party and paramilitary group. A key figure in the Afghan jihad against the Soviets and the main recipient of foreign funding for the cause, he is now waging a jihad against NATO forces in Afghanistan, who as far as he is concerned are foreign occupiers just as the Russians were. He is now wanted by the United States for participating in terrorism with al-Qaeda and the Taliban, and termed by the State Department a 'Specially Designated Global Terrorist'.

Pakistani Pashtuns living along the Durand Line, which (when it was drawn up in 1893 by the British to mark the border between Afghanistan and what was then British India) had split the tribes, have always felt the repercussions of the tumultuous events in Afghanistan. About 100,000 people a month cross to and fro, the border meaningless to them. People in the tribal areas therefore felt it their duty both as Muslims and Pashtuns to join their brethren in the fight against the communist infidels. There was a flood of weapons into north-west Pakistan. Sir Olaf Caroe, the last British governor of what was then the North-West Frontier Province (NWFP), described the Pashtun in the tribal areas as natural warriors with every man armed. Now the tribes had access to more sophisticated weapons. As arms went one way, heroin flowed the other. On their journey from the port of Karachi to Afghanistan, many of the weapons dispatched by the CIA disappeared into the local markets. Karachi ended up becoming one of the most violent cities in the world while Kalashnikov culture hit Pakistan in general, and the tribal areas in particular. The trucks which were used to carry the weapons were then filled with heroin extracted from poppies cultivated in Afghanistan and the Pakistani border area and sent back to Karachi. Pakistan became the world's largest conduit of heroin and the number of heroin addicts in the country rocketed.

By 1982 the Afghan jihad was receiving annual aid of $600 million from the United States and another $600 million from the Gulf states. The Saudis' funding for the Afghan jihad allowed them to promote Wahhabism, the doctrine of the dominant Islamic sect in Saudi Arabia. Over time its puritanical beliefs have influenced the tribal areas' longstanding Pashtun traditions. The growing number of madrassas or religious schools also affected local religious culture. According to a report by the International Crisis Group, between 1982 and 1988 more than 1,000 new madrassas were set up, many by radical Sunni parties – sponsored by various Arab countries – which were involved in the Afghan jihad or were political partners of Zia. Even US aid money was used to promote jihadi culture. Textbooks were published in local languages by the University of Nebraska at Omaha in the

United States to help indoctrinate young minds in the madrassas and refugee camps in the ways of 'holy war' and hatred of the Russians. The Pakistan government should never have allowed these outside influences in to establish these groups in the country; Shia–Sunni violence especially can be dated from this point and grew dramatically in Pakistan. This sectarianism did a lot to undermine the position of the jihadi groups at the end of the Soviet occupation. Three million Afghan refugees flooded into Pakistan, a country still ill-equipped to look after even its own people. Local living standards dropped as these huge communities of refugees competed for jobs and resources. Unlike Iran, where they were restricted to refugee camps, in Pakistan the refugees were allowed to move anywhere. I have to say though that the way ordinary Pakistani people shouldered the burden of such an influx of people puts to shame European countries for the fuss they make over accepting refugees. The Afghans themselves did their best to retain order in the camps through their powerful tribal structure.

Zia's eleven-year rule was a time of great prosperity but not because of any government policy; Pakistan averaged 6 per cent growth a year in the 1980s as the Afghan war brought dollars both in aid and easy credit. Moreover the remittances from hard-working Pakistanis abroad shot up during this period. It is estimated that between 1975 and 1990 some US$40 billion came into Pakistan. Had this money been invested in health and education rather than in useless consumption and extravagance, the country would not be in its present situation, but under Zia corruption passed manageable proportions. He used the money flooding in for the war to buy off political opponents and to fund new political cronies who would support his rule. Through complete control of information, the graft within the military hierarchy was hidden. But Zia's worst legacy was that in trying to keep Bhutto's PPP out of power he manufactured alternative political forces, strengthening both extremist groups and the military at the expense of democracy. In doing so he also allowed his own cronies to make money through corruption.

This was the period when Nawaz Sharif, twice prime minister of Pakistan (1991–93 and then 1997–99, after which he was forced into exile for some years), was literally manufactured as a leader. First the iron foundry his family had started and which was lost to nationalization under Bhutto was returned to his father by Zia, then he was allowed to build his business empire by using his position as Punjab's minister for finance. When he was elected Punjab's chief minister he did the same. Working from the principle that every politician has a price, he dished out state resources to buy politicians and become head of a political party, Pakistan Muslim League, and later the Islamic Democratic Alliance, which had been cobbled together by Zia's ISI. According to an affidavit to the Supreme Court by the head of ISI at the time, General Durrani, Nawaz Sharif (amongst other politicians) received 3.5 million rupees from them.

The general's 1985 non-party elections propelled corruption to heights then unknown in Pakistan. Since candidates were not affiliated to parties, they had to be lured into Zia's King's party through material incentives, like plots of state land, loans from nationalized banks, permits and lucrative government contracts. The polls were a disaster for Pakistan, creating a culture of corruption and sowing the seeds for much trouble to come.

I might have been more focused on my career at the time, but it pained me to watch the steady decline of my country from the 1970s. Spending my summers in the UK playing professional cricket enabled me constantly to compare Pakistan with a developed nation, and it was demoralizing. Whilst in the UK the institutions were stronger than the individual, in Pakistan powerful individuals abused the state infrastructure for their own ends. I know it hurt them to admit it, but often I would hear the elders in my family saying how things had worked better under the British. Rule of law, meritocracy, the bureaucracy – all were more efficient under the British, who on the whole had kept a tight rein on corruption. My parents' generation felt so let down by their ruling elite. They had had such hope and pride in Pakistan at its creation but each year their frustration and disappointment grew. Some of the first generation of Pakistani politicians, like Sherbaz Khan Mazari, the son of a tribal chief from Baluchistan, and M. Asghar Khan, the first head of the Pakistan air force, campaigned for years to keep the flame of Jinnah and Iqbal's dream alive. Both spent time in prison or under house arrest after opposing Zia and Bhutto and both have written about their bitter disappointment in the direction the country took.

Like many others from my background I would complain about the state of the country but would not lift a finger to do anything about it. I was from that privileged class that was not affected by the general deterioration in the country. The schools we went to had an imported syllabus, so if education for the masses stagnated we were not touched by it. We did not have to worry if the hospitals were going downhill because we could always afford to go abroad for treatment. And if there were power breakdowns, we could buy generators. (By 2011, most of Pakistan would go without electricity for twelve hours a day.) If the government departments were corrupt, then it was all the easier for us to bribe them and have anything illegal we wanted done. In any case we were always likely to have the necessary government connections to remove any stumbling blocks. If the general public suffered, well it was bad luck for them. I was even more fortunate than the privileged class, as being a cricket star in a cricket-mad country, all doors were open to me. So I did not have to struggle for anything and life for me could not have been easier.

Although I took pride in my Muslim identity, 'Islamization' in Pakistan did not bring me closer to my religion. In fact it had the opposite effect. By nature I always hated being forced to do anything so Zia's imposition of Islamic injunctions upon us just made me want to rebel. When I saw Islam being used for political purposes it only deepened my disillusionment. For someone like me who did not have much understanding about Islam, whenever the country's corrupt leadership professed to be devout Muslims, I felt it was Islam that was at fault, rather than the leadership. You see something similar happening nowadays where hardliners believe that only a radical form of Islam will save the country, arguing wrongly that we need to change the way religion is practised, rather than the way our country is run. Moreover, in the late 1970s and 1980s the government-controlled television channel constantly had so-called religious scholars talking about Islam. Most young people would simply switch it off. But it was the hypocrisy that put most of the educated youth off Islam. People expected an Islamic state to have high moral standards.

Events in Afghanistan and Iran dampened any hopes for an Islamic solution for Muslim countries still finding their way in the post-colonial world. In Afghanistan, infighting between the warlords amidst the mayhem left in the wake of the Soviet withdrawal in 1989 came as a bitter disappointment. The Afghan jihad leaders, glorified as religious warriors, now behaved like criminals – resorting to extortion and murder in their battle for personal power. So many had died, so many ordinary foot soldiers had made great sacrifices, but their leaders betrayed them. The Taliban, which as a group first rallied in order to rid the people of the chaotic tyranny of the warlords, initially gave a semblance of rule of law to the war-ravaged country. But with their unenlightened version of Islam, their inability to understand the essence of the religion, combined with aspects of the harsh rural Pashtun culture, they began to look increasingly oppressive. They refused to tolerate any other viewpoints. Somebody could be declared un-Islamic and punished for something as trivial as not having a beard. Meanwhile, the sorry descent of the Pakistani jihadi groups after the end of the war in Afghanistan into sectarianism and religious bigotry also took the shine off the religious idealism of the late 1970s and early 1980s. During the Soviet–Afghan war, both the Saudis and the Iranians had supported sectarian militant groups in Pakistan. In its wake these groups turned on each other, unleashing Sunni versus Shia violence. For most people this was completely against Islam, which preaches tolerance towards other creeds and faiths. Even Iran, which had aroused such expectations in the

Muslim world, disillusioned those looking to Tehran for a lead on democracy Muslim-style. In particular, people were nervous about the power of Iran's Guardian Council of ruling religious leaders – which had the power of veto over democratic decisions. Again, this was completely contrary to the democratic message inherent in the Prophet's (PBUH) teachings.

Democratic principles were an inherent part of Islamic society during the golden age of Islam, from the passing of the Holy Prophet (PBUH) and under the first four caliphs. But after the fourth caliph – Hazrat Ali, the fourth successor to Muhammad's (PBUH) leadership, who ruled over his vast empire, from Egypt in the west to the Iranian highlands in the east – democracy disappeared from the Muslim world. Hereditary kingship replaced the budding democracy of the Medina State and only in the twentieth century did it make a reappearance in the Muslim world. (In the eighteenth century, Shah Waliullah attributed the decline of the Mughal empire in particular and Muslims in general to the institution of monarchy, which, according to him, was degenerative and bound to decay.) Today in the majority of the Islamic world there are sham democracies which have not given freedom to the people, hence the urgency and anger of the revolutionary movements spreading across the Middle East in early 2011. An Islamic state has to be a democracy and a meritocracy. In an ideal Islamic society there should be no hurdles in the way of a man achieving his God-given potential. Islamic legal discourse covers both spiritual matters and the rights of an individual in everyday life. On the one hand it deals with prayer, worship, fasting and pilgrimage. On the other, it protects the most basic human needs and rights expected under civil law in the West – the rights to life, religion, family, freedom of thought and wealth. An Islamic state also guards against the executive accumulating too much power by emphasizing that even a ruler is not above the law. Of the first four great caliphs after Muhammad (PBUH), two ended up in front of a judge in a court of law. Hazrat Ali himself lost a case against a Jewish citizen because the judge refused to accept the testimony of Hazrat Ali's son. In Islam, since all sovereignty belongs to Allah both the executive and the people have to stay within the limits of His Laws. The founding fathers of the American constitution also strove to do the same by making the constitution supreme. This is why when Jinnah was asked in 1947 about the constitution of Pakistan, he said its basis would be the Quran.

Justice, compassion, welfare and equality, along with democracy, are at the heart of Islam, yet we saw non-Islamic Western states having greater ethical and moral norms. When I arrived in the UK in the 1970s it was the first time I had seen a proper welfare state. Coming from Ayub Khan's Pakistan, I was amazed by the level of social security. I felt like the Islamic scholar Muhammad Abduh (1849–1905), who said on his return from a trip to Europe to his home in Egypt: 'I saw no Muslims in Europe but I saw a lot of Islam,' and of his homeland, 'There are a lot of Muslims here but no Islam.' This quotation is perhaps even more relevant today, as the spirit of sharia (Islamic law) is more visible in Western countries than in the Muslim world. Until I started educating myself about it, like the majority of Western-educated people in Pakistan I too believed sharia to be some medieval set of laws irrelevant to our times. It conjured up images of fanaticism, women in veils, terrorism, intolerance and the abuse of human rights. Part of this stems from the prejudice in the Western media about Islam, a prejudice that dates back to the Crusades. Unfortunately it must also be blamed on the extremely unenlightened interpretation of Islam by certain Muslim regimes and groups.

In theory, the Islamic state should be a welfare state. That is why I find it strange that in Pakistan people who stand up for Islamic values are called rightist. Islamic values actually have more in common with leftist ideologies, in terms of social equality and welfare. Hazrat Umar, the second caliph of Islam, who ruled from 634 until his death in 644, set up the first true welfare state in the history of mankind, even introducing pensions. Widows, the handicapped, orphans and the unemployed were registered and paid from the state treasury. Moreover, the Quranic injunction of zakat, which exhorts Muslims to give 2.5 per cent of their wealth to the poor and to charity, meant that it was compulsory for citizens of an Islamic state to look after the vulnerable. The idea of setting up waqf (welfare trusts) that ran orphanages, hospitals, madrassas and *sirais* (free accommodation for travellers) long preceded the concept of trusts in Europe. Yet today Europe has the best social security system, particularly in the Scandinavian countries, and even the United States spends billions of dollars a year on the welfare of its people. Sadly the vast majority of Muslim countries have no welfare system at all. The poor in Pakistan have no safety net other than their own families or tribes. They cannot afford education, health or justice. According to the UNDP (United Nations Development Programme), 54 per cent of Pakistanis face 'multi-dimensional deprivation', meaning they lack access to proper education and health facilities and a decent standard of living. Almost two-thirds of the country lives on less than US$2 a day and about 40 per cent of Pakistani children suffer from chronic malnutrition. How can Pakistan be called an Islamic society?

Returning in the winter to Pakistan after playing cricket in England through the summer, I watched the changes in my country with the nagging anxiety of someone who saw it deteriorating each time I came home. Yet I never thought of leaving, I could never imagine another home but Pakistan. Nor did it even enter my mind at this stage to enter politics. In fact I could not think of anything worse. By the early 1980s, like most of the privileged class, I was coming to the conclusion that, since Pakistan's problems were so many and so insolvable, the best thing to do was to just look after myself. Besides, what could politics possibly give me? I had the life that many young people, in Pakistan and elsewhere, dreamt about – I was a rich and glamorous cricket star, jet-setting all over the world. Politics was considered a dirty business for those who could not do anything else. Most of the students from my school who went into politics were hopeless at both academic subjects and sports. Usually they belonged to feudal families with political ties. No one thought of politicians as selfless people who wanted to make Pakistan a better place to live in. Neither did I take much interest in social work or charity. Sure, I attended fundraising dinners every now and then, but hardly ever because I was touched by the cause of a particular charity; more because of the social occasion. I hardly ever gave zakat, feeling I had done my duty to society once I had paid my taxes.

Despite this, it was around this time I began to contemplate that there could be a God. It had nothing to do with Pakistan's 'Islamization' but it something to do with cricket. By 1982 I was close to my peak as a cricketer; I had been playing all year round for almost seven years. During this time I began to observe a phenomenon that players called luck. There were times when I would be in great form yet would not have much success, whereas at other times I would be feeling lousy and yet do well. I also found that in closely fought contests there was usually one point that would tilt the contest in favour of one team. Sometimes this would have nothing to do with playing ability. For instance, many times during my cricketing career an umpiring mistake or bias had cost one team the match – even the series.

There were other times when a contest was being won by a team and some non-cricketing phenomenon like rain would tilt the game in the other team's favour. The toss of a coin also sometimes made the difference between winning and losing. And a peculiar phenomenon which only pace bowlers would appreciate is that sometimes a ball just does not do anything, no matter how helpful the conditions, while at other times a ball will swing in unhelpful conditions. This was because of the way it was stitched together. Then of course a ball could become soft or out of shape and would not respond to the most skilful bowler, again influencing the outcome of the match. On several occasions I would also observe that a batsman would play as if he had a charmed life and was destined to score runs on that particular occasion. He would make mistakes, take unnecessary risks, invite catches, look as if he was about to be got out any second, but end up making runs and being successful. I began to realize that in sports no matter how good I was or how hard I tried, success was never guaranteed. It is important to stress, however, that players who had ability, guts, diligence and determination were consistently successful, but there seemed to be a zone beyond which players were helpless, and it was called luck. Over the years I began to ask myself the question – could what we call luck actually be the will of God?

The other thing that made me feel there could be a God was the vulnerability every sportsman feels regarding injuries. A sportsman can train for months to prepare himself for a big event, yet a slight muscle tear can result in all the hard work going down the drain. As a fast bowler I had to be in perfect muscle condition before a match. Several times I played with half injuries, not sure whether they would worsen during the match or gradually improve. This again was an area out of my control. In 1982 I was at my absolute peak as a fast bowler in terms of physical strength, experience and skill and was poised to go for the world record for the highest number of test wickets. I was so fit and strong that I felt nothing could stop me. This was a point in my life when I used to wonder how people could get old. I just could not imagine that I could ever lose my fitness and strength to age. I felt invincible. In one year I had got over ninety test wickets in just thirteen tests – almost a world record. I had got there through sheer passion and hard work and never relied on anyone but myself. If I had injuries, rarely would I go to a physiotherapist, relying instead on exercise to help me recover. The Pakistan cricket team was rapidly becoming a force in international cricket. We had just thrashed Australia and India comprehensively. Just at that point

I got a stress fracture in my shinbone and could not bowl for the next two and a half years. During this time the majority of the doctors I saw felt that I would never bowl again.

My whole world came crashing down. Only an athlete can understand the shock of a potentially career-ending injury. It was the most devastating thing that had happened to me in my life so far. I also lost the confidence acquired through my success in cricket. Success always creates jealousies in certain quarters and all this came out now. There was a spate of nasty articles against me. A couple of players who would not have dared to cross me when I was fit took the opportunity to put the knife in, feeling that I was finished and it was safe to vent their animosity. I used to deal with such people by performing on the field and shutting them up. Now I felt defenceless and had no clue how to deal with the situation. I became a recluse and in my mind made it into a huge crisis. But with hindsight it was a storm in a teacup. Much later I read a book by the eminent cricket writer and historian David Frith about how many cricketers had committed suicide once they could no longer play cricket. Whilst I was never in danger of that, I understood their torment; not knowing whether I would bowl again made me feel extremely unsure and insecure about my future.

In such a state of mind I saw an astrologer and a couple of clairvoyants. Until then I had never believed anyone who claimed to be able to tell the future and frankly I had never needed to. I had so much self-belief that I felt I could achieve anything through my own talent and hard work. I was never one of those sportsmen with trivial superstitions about objects or habits that would bring me luck in a match. My experience

with both the astrologer and the clairvoyants was highly
unsatisfactory; most of what they said was wrong. I vowed
that I would not bother with them again. In my state of un-
certainty and vulnerability, despite all my doubts, I would
turn to God, especially when, on the long and painful road to
recovery, I would start feeling twinges in my shinbone. Twice
I had bowled too soon without waiting for the bone to heal
properly and both times the crack reappeared. The third time
I was careful but whenever I felt pain I was never sure whether
I would make it or not.

Chapter Three

Death, and Pakistan's Spiritual Life, 1987–1989

PAKISTAN CAME INTO EXISTENCE AS A COUNTRY BECAUSE OF Islam, and the Islamic beliefs of its founders and citizens. Through circumstances I came to understand Islam better than I had done in my youth, which led me to understand Pakistan, to appreciate its history and the course it was taking. As I learned more about Islam, and about being a Muslim, it became clear to me that I was on a path, one that would lead me to greater engagement with the political life of my country. A spiritual person takes on responsibility for society, whereas a materialist only takes responsibility for himself.

In Pakistan I often came across people who had some sort of spiritual experience or were deeply religious. This was especially true of the elders in our family. My mother started to become more spiritual when I was about ten years old. She and her sister met a female Sufi from Sahiwal, a district south of Lahore, and used to travel to visit her quite regularly.

Spiritual guides, or *pirs*, are quite common in Pakistan. Millions of people, particularly in rural areas of the country, follow them, consulting them on everything from religious matters to sickness and family problems. My mother always tried to encourage me to follow my religion, but it was hard for her to relate to me in the way that I can relate to my children, as she had no way of really comprehending the impact of the competing cultural forces in my life. With my sons I can understand what it means to grow up a Muslim in today's Western society. Meanwhile, my father was also religious, but in a different way. While he had immense respect for the great Sufi saints of the subcontinent, he believed in a direct relationship with God, and didn't feel he needed a spiritual intermediary or a guide as my mother and her sister did.

I had my first spiritual experience when I was nearly fourteen and already quite sceptical about religion and God. My mother was so excited because her spiritual guide, Pir Gi, came to visit us in Lahore for the first and last time. She introduced me to Pir Gi, hoping she would pray for me and offer me guidance. The woman was sitting on the floor with three or four of her disciples, her head covered by a chador. She never looked up at me and I never saw her face. She did not say anything for a few minutes and then suddenly said I had not finished the Quran. I was utterly shocked. Only the maulvi who came to teach me the Quran knew that I had not finished it. My Quran lessons used to be after school and the last thing I wanted to do at the time was to read the Quran. All I wanted to do was to go and play with my cousins in Zaman Park. After a year, the poor maulvi accepted that I was a hopeless case, and one day we both schemed to tell my parents that I had finally finished the Quran. My mother looked at me and immediately knew from my shocked face that her spiritual guide was spot on. Pir Gi told my mother not to worry, that I was a decent soul and would turn out all right. I saw the relief pass across my mother's face. Pir Gi went on to say that I would be very famous and make my mother a household name. When my mother died twenty-one years later of cancer, I built a hospital in her name and today the Shaukat Khanum Memorial Hospital (SKMH) is renowned across Pakistan.

The sense of achievement I was to feel when this hospital opened was far greater than anything I had achieved in cricket. It gave me a surge of pure happiness. The overhaul of my lifestyle from that of a sports star to a humanitarian worker and politician initially met with some scepticism. But as I began my spiritual journey I started to discover happiness comes from all those things that are considered to be boring by the mass media and the culture of self-indulgence it promotes: giving charity, helping others, family life and achieving selfless goals. My mother's long and painful death in 1985 was the catalyst for this change in me, a turning point in my life, forcing me to face up to my utter helplessness as I tried to ease her suffering.

I first heard the news of my mother's cancer when my sister Aleema called me in the summer of 1984. What had been initially diagnosed in Pakistan as a stomach infection had turned out to be cancer of the colon. I was in England at the time recovering from the stress fracture in my shinbone. I brought my mother to the UK for treatment but by the time we took her back home in September the cancer had spread to her liver. Her last six weeks were very painful and even today I have to block from my mind the memories of this time. Out of sheer desperation and helplessness I would beg the Almighty for help. All my family prayed for her too. So vulnerable was I that I even brought home a faith healer, who turned out to be a complete quack – there was, I soon realized, a whole industry existing in Pakistan of quacks, faith healers and fake spiritualists who prey on vulnerable people.

For a few months after my mother's death I completely removed from my mind the idea of God. However, my internal debate about whether He existed or not later resumed. I had become embittered towards God. If he did exist, how could he have put my mother through so much pain? She was very religious and had been such a selfless mother. The experience of my mother's death coupled with my stress fracture had made me realize how vulnerable I was. The complete faith I had had in my own strength and capabilities was no longer there. It was almost as if someone had put me in my place by making me aware of my many limitations. I again started saying my prayers every morning. This was really like an insurance policy – a sort of safety net in case God really did exist. It is possible that many Muslims suffer from this dilemma. They pray not because they know that there is a God, but because they cannot be certain that there is no God. By this point, my leg had healed and I threw myself back into cricket with all my stored-up enthusiasm. Soon I started having the same degree of success as when I had left off. In fact the long, hard road back to fitness had toughened me up mentally and what I had lost physically during the two and a half years I had been out as a bowler because of my injury I now made up for with much greater mental strength. Just as the body gets stronger by exercise, so does the mind when it encounters resistance.

By this time I had come to the realization that the hedonistic lifestyle that had seemed so appealing from the out-side was a mirage. The hurt I caused and the feeling of emptiness I experienced in transitory relationships far out-weighed the moments of pleasure. Most of the jet set I knew and socialized with in the 1980s could not face a party unless they had enough alcohol or drugs in their system. It was a world completely cut off from the rest of humanity. I also began to question the things I had always assumed were great fun. The people I was hanging out with had been conditioned by Hollywood-led trends and peer pressure to believe night-clubs, beach and yachting holidays, expensive restaurants and designer clothes made you happy. But parties and nightclubs began to bore me, as did eating out, which had once seemed so much fun. I began to crave home cooking, while years of cricket tours made me hate the sight of hotels. Once I began to change my lifestyle I realized there was a world of difference between happiness and pleasure-seeking. I had mis-taken pleasure for happiness but the former does not last long and the activities that give it have diminishing returns. Over the years I had seen so many destroy their lives through hedonism. Alcoholism and drug addiction have ruined the potential of so many pop, film and sports stars. I could easily have slid down that slippery slope, entering that world as I did as an impressionable eighteen-year-old just as the sex, drugs and rock and roll revolution was at its peak. What saved me from disaster was cricket. I had to be fit to perform at the highest level, and therefore never indulged too deeply in that lifestyle. I also had too much self-respect to allow myself to be humiliated on the cricket field due to over-indulgence else-where. My strong family roots, and above all my mother's powerful influence and the fear of humiliating both my imme-diate and extended family, helped me exercise self-control.

I discovered that it is the environment we grow up in that influences what we enjoy in life and I began to rediscover how much I loved trekking in Pakistan's northern mountains in the summer and partridge shooting in the Salt Range in the winter. Similarly, after all the fancy restaurants I have eaten in, what I really enjoy is the food in the cheap truck drivers' cafés on the intercity highways in Pakistan. This is where the men who drive the famously colourful Pakistani trucks stop to sit on *charpoys*, bed frames strung with rope, and eat spicy food with mugs of hot, sweet chai. The dishes are simple – daal, mutton or chicken cooked in *desi ghee* (clarified butter). They are typically all made from local ingredients and freshly cooked, which is why they are so good. Even better is the food I have eaten in the old city of Lahore. No food in the entire Indian subcontinent can match that.

Perhaps it's no surprise, then, given my love for it, that it was while I was in the Pakistani countryside that I met the first of the men who would become my spiritual guides. The first man I met was not exactly a guide but the encounter, and what he told me, so astonished me that it led to my next encounter as I became more open to the ideas these extra-ordinary men introduced me to. The spiritual journey I embarked on I regard as intrinsic to my history of Pakistan because it was only when I understood fully the spiritual inheritance of the nation, from the principles of Islam expounded by its founders, that I was able to see and comprehend the nature of the history unfolding in front of me, and my place in it.

In 1987, the year I had announced my initial retirement from cricket, I was on a shooting trip with a couple of friends some 100 miles north of Lahore. After the shoot, our host suggested that I meet a spiritual man who lived in a village on the way back home. I saw no point in it but at the others' insistence I agreed to see him. The man, whose name was Baba Chala, lived in a little village just a few miles from the Indian border. He was short with piercing eyes and a happy face. He did not know who I was as nobody in the village had a television and, besides, he did not look like the type of person who would be into cricket. He certainly had not heard about my retirement despite it having been headline news. My host asked him what I should do after cricket. The man looked at me and said I had not left my profession. We all told him that I had retired and had no intention of playing again. The man said, 'It is the will of Allah; you are still in the game.' Next he told me how many sisters I had and what their names were. He then turned to one of my friends, Mohammed Siddique, and told him that he would be double-crossed in a business deal and that he should immediately take his money out of the project, but that things would eventually be resolved. He shocked him further by telling him the actual amount of money involved. We left his place perplexed. What was the trick? On the way back we discussed how he could have known the names of our family members. What we found most difficult to comprehend was how he knew the exact amount of money involved in Siddique's project. Three months later at a dinner given for the cricket team in Islamabad, General Zia asked me to take back my decision to retire for the sake of the country, and again captain Pakistan. Within weeks I was leading the national team on a tour of the West Indies, and my friend's business dealings unfolded as Baba Chala had predicted. How could that man in the village have known, I kept thinking? My mind also went back to my mother's spiritual guide, who had been able to tell that I had not finished the Quran.

Just over a year after that I came across someone who would become the single most powerful spiritual influence on me and completely change my direction in life. A friend in Lahore had invited me for lunch. The only other guest was a frail-looking, clean-shaven man in his sixties by the name of Mian Bashir. The lines on his face showed that he had seen a lot of suffering. He was a retired junior civil servant who I was told was struggling to make ends meet on his meagre pension. The man sat quietly throughout lunch with a disinterested look on his face. After lunch he politely asked me if I con-stantly read a certain verse from the Quran. I told him I hadn't even heard of the verse. His face went into a deep frown. He closed his eyes, took on an expression of concentration and then said: 'Sorry, it was your mother who would read that verse for your protection.' With astonishment, I realized that he was absolutely right. When I was a child, before I went to sleep, my mother would repeat a verse from the Quran three times and blow on me. He went on to say that I was protected because of it. Then he told me a couple of incidents about my family, about which no one else could have known and too personal to relate here. I asked him how he acquired this skill. 'It is the will of Allah, at times He shows me something even without my asking for it. Other times I beg him for knowledge about some subject and He refuses me,' he replied. I was really curious. I wanted to know more.

Mian Bashir's father had died when he was barely two years old. His mother really struggled to look after him as the father's share of the family property was fraudulently acquired by his uncles. From the age of about seven Mian Bashir would occasionally see visions, which he could not interpret properly. He met a man at this juncture who told him to read the Quran and spend more time praying and meditating about Allah. 'There are no coincidences in life, that man was meant to guide me towards Allah,' he told me. By the time he was twelve, even the schoolteachers were over-awed by his power to see what others could not. He dropped out of school and for the next few years made it his mission to expose professional pirs who, like the commercial Indian gurus, make money off insecure and vulnerable people. He would put out newspaper adverts issuing a challenge to match their spiritual powers with his and expose these frauds who thrive on the poor villagers of Punjab and Sindh.

Over the next year or so, I met Mian Bashir a few times; he fascinated me. Like my mother's guide, he was an unassuming and unprepossessing person, who wore his wisdom lightly. He was extremely humble and would take great pains to tell me that he had no such art of looking into the future or the past. Instead, he said that when he meditated and begged Allah to help him, He would occasionally 'lift the veil', but it was always to help people in distress. 'Nothing,' he said, 'can happen without Allah's will.' Each meeting with him would leave me more convinced about the existence of God. I had been so angry since my mother's death, and here was a man helping to answer many of the questions that had been torturing me. Over a period of two or three years he resolved many of the issues which for me had been an impediment to faith. The difference between the way I learned about Islam from him and the way I had been taught at school or by the maulvis who used to come and teach me the Quran at home, was that he never insisted on any religious rituals. He never told me to pray five times a day or to fast at Ramadan, never insisted I read the Quran. Instead he explained what lay behind the rites. He knew that one cannot force external demonstrations of religiosity as otherwise they are just empty rituals. The internal change must come first. And he let me develop my faith in my own time. Sometimes it took six months for me to truly understand something he had said, but he never hurried me.

What appealed to me about him was that he had no ulterior motive; the only reason he was leading me towards spirituality was for my own good. Rather than making himself indispensable to me, as some fake religious gurus do, he told me that he could only help me so far. I would ask him to pray for me and he would insist that I pray myself, or I would ask his advice and rather than giving it to me he would tell me to pray to God for direction. He never asked for a thing and would say that any religious person who charged people money was a quack. Just as somebody who is blessed with wealth is morally obliged to share it with others, Mian Bashir believed that somebody with his kind of blessing was obliged to use it to help people.

Mian Bashir, who died in 2005, also had a very poor opinion of those preachers who, by laying so much emphasis on rituals, would completely miss out on the essence of religion. Some, according to him, had made religion into a profession and were there not to guide people but to profit from them. He also felt that they condemned people too quickly and actually made them scared of religion. 'The Quran,' he said, 'was supposed to be a blessing for mankind. It was not to make life more difficult. You cannot drill people to have faith; their hearts and minds have to be penetrated. Faith is the greatest gift of Allah.' He also taught me that any belief system that failed to instil compassion was not real religion or had failed to touch the person internally. So much harm is done in the world by people who treat religions as competing ideologies, yet all religious messages teach humanity, selflessness and justice. People who kill in the name of religion are no different from the materialists who fight in the name of communism, national socialism or capitalism.

So now I had come to the realization that there was a God, but I had to do the reading, to understand the religion that had been sidelined in my Western-style education. Mian Bashir had never finished school, so other than the Quran, he was not in a position to advise me on what to read to deepen my knowledge. My need to explore the religion was spurred on by the furore in 1988 and 1989 over Salman Rushdie's *The Satanic Verses*. Muslims understandably found the book deeply offensive in its satirical portrayal of the Prophet Muhammad (PBUH). It hurt even more because Rushdie was from a Muslim Indian family and must have known the outrage it would cause. You cannot hide behind freedom of speech to humiliate an entire religion and cause so much hurt. Most Muslims felt insulted and responded by refusing to read the book but there was always going to be an extreme reaction from certain quarters. Every society is made up mainly of moderates but has its extremists and the extremist elements of the Islamic world erupted. Only a minuscule proportion of the international Muslim community reacted with violence but all 1.3 billion Muslims were tarnished. Translators of the book were killed or attacked in Japan, Italy and Norway. In Pakistan, several people died when Islamists attacked the American Cultural Center in Islamabad. In Bradford, Muslim immigrants, many of them British Pakistanis, burned copies of the book. British Muslim groups campaigned unsuccessfully to have the book banned in the UK as the country's blasphemy law protected only Christian beliefs. Most famously, Iran's Khomeini declared a *fatwa*, or religious ruling, condemning Rushdie and the book's publishers to death and calling on Muslims 'to execute them immediately wherever they might be'. An Islamic charity in Tehran put up a bounty for Rushdie's head. Khomeini's fatwa was condemned by a variety of religious scholars, leaders and groups, including the Organisation of the Islamic Conference, the inter-governmental body that represents Muslim countries. While blasphemy, according to some interpretations of the Quran, is punishable by death, the fatwa violated various laws in Islamic jurisprudence, which states the need for a fair trial to allow the accused to defend themselves and repent.

The Western public was puzzled by such fury, being

absolutely clueless about how much love, respect and reverence Muslims have for the Prophet (PBUH). Our faith depends on his credibility because he is the witness to the Quran. If his credibility is questioned then so is the Quran. Most Muslims live by this book of guidance so therefore take any criticism of it as an attack on their whole way of life. I blame the intelligentsia and leaders of the Muslim world for not making clear to Western countries how hurtful the *Satanic Verses* affair was. The OIC (Organisation of the Islamic Conference), an association of Muslim states, should have sent a delegation to the European Union and US Congress to explain to them the offence caused by slandering the Prophet (PBUH). Otherwise, how could the West understand, when in many Western countries people are allowed to make fun of religious figures? The Jewish leadership has been very effective in making it clear that the Holocaust, which understandably causes them so much pain, cannot be ridiculed. The Muslim elite should have followed their example.

There was nobody to defend the religion, though, and Islam was under attack, with people in the West drawing comparisons with the book-burning of Nazi Germany. I didn't have the depth of knowledge to defend it either. While leading Pakistan on a tour of New Zealand at the time I was constantly being asked about whether Islam was a violent religion. So I started reading books about Islam and found that my mind was more stimulated than it had ever been. I was inspired by the writings of great scholars like Iqbal, the poet-philosopher integral to the founding of Pakistan, and Ali Shariati, an Iranian writer and sociologist, who regarded himself as a disciple of Iqbal. Both believed in Islam's potential for creating a just society, as had been seen during what is known as the Golden Age of Islam in the first five hundred years after the Prophet's (PBUH) death. The more I read, the better I could understand the Quran, which has many layers of meaning. The more devoted and learned the interpreter, the more the meaning of each passage expands. I was also drawn to the writing of Charles Le Gai Eaton, a British convert. A former diplomat, writer and broadcaster, Eaton was one of the foremost Muslim intellectuals of the West. His writing did much to emphasize Islam's spirituality and undermine the religious arguments of ideologues and extremists, and, together with the example of his own life story, provided a bridge between East and West and demonstrated how Islam could contribute positively to British society. As his obituary in the *Guardian* put it: 'Refusing to conform to the dictates of any ethnic or cultural model imported from abroad, this impeccable Englishman showed far more effectively than any amount of theory that Islamic faith is fully compatible with British identity.'

Because my roots were Islamic but my education was Western, what appealed to me about Eaton was his experience of and views on Islam as a Westerner. A convert's experience of Islam is purely spiritual, rather than cultural. A lot of scholars in the Islamic world labour under the burden of culture and history and can be too influenced by both. As Eaton himself says in his introduction to his book *Islam and the Destiny of Man*: 'One who enters the community of Islam by choice rather than by birth sinks roots into the ground of the religion, the Quran and the traditions of the Prophet; but the habits and customs of the Muslim peoples are not his. He lacks their strengths and is immune from their weaknesses; immune, above all, from the psychological "complexes" which are the result of their recent history.' Besides Eaton, another convert who fascinated me was Muhammad Asad, who was born an Austrian Jew under the name Leopold Weiss in 1900. Asad was a scholar and diplomat who was given Pakistani citizenship and advised on the drafting of Pakistan's first constitution.

My greatest influence at this time though was Iqbal, a philo-sophical descendant of the Eastern sage Rumi, the renowned mystic and poet-philosopher of thirteenth-century Persia. One of the greatest thinkers of modern Islamic history, Iqbal had studied in both East and West and inspired in a generation of Indian Muslims an ardent desire for change. Central to his vision is his philosophy of *khudi* (ego or 'selfhood'). According to this philosophy, the development of khudi comes about through 'self-reliance, self-respect, self-confidence, self-preservation, and self-assertion when such a thing is necessary, in the interests of life and the power to stick to the cause of truth, justice, duty'. Iqbal ardently believed that human beings were the makers of their own destiny and that the key to destiny lay in one's character. His philosophy was essentially a philosophy of action and it was concerned primarily with motivating human beings to strive to realize their God-given potential to the fullest degree. This he likened to the eagle, the *shaheen*, an emblem of royalty which denoted a kind of heroic idealism based on daring, pride and honour. It is the king of the birds precisely because it disdains any form of safety or ease. He reminds the younger generation:

Tu shaheen hay, parwaaz hay kaam tayra
Teray saaminain aasmaan aur bhi hain
You are a *shaheen*, your work is to fly
There are other skies in front of you

and:

Naheen tayraa nashayman Qasr-e-Sultani kay gumbad pur
Tu shaheen hay, basayra kur paharon ki chattanoon main
Your abode is not on the dome of the palaces of kings
You are a *shaheen*, live on the mountain-cliffs

The second major theme of Iqbal's philosophy that appealed to me – child of a post-colonial world as I was – was his strong affirmation of freedom and justice. Throughout his life, Iqbal identified himself with the oppressed people of the world, and urged his fellow Muslims to rebel against all forms of tyranny – be it religious, political, cultural, intellectual, economic or any other. For Iqbal, Islam – whose very name means the submission or surrender of oneself to God – implied that Muslims should not surrender their freedom to anything except God. He believed a large part of the Quran's teachings were aimed at freeing human beings from the chains that bound them: traditionalism, authoritarianism (religious, political or economic), tribalism, racism, classism, caste and slavery. This concern is reflected in much of Iqbal's writing. He believed passionately in freedom, which he considered to be 'the very breath of vital living'. In his eyes, a slave nation had no future. 'In Servitude, it is reduced to an almost waterless stream, but in Freedom, Life is a boundless ocean,' he wrote. Each country had to chart its own path.

On 1 January 1938, amid the build-up to the Second World War, Iqbal made a passionate condemnation of imperialism in a New Year message broadcast on All-India Radio. It was just a few months before his death.

> The tyranny of Imperialism struts abroad, covering its face in the masks of Democracy, Nationalism, Communism, Fascism and heaven knows what else besides. Under these masks, in every corner of the earth, the spirit of freedom and the dignity of man are being trampled underfoot ... The so-called statesmen to whom government and leadership of man were entrusted have proved demons of bloodshed, tyranny and oppression. The rulers whose duty it was to protect and cherish those ideals which go to form a higher humanity, to prevent man's oppression of man and to elevate the moral intellectual level of mankind, have in their hunger for dominion and imperial possession shed the blood of millions and reduced millions to servitude simply in order to pander to the greed and avarice of their own particular groups. After subjugating and establishing their dominion over weaker peoples, they have robbed them of their religions, their morals, of their cultural traditions and their literatures. Then they sowed divisions among them that they should shed one another's blood, and go to sleep under the opiate of serfdom, so that the leech of imperialism might go on sucking their blood without interruption. This message is even more relevant today.

Reading and understanding all this was an exciting time of discovery for me but others were rather perplexed. My sisters and particularly my father were amused as they looked upon me as someone who was totally immune to religion. As for my friends, both in Pakistan and England, they started wondering if I had gone a little crazy. They could not understand what had come over me. I didn't fall out with people over it, but after too many passionate arguments I became frustrated, and decided I could not explain faith to people who believe that if something cannot be explained scientifically, then it cannot exist. Faith is something you feel, you cannot explain it. Many assumed my transformation was a result of the trauma of reaching the end of my long-running career. My friends knew me to be a rational and completely non-superstitious person, so this passionate belief in the unseen was a mystery for them, as was my complete change of lifestyle. One of my closest friends, Yousaf Salahuddin, grandson of the great Iqbal, thought I had become a fundamentalist. Amongst sections of the westernized elite in Pakistan, if you start to talk about religion you are automatically branded a mullah. Years later I was speaking to Yusuf Islam (the former Cat Stevens) and he told me how difficult it was for him when he discovered God. He cut himself off from his past life, stopped singing, dumped his old friends and changed his clothes. It took him a while to come to terms with the change in his thinking and to reconcile it with his environment.

It was hard enough for the people who knew me intimately – for the ones who only knew me as a sports star with a playboy reputation, the reaction was even more extreme. I was accused of being a hypocrite or of suffering from a midlife crisis or a nervous breakdown. I remember an article in an English-language Pakistani newspaper that compared me with another Pakistani cricketer, Fazal Mahmood. He was the pin-up sportsman of his time, and led a glamorous life until his retirement, when he turned to God. I suppose people thought that sometimes a professional sportsman needs to replace one passion in his life with another, and often religion can fill that void. (My internal journey had started before I left cricket.) I too used to think Mahmood had become a bit weird. Now I realized that, like me, he saw through the glamour of the fast life and began to search elsewhere to satisfy his soul.

There is a section of Pakistan's westernized class that is not just secular, but actually anti-Islamic, and they use the figure of the mullah or the fundamentalist to attack Islam. Former Turkish prime minister Necmettin Erbakan talked about a similar attitude amongst the anti-Islamic elite in Turkey. In an interview he once described how they started booing and thumping their desks whenever the Prophet (PBUH) was mentioned in parliament. This part of Pakistani society and its media really went for me, accusing me of being a 'born-again' Muslim. Yet no spiritual transformation happens overnight or comes out of nowhere. It is an inner journey that takes time and is shaped by various events in your life. Neither is it a straightforward journey and there were times when I relapsed or had doubts. The Quran warns the believer that their faith will be tested by crises.

My mother always knew that one of the things I hated most was being forced to do something. The more somebody tried to make me a better Muslim through fear or pressure, the more I would resist. The Quran specifically states: 'There is no coercion in religion.' You can't force somebody to have faith because it is ultimately a battle for the heart and mind. So if I became a practising Muslim, it was because it was a decision

I came to by myself, after much thought and reflection. I believe that people only really change when their belief system changes. I don't believe that people change because they ever have enough of a pleasure-seeking life. People said that having satiated myself with the life of fun, I had now turned religious. I disagree. In my experience people never have enough of a fun life, they just get more and more debauched in search of pleasure. Besides, these accusations implied that humans cannot evolve and reform. It is only the strengthening of the will through faith that enables a person to conduct the struggle against earthly desires; what the Prophet (PBUH) called the greater jihad. This struggle continues all one's life. This is one of the mistakes atheists make; they think that a religious person should be immune to temptation, that the moment he claims to have faith he should transform into an angel, but actually the battle has only just begun. It is the beginning of the battle for the soul. When a Muslim prays five times a day he is making a constant plea to God to help him stick to the right path. For saint or sinner, the prayer is the same call, five times a day, day after day, year after year, for ongoing guidance. 'Guide us the straight way – the way of those upon whom Thou has bestowed Thy blessings, not of those who have been condemned (by Thee), nor of those who go astray' (Quran 1: 6). It is a constant reformation of one's character.

I have rarely seen people be changed by seeing psychiatrists. According to Charles Le Gai Eaton, 'Psychiatry is the study of the soul by those people who have no understanding of the soul.' Most drug addicts and alcoholics struggle to control their habits despite repeated visits to rehab clinics. My friend

Prince Jagat Singh of Jaipur died in his forties after struggling with alcoholism and going in and out of such expensive facilities. His problem was that he had a directionless and meaningless life and a dissatisfied soul. No rehab clinic is going to help with that. But I have met a lot of people who have changed completely when their souls have been touched by faith. I benefited hugely from the direction of Mian Bashir during this journey of mine. Faith without direction and especially wisdom can produce fanatics, self-righteous bores, even ascetics. Guidance from a proper scholar is most important, hence the tremendous respect given to scholars in Islam. Taimur, or Tamburlaine, the Turco-Mongol conqueror who was one of the greatest butchers in the history of mankind, would ensure that all the scholars were protected before massacring a city's population. Throughout Muslim history scholars could travel to any part of the Islamic world and be received with great respect wherever they went.

Mian Bashir used to laugh at me and say: 'Think how long it took you to believe. You want others to understand you in a few minutes.' He would urge me to recall these words from the Quran: 'Say: I worship not that which you worship. Nor will you worship that which I worship. Unto you your religion and unto me my religion' (Quran 109: 1–6). He explained to me that the basic requirements of the Quran are that a human believes in One God, the day of Judgement, the hereafter, and does good deeds to help others. Several times the Quran refers to Muslims as 'those who believe and do good deeds'. Following religious rituals without doing good deeds makes them meaningless. Inspired by this idea, after my final retirement from cricket I began to work on building the hospital in my mother's name in earnest. However, my way of life was still not exactly Islamic. Mian Bashir, despite being well aware of this, never told me to change my ways. Not once did he give me a sermon about praying, reading the Quran or living a pious life. All he would say was that nothing would please Allah more than the hospital I was building for the poor. When he used to see me worrying about the project's many obstacles, he would reassure me by saying Allah would solve my problems and that He always rewarded good intentions backed by effort. He also reassured me when every now and then my faith wavered. 'Even the Prophet had doubts in the beginning. It was his wife Khadija who assured him that his meeting with the angel Gabriel was real and that he was not going mad,' he told me.

Mian Bashir may have had an ability to see into the future, but it was his wisdom and absolute belief in the existence of God that had a real impact on me. He also helped in removing one of the biggest impediments to my having faith in God. I simply could not picture Him. As a child I would imagine a grand old man with a huge white beard. As I grew older it became much harder to believe that anyone could be so powerful as to create the entire universe and control everything that happened with His will. Mian Bashir simply quoted the Quran: 'Far Exalted is He above all that you attribute to Him', and told me that the human mind is not capable of comprehending Allah, so it was futile to try to picture Him; instead one should try to understand Him through the ninety-nine names given to him in the Quran describing His qualities. He told me that it was also impossible to imagine the angels, Hell or Heaven.

I also discussed with Mian Bashir an issue that had bothered me for a long time; it was about the immoral believer and the moral atheist. I had met so many moral and principled people in the West who did not believe in God – and in Pakistan there was no dearth of believers who prayed five times a day and yet indulged in every immoral activity. His answer was that when prayers become a mechanical ritual and fail to touch the soul, a man can struggle to resist his material and animal desires. A lot of people who are religious are not actually convinced that there is a God. As for those who do not believe in God and yet are moral – he felt that morals are engrained into a person by their parents, school or even society, but that ultimately all morality originates from religion. According to him there is no such thing as moral atheism. Once people are cut off from religious values a society's morals will eventually degenerate.

I asked Mian Bashir how he could tell which verse of the Quran my mother would read to me when I was a child. He stressed over and over again that he could only see what Allah allowed him to see. He told me there were times he would meditate and beg Allah for some knowledge to guide someone but it would be denied to him. When I asked him about how he acquired these powers, he simply said: 'Through devotion to Allah.' He would go on to explain that since He has all knowledge, when a man gets close to him, He allows him to see what others cannot (Quran 3: 179 and 72: 26–27). He said not everyone can acquire this knowledge though. Some can try as hard as they can and still not get anywhere. Others, such as God's Prophets, can be shown this knowledge without much effort. For ordinary mortals this knowledge can be acquired through isolation and ascetic discipline. Reading the biography of the twelfth-century Andalusian mystic Muhammad Ibn Arabi helped me understand Mian Bashir's gift better. Ibn Arabi referred to those 'that see with two eyes'. He believed that after a process of spiritual discipline somebody could reach a state during meditation in which they received direct knowledge from Allah.

I also started to read about Sufism, and discovered there was a whole world of spirituality about which I was completely clueless. Sufism is too big a subject to delve into in this book, but these beautiful lines from the mystic poet Rumi reflect what he calls the inner journey of man, and the ascent of the human soul. People who know about mysticism will understand about the journey of the soul towards God.

> Low in the earth
> I lived in realms of ore and stone;
> And then I smiled in many-tinted flowers;
> Then roving with the wild and wondering hours,
> O'er earth and air and ocean's zone,
> In a new birth,
> I dived and flew,
> And crept and ran,
> And all the secrets of my essence drew
> Within a form that brought them all to view –
> And lo, a Man!
> And then my goal.
> Beyond the clouds, beyond the sky,
> In realms where none may change or die –
> In angel form; and then away

Beyond the bounds of night and day,
And Life and Death, unseen or seen,
Where all that is hath ever been,
As One and Whole.

Mian Bashir taught me to deal with aspects of Sufism that I couldn't understand by accepting that we are not all-knowing, that we need to have humility. The arrogance that we are meant to know everything only demonstrates the superficiality of our knowledge. Throughout the history of mankind, people have claimed absolute truths – things later proved to be wrong. There is a dimension that is beyond science, logic and modern education, and we should not assume that what cannot be proved does not exist. The more knowledge you have the more you should realize how little you know. I find that people who are deeply knowledgeable, like Mian Bashir, are deeply humble. For me the internal conflict was over from this point onwards. Now there was just this burning desire to understand God. I asked Mian Bashir where I should start. 'Read the Quran,' he said. 'Why did you not ask me to do so before?' I asked. 'You were not ready,' came the reply. 'The Quran only makes sense to those who are searching for the Truth; not those cynics who read it to disprove it.' For someone who believes in reason and logic it is difficult to blindly believe that the Quran is the word of God. It was simultaneously reading the Quran and the fascinating life of the Prophet (PBUH) that convinced me about its divine origin.

Whenever I did not understand anything in the Quran I would ask for Mian Bashir's guidance. He would explain

111

complex issues in very simple terms. Over a period of time he answered most of the questions that had been bothering me about the existence of God. One of these was why, if there is a God, was there so much suffering in the world? The answer came, when you have faith there is a hereafter which is eternal; God is not here to save us from difficulties but to give us the strength to overcome them. (Years later, my son Sulaiman, when aged about twelve, asked me the same question.) This life is just a test for that hereafter. Other questions that I had were answered by reading the Quran. The book that had seemed so difficult to get interested in now offered jewels of wisdom on every page. Having said this, I admit in all humility that I do not have answers to all the questions and I would like to think that, as the Prophet (PBUH) stated, I will keep learning from the cradle to the grave.

Neither do I claim to be an Islamic scholar, but I would like to use the example of my spiritual journey to put right some of the myths and misconceptions about Islam in the West. A great religion has been maligned thanks not just to ignorance in the Western world, but also ignorance amongst Muslims about Islam's true essence. There is so much debate about moderate and radical Islam but there is only one Islam. People can be moderates, radicals or liberals in any human community but all the world's great religions have at their heart a message of compassion. Faith should be about encouraging all that is noble in a human being. It should enhance both the individual and the community, and is not to be used as a political tool by those greedy for power, as it has been in Pakistan and other Muslim countries, or in medieval Europe. I also want to show that terrorism has nothing to do with religion and certainly nothing to do with the true teachings of Islam. How can mindless butchery and killing be attributed to faith? Islam, like many religions, and for that matter political ideologies like socialism or communism, has been misused by humans for personal and political gain.

For a start, as my faith grew my entire outlook on life changed and I began to reform my character. Those who believe that they will be judged by their conduct on this earth in the hereafter will lead their lives differently to those who only believe in the present life. Had this inner transformation not taken place I would have continued to live a pleasure-seeking existence. I had everything I needed and with a few months of cricket-related work like commentary or journalism I could earn enough money to live a life of complete leisure for the rest of the year. I had always led a self-centred life. I had a handful of friends in Pakistan and England and made no effort to meet new people and enlarge the circle of people I mixed with. Being shy I found it difficult to open up with those I did not know very well. My bachelor life suited me well as not only did it give me a self-contained way of life without any responsibilities but it also fitted in well with my hedonistic philosophy. I had no desire to have children as they did not fit in with the way I wanted to live. Most of my married friends had struggled with their marriages, not spent enough time with their children and had ended up going through really ugly divorces. My future plans had always been based around how I could maximize this existence: winter months to be spent in Pakistan with family and friends and partridge shooting; the months of June and July in London for the hectic peak of the social season, as well as Lord's test matches and Wimbledon. Then in August I would be back in Pakistan for travelling in the Karakoram. However, as my faith grew stronger I began to feel that I had a responsibility to the society I was living in. I found that there were greater goals in life than material and sensual pleasures. I also started to become aware of the fact that the Almighty had been extremely kind to me. I used to always think of all those things that I did not have, but now I realized I had been blessed with so much and needed to give something back.

I was heavily influenced by the Quranic injunction 'Keep the money you need and give the rest away.' It took me quite a long time to understand this, yet within it lies the key to human contentment. Most people cannot distinguish between wants and needs because wants can be limitless. I would see cricketers I had played with – some of whom came from very humble backgrounds – striving to make more and more money even after they left the sport. I realized that it was out of insecurity. For a sportsman in particular there is usually only a limited time in which one can make a lot of money. These people were caught in a never-ending race where no amount of money was ever going to be enough. It is the same with Pakistan's ruling elite. Some of our politicians are dollar billionaires yet there is still no end to their greed. What I realized whilst raising funds for the hospital was that the unhappiest people are those whose goals are entirely material. The people who had donated the most were also the ones who were spiritual and seemed most content. In the same vein, the greatest scenes of happiness and contentment I had ever seen were in the villages and homes of rural communities of Pakistan. I have long since believed that the people who are richest are the people who cannot be bought, for any price.

The forefathers of many Pakistanis in Sindh and Punjab were Hindus and before Partition the area that is now Pakistan was a more religiously diverse society, with communities of Muslims, Sikhs, Christians and Hindus living side by side. Now it is about 95–97 per cent Muslim. But there is an especially strong Hindu influence in Sindh, still home to the majority of Pakistan's Hindus. There is an acceptance of life's lot as a part of the journey in Hinduism, as part of karma, so in Sindh a peasant typically accepts this, despite being treated almost as a slave by some Sindhi landlords. In parts of Pakistan, especially Sindh, a sense of Hindu fatalism lingers amongst the peasants. Contrary to the impression some Westerners form from the frequent use of the word 'inshallah' (by the will of God) in the Muslim world, fatalism is not part of Islam. You learn to accept what is past, but you retain control of your future. Iqbal ardently believed that human beings were the makers of their own destiny and that the key to destiny lay in one's character. 'Your *Khudi* elevate to such a height that ere each Judgment, / God Himself asks of His creature, "What is your desire?"' he wrote in one of his best-known couplets: '*Khudi ko kar buland itnaa, kay hur taqdeer say pehlay, / Khuda banday say khud poochay buta tayree raza kya hay?*'

In other words, we are masters of our own destiny. The goal of Iqbal's philosophy was not only personal but also social transformation, inspired by the Quranic proclamation, 'Toward God is your limit' (Surah 53: *An-Najm*: 42).

Like many people I used to torment myself with regrets, obsessing about my mistakes in cricket, racking my brain about what I could have done differently. With faith I learned to let go of what had already happened, something I've been able to do at two different and very painful times in my life, after the death of my mother and then again following my divorce. The Quran states that those who believe in God will be blessed and protected by God: 'Surely those who believe, and those who are Jews, and the Christians, and the Sabians, whoever believes in Allah and the Last day and does good, they shall have their reward from their Lord, and *there is no fear for them, nor shall they grieve.'*

And indeed the greatest blessing faith gave me was that it liberated me from my fears: fear of failure, fear of death, fear of losing my livelihood, fear of being humiliated by others. 'Don't fight destiny, because Destiny is God,' said the Prophet (PBUH). This text means the past is only to learn from and not to live in, and that the future is to be looked forward to and not feared. You try your best in the given circumstances; whatever happens after that, you accept as the will of God and come to terms with it.

Because my profession, rather like that of actors and models, depended so much upon my youth I used to worry about both ageing and dying. What was I going to do after cricket? But I came to realize that your livelihood, your health and the time of your death were in God's hands. This was all of great help to me during the last two years of my sports career. It is very difficult to play professional cricket well if you are not playing all the time. I was only participating in international cricket by that time to help raise funds for the hospital. So it was hard to keep my skills honed and I was past my prime. And yet I had more acknowledgement and respect in the last two years of my career than before. I only managed to overcome injury and play in the 1992 World Cup because I had lost my fear of failure and leaving cricket in humiliation. In the past I would never have risked playing in such a high-profile tournament so injured and so out of form. As the Quran says, 'If anyone puts his trust in Allah, sufficient is He for him.' Within me grew the innate confidence of knowing that respect and humiliation are in God's hands. I used to be so sensitive to criticism; I'd fight with people if I thought they were rude to me, I'd never speak to a journalist again if they wrote something negative about me – a couple of times I'd even slapped one when they were rude to me in public. I masked my shyness with aggression. But my belief in God made me become immune to ridicule. According to the Quran, no human being can humiliate another decent human being. The Greek scholar Socrates, when he was sentenced to death, said more or less the same thing, 'No evil can happen to a good man, neither in life nor after death.'

I was always a risk-taker and faith enhanced that. Fear is the biggest impediment to a human being achieving their potential and dreams. During my cricketing career a lot of talented cricketers never realized their potential because of the fear of failure. Less talented players got far better results simply because of a positive attitude. Some hugely talented batsmen could not do justice to themselves because they were physically scared of getting hit by fast bowlers. In fact, in all aspects of life fearlessness is an essential quality for success. A soldier who is scared of dying is unlikely to win any medals. A businessman who does not take risks is unlikely to succeed. A leader who lacks courage can never command respect and hence never inspire his team. Most crucially, a leader needs courage to take the big decisions, and big decisions always carry big risks. The difference between a good leader and a bad one is that the former takes huge risks while fully grasping the consequences of failure, while the latter takes risks without a proper assessment of the pitfalls. Successful people never make decisions based on fear. Leaders of a country shaping policies out of fear of losing power have always proved to be disastrous. Great leaders always have the ability to resist pressure and make policies according to their vision, rather than fear. As Iqbal said, the punishment for the crime of cowardice is death: *'Taqdeer kay qaazee ka yeh fatwa hay azal say, / Hay jurm-e-za-eefee ki sazaa murg-e-mafajaat.'*

Once you learn to overcome your fears, your life transforms because fearlessness breeds idealism. On the other hand, so often have I seen materialism forcing people to be more pragmatic. I am not of course saying that people should not be aware of their limitations. In cricket the first thing I feared was that one could not be successful unless one played within one's limitations at a given point in time, but one should always strive to overcome them. I have always been something of an idealist, never content to accept my apparent limits. When I was just starting out at international level at cricket, I was so inspired in 1972 by watching a fast bowler for the first time – Dennis Lillee – that my ambition became to emulate him. The senior players and my coach at Worcestershire insisted I had neither the physique nor the bowling action to become a fast bowler and that if I tried to change I could ruin my career. It was idealism that dared me to take risks. Not only did I completely remodel my bowling action to become a fast bowler, but my body also became stronger for me to bowl fast. (No one in international cricket has completely changed their bowling action as I did.) As Iqbal says, 'Gabriel told me at the beginning of time, Do not accept the heart that is enslaved by reason.' Had Sir Edmund Hillary been a slave to reason, he would never have climbed Mount Everest.

Lastly, faith helps you to control your material desires and steels your will. This is part of the inner jihad – the battle between soul and body. I used to consider fasting to be a ritual that was inconvenient and a hindrance to my routine. I would not fast if I was in training as I would be worried about getting dehydrated. After retiring from cricket I decided to try and stick to my daily routine (including exercising) during Ramadan. By the end of the month of fasting I felt I had much more endurance and stamina and felt physically cleansed. Much more significantly it made me realize just how powerful the human will really is. The more you exercise it the stronger it gets. Fasting, if done in the right spirit, can be of immense value. There are a lot of Muslims who destroy Ramadan's value by sleeping during the day and staying up eating all night. During the long, difficult years I was building the cancer hospital, praying became to me more than a meaningless ritual. I found that prayers were the best way to relieve stress – provided one prayed with the knowledge that there was a God and He was listening. Previously the only way I would fight stress was by exercising. I remember so many times coming out of the hospital's board meetings, weighed down by some new crisis we were facing. Since the entire burden of fund collection was on my shoulders I would always assure the senior staff at the hospital not to worry as I did not want to demoralize them. Then I would head straight to the beautiful mosque in our hospital and pray for help. I always felt relaxed afterwards. Soon praying five times a day became a need rather than a duty.

I never took for granted the knowledge I'd gained from being placed on the path by Mian Bahir, as I know from my own experience that it can be argued that just because someone has an extra sense or an ability to predict the future, it doesn't prove that there is a God. After all, some psychics and clairvoyants can get quite a few things right about the future. But never, in the almost twenty years that I knew Mian Bashir, were one of his prophecies ever wrong. Like most people brought up in the West, my ex-wife Jemima was also quite sceptical about this talent. When she first met him he asked her to write down three things she wanted more than anything in her life. He left her completely awestruck when without even looking at the piece of paper (he could not read English in any case) he told her exactly what her three wishes were.

All the truly great people in history – Jinnah, Gandhi, Mother Teresa, Nelson Mandela – have had a vision and ambition beyond themselves, often achieving more than others not because of more talent but because they had bigger ambitions and selfless dreams. The idea of constantly striving towards ever higher goals struck a chord with me, dovetailing with my own philosophy that I had developed through sport – the more you challenge yourself, the more you discover greater reserves of strength within you. The moment you relax and stop pushing yourself is the moment you start going downhill. I first strove to play cricket for Pakistan, then my goal became to be my country's best all-rounder, then the best

Top left: A moment of family pride: my grandfather, Ahmad Hasan Khan (*second from right*) hosting Jinnah in Julunder, India, 1946.

Below left: With my grand-mother, who lived to be one hundred, Lahore, 1982.

Below right: With my mother and father in Lahore.

Above left: With my sister Rubina, aged one and a half, Lahore, 1958.

Above right: With my sisters Noreen and Rubina, Lahore.

Right: My family home in Zaman Park, Lahore.

Left: A drawing of Allama Muhammad Iqbal, whose words constantly inspire me.

Below: Nehru (*left*) and Jinnah (*right*) sit on either side of Lord Mountbatten and his councillor Lord Ismay, discussing the British exit from India and the partition of the sub-continent into two separate nations.

Bottom: Partition was a 'massive exercise in human misery', with thousands dying on both sides. Here packed trains are transporting Muslims north to Pakistan.

Left: During my youth the smouldering tension with India over Kashmir occasionally burst into open war. This Indian jeep was recovered just outside Lahore after I'd been evacuated from the city, even though – aged thirteen – I'd been ready to fight.

Below, clockwise from top left: Pakistan's leaders: President Ayub Khan (1958–69); President Yahya Khan (1969–71); President Zia (1978–88), who had overthrown the civilian leadership of Zulfikar Ali Bhutto (1971–3).

Above: Afghan refugees escaping the fighting in their country in 1983, during the years of occupation by Soviet forces. Pakistan provided a home for them.

Main picture: The Hunza valley, a stunningly beautiful place far to the north of the country. I always felt at peace in the mountains.

Below: With Sir Jimmy Goldsmith and my friend and host Fareedullah Khan, former senator, who was the Malik of his Waziri clan in South Waziristan. He was assassinated by the Taliban in 2005.

Above: The tribal areas on Pakistan's northern border are places where I always felt welcomed. Everyone was armed – even the young boys.

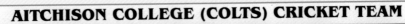

AITCHISON COLLEGE (COLTS) CRICKET TEAM

Above: Aitchison College cricket team in 1964. I'm seated second from the left.

Left: Playing cricket for Pakistan at Lord's in 1971; I am introduced to Her Majesty the Queen.

Below: Captain of the team in Oxford in 1974.

Above: Bowling for Pakistan against England, Edgbaston, 1982.

Above right: At Lord's in 1987 for a Rest of the World XI against England.

Right and below: After some testing games, during which even Pakistanis doubted we could win, Pakistan triumphed at the 1992 World Cup in Australia. I played the whole tournament with a ruptured cartilage in my shoulder.

Above: Nawaz Sharif, twice prime minister of Pakistan, pictured here in the 1990 election campaign, which he won.

Left: Benazir Bhutto, also twice prime minister of Pakistan. She returned to the country, assured of her safety, but was assassinated in 2007. I'd known her since we were together at Oxford University.

Below: With President Pervez Musharraf in 2002 when he visited the Shaukat Khanum Memorial Hospital, before our parting of the ways.

fast bowler. From there I wanted to become the best all-rounder and the best fast bowler in the world. When I was made captain the ambition became turning the team into the best in the world. And once the cancer hospital I founded in memory of my mother became a success I set about building two more hospitals, one in Karachi and one in Peshawar. Now my challenge in life is to bring about a socio-economic revolution in Pakistan. I am also building a knowledge city on the pattern of Oxford University in Mianwali, the first private-sector university in the rural areas of Pakistan. After one goal has been achieved, there are always more to conquer. As Iqbal says: 'Other worlds exist beyond the Stars / More tests of love are still to come.'

My ex-wife Jemima used to ask me how long I would keep pursuing politics without succeeding, at what point would I decide it was futile. But I couldn't answer, simply because a dream has no time frame. It does not matter what your education or social background is, you can only fulfil your human potential if you never give up on the pursuit of your dreams. Human contentment is connected to knowing the purpose of one's existence. When one is pursuing one's dreams, even when one is going through outer turbulence, there is always inner peace. During the last decade I went through some of the most painful and difficult phases in my life, but I always slept well, confident within myself that the resistance I was facing was to strengthen me to achieve my goals.

Faith answered two of the most important questions, which had always nagged me. Questions that science could never answer. What is the purpose of existence? What happens to us after we die?

Chapter Four

Our Failed Democracy, 1988–1993

A S THE COUNTRY CONTINUED ITS DOWNWARD TRAJECTORY IN the 1980s and 1990s, crippled by its own leadership regardless of dictatorship or democracy, about the only thing we still did well was play cricket, hockey and squash. My one contribution to restoring some of our battered national self-esteem was to lead our team in winning the World Cup in 1992. While I think the lowest point for the country's morale was when we lost East Pakistan, the highest was winning the World Cup. It was perhaps the last time Pakistan was united as everyone joined together to celebrate. When we arrived back in Lahore with the trophy, people lined the streets for miles. Watching the sheer joy on their faces gave me a tremendous feeling of satisfaction. I led the country to victory on the cricket field, but had yet to feel the need to mirror that leadership in politics.

In July 1988 while I was playing for Sussex and living in London, I got an unusual call from Pakistan. It was my friend Ashraf Nawabi, who was close to Zia. He asked if I would

become a minister in the general's cabinet. Zia had just dismissed the elected government of Muhammad Khan Junejo,
who was probably the most decent prime minister Pakistan
had ever had. Junejo was from Sindh province, and Zia had
assumed that he would be very pliable and docile. But Junejo
made the mistake of trying to assert himself, including on the
issue of Zia's refusal to sign the Geneva Accords that would
end the Soviet war in Afghanistan. He also tried to introduce
an austerity campaign. Unlike many of Pakistan's rulers, who
seem to want to live in the grandeur of Mughal emperors,
Junejo led by example, driving a Pakistani-made Suzuki in an
attempt to encourage cabinet members and the military to
ditch their luxury imported cars. Nawabi's offer took me completely by surprise. I declined it politely, saying that I was not
qualified for the job. A day later Dr Anwar ul-Haq, Zia's
younger son, called me up and urged me to join the government for the sake of the country. He said his father was sick
of corrupt politicians who were only in politics to further their
personal interests. People of integrity like me were needed in
the cabinet, he said. This seemed rather ironic given that Zia
had done so much damage to democracy and rule of law in
Pakistan, particularly with his non-party-based elections. I
was flattered but again declined.

Shortly after that phone call, Zia died, killed, along with the
top ranks of his army and the serving American ambassador
to Pakistan, in a mysterious plane crash. I was in the south of
France on holiday when I heard. It was quite a shock. Almost
as much as with Bhutto. The cause of the accident remains
a mystery but there are plenty of conspiracy theories. In
Pakistan there was a suspicion that the CIA had a hand in it,

that Zia was bumped off the moment he moved away from Washington's script and no longer served its purpose. After his death there was the same feeling as, years later, after Musharraf left – euphoria that we would be free again from dictatorship, corruption and media suppression to resume our journey towards true democracy. The election three months later of Zulfikar Ali Bhutto's daughter Benazir as prime minister, the first open elections in a decade, ushered in a new period. Like all Pakistanis I had great expectations of her. With her understanding of Western democratic societies and her education at Oxford and Harvard, she was ideally placed to bring in a new era for our country. She was well off and didn't need the money that came with power – or so we thought. She had everything going for her. She was popular in Pakistan and one of the best-known Muslim faces in the West. In fact the Western media was totally enamoured of her – the glamorous daughter of a charismatic democratic leader who had been hanged by a military dictator, and, to top it all, the first female prime minister of a Muslim state. In front of the Western media, Benazir played the role of being the exotic 'daughter of the East' to perfection.

Of course there was an early warning sign even before she came to power. Her greatest betrayal was of the thousands of people who worked for the party founded by her father, the PPP, who had endured years in jail striving for democracy during Zia's martial law, in completely abandoning the mission statement of the People's Party, of having a 'just and egalitarian society and having social justice' – all that was cast off. She further made a mockery of democracy by competing with Nawaz Sharif, then chief minister of the Punjab and later to be her successor as prime minister, to buy off independent MPs. In the absence of ideology, politicians were auctioned and independents were bombarded with lucrative offers for them and their families. The term 'Changa Manga' politics or culture in Pakistan stems from Sharif paying off and then literally locking up a group of provincial MPs in an isolated rest house in the forest of Changa Manga outside Lahore so that the PPP could not make them a counter-offer.

It was not long before all of us were disappointed by Benazir. She began to behave more like an empress than a democratically elected prime minister. After her death William Dalrymple described finding her 'majestic, even imperial' on interviewing her when she was prime minister. 'She walked and talked in a deliberately measured and regal manner and frequently used the royal "we",' he noted. I have to say that these imperial traits were already evident when she was young. The first time I met her she was tearing a man to shreds for daring to question her socialist credentials. As a student at Oxford I shared a house with Zia Malik, the brother of the actor Art Malik. One day I came home and could hear a woman's voice arguing as I locked up my bike outside the house. Zia had invited some of the other Pakistanis at Oxford round to meet Benazir. However, he had managed to enrage the guest of honour by complaining that effective land reforms had not been implemented in Sindh. It was obviously a sensitive topic for Benazir, as her father had made a token attempt to undermine the power of the feudal landlords with some limited land reform in 1972. I tried to calm Benazir down and after that initial meeting we became good friends. She had a reputation for being polite to the

English and imperious with fellow Pakistanis. I remember seeing her at a reception in 1974 held by the Pakistani embassy in the Netherlands in honour of the visiting Pakistan cricket team. Aged only about twenty, she was ordering the ambassador around as if he was her personal servant. To the bemusement of me and the rest of the team, the poor man was scurrying round moving chairs and tables for her.

It was also quite obvious that Benazir was ambitious from a young age. She stayed on at Oxford for an extra year after I left and I always presumed it was because she was so determined to become president of the Oxford Union. Benazir's problem, though, was that her first ever job was being prime minister. And she only became prime minister because she was her father's daughter (just as her son Bilawal became chairman of the PPP at the age of nineteen because he is his mother's son). Benazir had struggled, spending six months in jail and several years in and out of house arrest, but she had not had to fight her way to the top of her party, nor spend years in the political frontline, fighting her party's cause. That is not to underestimate the suffering that years of confinement must have caused such a young woman, but it is not preparation for leading a country. How on earth can you run a country when your first job is to be prime minister? She had not been tested by the rigours of the journey towards leadership, nor developed a vision or ideology, nor learned about management or institution building. To become a general in the army, or a chief executive of a company, there is a long process of acquiring skills and accumulating responsibilities. Family dynasties in politics inevitably lead to incompetent leadership and decay. Their dominance of South Asian politics is precisely why true democracy has foundered in the region. A meritocratic system is vital for democracy. In some ways dynastic politics is even worse than a monarchical system. At least with a monarchy a prince or princess is given a grounding in the art of leadership. Bilawal Bhutto, a young man who has spent half his life outside Pakistan, is far less equipped to lead than, for example, the UK's Prince Charles.

If Benazir was woefully inexperienced for the job, she was also unfortunate in her choice of husband, Asif Ali Zardari. The son of a feudal family, he had achieved little in life off the polo field. In her defence, Benazir's position did not make it easy for her to find a decent husband. By the time she came to marry, at the age of thirty-four, she was already considered old by Pakistani bride standards. Besides, her family was hounded by the Zia regime, so people were terrified of associating with them. It is very dangerous to be on the wrong side of politics in Pakistan. It was therefore difficult for her to meet normal people. I introduced her to a cousin, Qamar Khan, at one point and they thought about marriage but then Al-Zulfiqar, the organization set up by her brothers to avenge their father's execution, hijacked a Pakistan International Airlines flight in 1981 and she was thrown back in jail. By the time she emerged, Qamar Khan had married a wife chosen by his family. So she ended up with Zardari, whom she loved so much that she gave him free rein to use his position to amass as much power and money as possible. He treated Pakistan as his personal estate and considered it his feudal right to abuse power and take commissions on government contracts (with estates in France and – though now sold – in Surrey, it was clear where the money was going). Soon he was known as

Mr Ten Percent, although from my one and only meeting with him I can say his price was double that.

The construction of the hospital, about which more later, gave me an insight into the way he worked. In 1989, I went to Benazir's home, Bilawal House, in Karachi to ask for assistance in raising funds for the hospital. Since I was trying to help compensate for the lack of social services provided by the government, I thought I would get help in kick-starting the project. She was busy, so we were given an audience with Zardari. Since I had been friendly with Benazir at Oxford, I expected a sympathetic hearing. He was charming and extremely flattering towards me. However, he offered no help, and instead spent most of the time talking to my friend Tariq Shafi. Tariq comes from one of Pakistan's most powerful textile-industrialist families and Zardari asked him to set up a couple of factories in Sindh, PPP's stronghold, saying he needed to provide some employment in the province. He suggested that if 20 per cent of the shares in the business were given to him, he would remove all 'bureaucratic hurdles' and help obtain loans from the nationalized banks. Needless to say, no help on the hospital was ever forthcoming, either from Benazir or her husband.

So imagine my surprise five years later when a week before the opening of the hospital I had an unexpected visit from an old friend called Navaid Malik, whom I had not seen for years. Bhutto was at that point in her second term of office, after being dismissed in 1990 on charges of corruption and incompetence and then voted in again in 1993. Navaid brought a message from her and Zardari saying they wanted to honour our hospital by cutting the ribbon. Although the hospital had already started operating on a small scale, we had set the official opening date for 29 December 1994 and had decided that the ribbon would be cut by our first cancer patient, a ten-year-old girl from a poor family called Sumera Yousaf. Ordinarily it would be flattering for any institution to have the prime minister opening it, but of course I refused. I was later to learn the cost of snubbing the royal couple's request. Benazir had become quite unpopular because of corruption scandals surrounding her husband and had presumably wanted to cash in on the euphoria in the country surrounding the opening of the hospital. Besides, my recent six-week campaign around Pakistan to raise money for the project had been seen by her and Zardari as politically threatening. The trip had in fact been a little like an election campaign, with thousands of ordinary Pakistanis turning out on to the streets to give me money. Some of them asked me to come into politics as they made their donations; and for the first time the media started talking about my entering the political fray.

In between Benazir's two terms in office, Nawaz Sharif had come into power. After two years of her and Zardari, people thought he could only be an improvement. However, rather than building up the country, he expanded his own industrial empire. It grew at a phenomenal rate under government patronage – a staggering 4,000 per cent from 1985 to 1992. He was just as corrupt as Benazir and Zardari; he simply went about it in a different way. He perfected the art of buying politicians. When I first met Sharif in the late 1970s at a cricket club, he seemed like a regular guy with little drive or ambition, more interested in cricket than politics. I think his real dream would have been to be captain of the Pakistani cricket team. He just loved the glamour of the sport.

An incident happened in autumn 1987 which illustrates Sharif's mindset. Just before the World Cup in October 1987, when I was captaining Pakistan, we played a warm-up match against the West Indies at the Gaddafi stadium in Lahore. Moments before the match, the secretary of the cricket board, Shahid Rafi, informed me that the Chief Minister of Punjab, Nawaz Sharif, was going to captain the team that day. I was taken aback but then assumed that he would have a non-playing role and wanted to watch the match from the dressing-room. Therefore I was shocked to see him walk out to toss the coin with Viv Richards, the West Indian captain, dressed in his cricket whites; but there was a bigger shock to come. He won the toss, and returned to the dressing-room and started putting on his pads. None of the team could believe what we were seeing; he was going to open the innings with Mudassar Nazar against the West Indies, one of the greatest fast-bowling attacks in cricket history. Nazar wore batting pads, a thigh pad, chest pad, an arm guard, a helmet and reinforced batting gloves, while Sharif simply had his batting pads, a floppy hat – and a smile.

For those who are not conversant with cricket history, it is important to know that this was a fast-bowling attack not seen before or since in the cricketing world, such was the West Indies' blistering pace, with four bowlers bowling above 90 mph. It was the sort of attack that had destroyed the careers of many a talented batsman; international batsmen, professional cricketers, who would have sleepless nights when they were due to face the West Indies. And here was Nawaz Sharif, who had no experience of playing at this level of cricket, walking out, unprotected, to face this deadly attack. Clearly he would not have the reflexes to defend himself if a short ball was aimed at his body, so there was a risk of a serious injury. I quickly inquired if there was an ambulance ready.

As we watched the first ball – by a 6ft 6 inch West Indian fast bowler – hit the wicketkeeper's gloves even before Sharif could lift his bat, the team sighed with relief that it wasn't straight. Mercifully for Sharif, the second ball was straight at the stumps, and before he could move his stumps lay shattered.

For those who don't understand cricket, Sharif was trying the equivalent in academic terms of a child, having just finished primary school, attempting to write a PhD thesis. When I was a schoolboy I indulged in a daydream; that I would be at a test match, the team would discover they were a player short, I would put up my hand and be brought on to suddenly become a hero. This seemed to be Sharif's dream too, as if he could by-pass the whole process of working your way up the ladder and become a hero. It was only when I started growing up, as a teenager, that I learned there are no shortcuts to achieving big dreams, there is a whole struggle a person has to go through to reach the top in any profession. Here we are talking about the chief minister of the biggest province of Pakistan having such fantasies.

Sharif had been forced into politics by his father, who wanted to protect his business interests. Sharif had a similar handicap to Benazir, in that he was given power without ever having earned it the hard way. Through his complete loyalty and subservience to Zia, rather than experience, he proceeded quickly through the ranks of the Punjab government, progressing from finance minister to chief minister in 1985. Military dictators always look for pliable politicians and he fitted the bill perfectly. Sharif appeared to view public office not as a responsibility but as a means to get rich and once he became prime minister in 1990 many of the family assets were acquired through loans from nationalized banks that have never been paid off. The Pakistani press soon started to print allegations that senior politicians were trying to bully banks into giving them multi-million-dollar loans. Under Sharif's government, the culture of 'lifafa journalism' also sprang up – a *lifafa* is a packet, or bribe. Journalists were bought off with cash while politicians were bribed with plots of government-owned land. Sharif, like Zardari, is rumoured to be one of the richest men in Pakistan. He was dismissed amid charges of corruption after three years, only to be replaced by Bhutto in her second term. He returned to power for his second term in 1997 after Bhutto was again forced to step down – the merry-go-round of corrupt government was as dizzying to the public as to the politicians themselves. Zardari's political life is an indication of how Pakistan's political system worked; when Benazir's government was dismissed in 1990, he went straight from the PM's house to jail. When she came back into power in 1993, he went straight from jail to the prime minister's house; and in 1996 he went from there back to jail. The moment he came back into power, all charges were dropped; our justice system could only act against those out of power. In power, the justice system became part of the executive.

Every time Benazir or Sharif came back, one hoped that maybe they might have learned something in opposition or in exile, but to no avail. Like most people, I watched the descent of our country into corruption and lawlessness with dismay. It was in the 1990s that Pakistanis really started to lose hope in the country and there was a great brain drain as the country plunged into semi-anarchy. More or less every institution was destroyed. Corruption permeated down from the prime minister to government ministers to members of parliament, the bureaucracy, the judiciary and the police, into every stratum of society. When the Punjab inspector general of police Abbas Khan was asked by the Lahore High Court in the 1990s why the city's police were so corrupt, he reported that 25,000 policemen had *not* been recruited on merit and amongst them were known criminals. He blamed the situation on Nawaz Sharif's Punjab government. In Sindh, the PPP and MQM (Muttahida Qaumi Movement, the United National Movement) governments had done exactly the same, filling the police up with their party cadres, even though some of them had a criminal past. This destruction of our police system was done at the cost of law and order in Pakistan and it was deliberate because the police typically play a major role in manipulating the elections and intimidating the opposition. The whole moral fabric of the country began to fall apart. In 1996 Transparency International (an NGO that rates political corruption in an annual index) rated Pakistan to be the second most corrupt country out of fifty-eight. The economy fared no better. Unemployment coupled with inflation (due mainly to indirect taxes) forced people to turn to crime. The drug mafia boomed. During the 1990s economic growth, exports, revenues and development spending slipped while poverty levels rose. Economic sanctions slapped on the country following Pakistan's first nuclear test in 1998 only added to our woes.

What pained me in particular was the environmental and cultural destruction. For me, the beauty of Pakistan was never in our cities, it was in the mountains and the wilderness. In the UK the environmental movement had got into full swing by the 1980s while in Pakistan we were destroying everything worth preserving without any concern for future generations. I could not bear watching our forests decimated, our rivers polluted, historical monuments destroyed and above all our wildlife disappearing. Our tree cover suffered more under democratic governments, because members of the 'timber mafia' would fight elections with money made from cutting forests. 'One of the most powerful and ruthless organizations within Pakistan, the timber mafia engages in illegal logging, estimated to be worth billions of rupees each year,' wrote the British newspaper the *Guardian*. In the summer of 1993 I was driving along the Karakoram Highway and saw timber – the remains of conifers hundreds of years old – lying on either side of the road for around fifty miles. I was so upset about it I wrote an open letter to the caretaker prime minister at the time, Moeen Qureshi, who had taken over after Nawaz Sharif resigned from his first term in office as prime minister. He did take measures to crack down on illegal logging but they didn't last long. The problem is that Pakistan hasn't changed the law since the days of the British – the fine is a few hundred rupees. Pakistan has one of the lowest percentages of forest cover in the world – 2.5 per cent according to a 2009 study by the UN's Food and Agriculture Organization. The deforestation rate stands at 2.1 per cent a year, the highest in Asia. Already limited by an arid or semi-arid climate in parts of the country, our forestry has been further decimated by large-scale deforestation and degradation. Not surprisingly floods are now a problem in many areas as a result. Successive governments have allowed Pakistan to squander both its forests and its water supplies as a growing population competes for dwindling resources. But politicians in Pakistan have no sense of the environment or of aesthetics; most of them are only interested in making a quick buck. They have houses in fancy foreign locations, their wealth is stashed abroad, they educate their children in the UK, Canada or the United States – they have no stake in the nation's future. Every time the government changes in Pakistan there is an exodus of crooked politicians who scuttle away to their safe havens abroad. There they bide their time till the new government has been discredited and then come back to start their looting and plunder again. Nor do they have any knowledge of the Pakistani countryside, rarely venturing beyond the cities. They are ignorant of Pakistan's natural treasures, and yet Islam instructs Muslims to care for the environment.

Amidst the destruction being wrought by our politicians, Pakistan's World Cup win was a much-needed boost for national morale. The irony was that I had never planned to stay in cricket into the 1990s. I had already retired following the 1987 World Cup but a year later General Zia requested my return to the sport on national television. At a dinner organized for the team he took me into another room and warned me about what he was going to do. 'Don't humiliate me by saying no,' he said. 'I am going to ask you to come back for the sake of your country.' Touched by the appeal to my sense of patriotism, I of course had to say yes. The other reason for my return, though, was that I still had an unfulfilled longing to have a last bash at the West Indies. This was one of my great cricketing ambitions – along with winning the World Cup, and beating England and India on their home turf. I wanted to leave on a high and the chance to have another crack at the West Indians came up because Australia cancelled their tour of the West Indies in 1988 and Pakistan was invited instead. The main aim when playing them was to lose with dignity; winning was not even considered an option such was the destructive power of the West Indies juggernaut. But we were the first team in fifteen years to play them on their home turf (with home umpires) and come back with the honours – getting the better of a one-all draw. By the following year, however, I began to cut down on my cricket commitments and seriously concentrate on the hospital project. Then in 1990 Pakistan toured Australia and it was now that I noticed that running around for the hospital and not playing any first-class cricket had taken its toll on my game. I could not perform at the level that was expected of me, especially as a bowler. Yet if I flopped it would have disastrous consequences for my recently begun fundraising campaign. The problem was compounded by the weak team I was leading. A couple of top players had retired and the new ones were not up to the mark. Although we lost the series, I personally had a successful tour and went on to win 'Cricketer of the Year' in Australia as a batsman.

I learned a lot, as the leader of the team. Cricket is the only sport where you need leadership on the pitch; no other sport gives so much of a role to the captain as in cricket, in all other sports it is the coach who is crucial. A leader on the cricket field can raise the performance of an ordinary team, whereas a poor captain can prevent a talented team from fulfilling its potential. A cricket captain, to be leader, has to lead by example – he has to show courage if he wants his team to fight. He has to be selfless if he wants his players to play for the team. He has to have integrity if he wants to command the respect of the team. Above all, in times of crisis, he must have the ability to take the pressure – that's when a team needs the leader most.

People come under pressure when they fear failure, but it is all in the mind. Striding out to the crease, when you can be out first ball (especially when your team is in deep trouble), if you allow yourself to feel fear, you will freeze. The fear of failure clogs the mind with negative thoughts. Even before I walked out, I would be prepared for a crisis so I would not be taken by surprise. I concentrated only on how I was going to build my innings, I would block out any thought of failure. I knew that someone who was afraid would find their hands tensing up, so I would relax my hands, keep my focus on how to organize my innings, and consciously ignore any hint of fear. When as a bowler I was at my fastest, I would watch the body language of an incoming batsman, especially the eyes, as they would reveal any traces of fear. Very rarely did they not succumb. From the middle of my career I became an expert at dealing with pressure.

When I became captain, the great players had left and I had to lead a very inexperienced team; before entering a match, I knew that if I did not perform, the team would not win. It didn't mean I always ensured the team won, but it meant I automatically put myself under pressure. If a captain shows any weakness or buckles under pressure, the team collapses, and I knew that without my performance the team wouldn't succeed. I discovered that the most crucial time for a leader is when there's a crisis, and by constantly playing under pressure, I learned to cope with crises. The West Indies of the 1980s would always target the opposing captain, knowing that the moment the captain collapsed, so would the team. I feel my greatest achievement in my cricket career was that I was the only captain in the 1980s who played three series against the far superior West Indians and who did not lose. Every other team was crushed by them.

When I got back from Australia in 1990 I decided I would give up the sport. I thought it best to leave on a high and I wanted to concentrate on the hospital. I simply could not risk another series and wanted to leave on my own terms rather than putting myself at the mercy of the selectors. Hardly anyone in international cricket, and particularly Pakistani cricket, leaves with dignity. Without officially announcing my retirement, I stopped playing, and spent the next six months working on the hospital and doing the things I had missed most while being on the cricket circuit – trekking in the mountains and shooting partridge. However, when I returned and told the hospital board members about my retirement plan, they were horrified. They all felt there was no way we would be able to collect significant funds for long once I was out of cricket. None of them had any idea about the game; all they noticed was the publicity in the press. I knew nothing would give more pleasure to the cricket-mad Pakistani nation than winning the 1992 World Cup held in Australia, which was at that point more than two years away. I also realized that in order to collect the vast sums of money required by the hospital my only chance lay in doing something dramatic like winning cricket's most high-profile tournament. So I started preparing a year in advance – meticulously planning the team I would need to execute my strategy. Knowing that it would be the last time I would play international cricket, I put everything into getting as fit as I could despite being thirty-nine and way past my physical prime.

Since I knew that the hospital's future depended upon our World Cup win, before leaving for Australia I told the hospital marketing team to prepare a strategy for fund collection in case we came home with the trophy. This was my fifth World Cup, and my third as captain. It was the only time I told the press that we would return victorious. Unfortunately my plan started going wrong the moment we landed in Australia. Our star one-day batsman Saeed Anwar and our fast bowler Waqar Younus, both key players in my strategy, both match-winners, got injured and were ruled out. (A good team is lucky to have four match-winners.) Then two days before the World Cup was to begin, I ruptured a cartilage in my shoulder. It was only when a Melbourne specialist examined me that I realized the true extent of the injury. He said I had to rest it for at least six weeks. I was shattered. It was a disaster on so many levels. Only a sportsman can understand the utter disappointment and demoralization of getting an injury after all the hard work and training that goes into preparing for a major tournament. I also realized that my not being able to play would have a devastating impact on the morale of my young team. What's more, I had staked the hospital on winning. The manager Intikhab Alam and I decided to keep my injury a secret from the team.

My worst fears were realized when the team did disastrously without me in the two opening matches against the West Indies and England. Although over the years I had become mentally strong by taking on challenges, especially my comeback from the stress fracture in my shinbone, I would never normally have played with such an injury – mainly because I would have been too scared to fail. I would certainly not have played if the team was good enough to win without me. So I began to play by taking cortisone injections to the shoulder as well as oral painkillers. Never had I played in my 21-year career in such a bad way. So serious was my injury that after the tournament it was fully six months before I could lift a glass with my right hand without feeling a shooting pain from my right shoulder to my neck.

Those who remember that World Cup will recollect that mid-way through the competition we were third from the bottom; the bookies rated our chances fifty-to-one. My cousin Javed Burki, who was the chairman of the selection committee as well as my childhood hero, called me up regarding the issue of sending a replacement for another injured player. He seemed to have given up on us from the tone of his voice. I told him we would win. There was silence at the other end. Later he told my sisters that he was convinced I had finally flipped. My closest English friend, Jonathan Mermagen, called me to cheer me up – as a true friend would do in bad times. It was he who broke it to me about the fifty-to-one odds. I begged him to put money on us. He did not share my faith and regrets it to this day. One of my oldest friends, Mobi, advised me not to come back to Pakistan afterwards, telling me to take a holiday in Europe for a while to let the country cool down; such was the growing hostility against me. I'm afraid every top sportsman has to accept this – the greater the public expectations, the greater the public disappointment. In the beginning when I failed to perform to the crowd's expectations I would feel self-pity and hurt when I was criticized but with time I became resigned to the roller-coaster that is sporting fame.

In Perth the Pakistani ambassador had a dinner for the team. It was more like a funeral wake. I gave a speech and told them that I had no doubt we would win. I can still picture the look of complete bewilderment and bemusement on people's faces as I said it. I concluded by saying that hopelessness was a sin in Islam, because it meant one had no faith in Allah. This was widely reported in the Pakistani press and ridiculed. Meanwhile I received bad news from my sister Aleema, who was managing the hospital's marketing campaign. Fundraising had virtually collapsed because of the team's poor performance and the press had made me the scapegoat. Nevertheless I told her to prepare for a renewed campaign once we came home with the cup. Unfortunately she did not take this suggestion seriously either and nothing had been prepared when we returned to Pakistan victorious. My complete belief that we would win boosted the team's confidence and helped prevent it from falling apart. At times of crisis the entire team will look to the captain, but they do not so much pay attention to what he says as to whether he believes in what he is saying. They watch his body language rather than listen to his speeches. My conviction gave me the right body language. It helped too that in the previous three years we had won many times from impossible situations. (In

1989, we had won the Nehru Cup in India, after being on the brink of elimination mid-way through the competition. We won the final in Calcutta in front of 100,000 Indians who were egging on the West Indians to win.) We were also lucky in the World Cup when on two occasions rain was forecast while we were batting second. It only had to rain on one of those occasions for ten minutes and it would have been all over for us. In that tournament the laws were such that a team batting second had no chance of winning if the match was interrupted by rain. In the semi-final in Auckland, the clouds came but it did not rain. From the mid-way point we came from behind and went on to win. Twenty minutes after the match finished it started to rain, and it rained for the next 24 hours.

My love affair with cricket had been over since 1987; after that I had played only for the hospital. So happy was I for this dream of mine that at the presentation ceremony after the game, I forgot to thank the team for their brilliant performance. I was criticized for it and I must confess the speech was terrible; thinking about it still makes me cringe. But quite frankly I had other things on my mind than making a speech. It also has to be said that I was the kind of person who had trouble speaking to a small room of people and suddenly a microphone was thrust in my face without warning and I was expected to address a crowd of 90,000 people and hundreds of millions of television viewers around the world.

However, something bizarre happened after the World Cup. For some reason several players in my team began to think that the money the ecstatic Pakistani public would shower on them for winning the tournament would somehow be diverted by me to the cancer hospital. I am still puzzled about how they came to this conclusion. When we stopped in Singapore on the way home from Australia, the Pakistani ambassador presented me with some money for the hospital. I guess that might have sparked off this idea, and that the team might have thought this money should go to them. Then when we returned to Pakistan, the traders of Lahore threw a function in the city's Shalimar Gardens in our honour. In the beautiful setting of the formal gardens, built by the Mughal emperor in the mid-seventeenth century, they announced they too had raised some contributions for the hospital. To my amazement the rest of the team walked out of the party in protest. I had had several great shocks in my life by that point: my mother's death; hearing about the massacres in East Pakistan from Ashraful Haque; breaking my leg at the peak of my career. But learning that players I had hand-picked and nurtured could think I would divert their winnings took me by complete surprise. It disappointed me intensely. Awards were always divided up evenly. If you were 'Man of the Match', the winnings were shared amongst the team – for ten or eleven years I had been 'Man of the Series' almost every series and I had always shared everything. Most of the team were later to apologize for their behaviour; a few of them said they had been misled and they all blamed each other. I can't help feeling that the seeds of greed were sown after the 1992 World Cup. Altogether the winnings were 90,000 pounds each. No Pakistani cricketers had ever made so much money. The team that I left in 1992 was the best team in world cricket and should have dominated the sport for the next decade, and they were the favourites to win the next two World Cups of 1996 and 1999 but that team never lived up to its potential. From

1993 this great team was dogged by match-fixing allegations, culminating in the ultimate disgrace of sport-fixing in 2010.

The three tours where I was tested the most as a captain were India in 1987, the West Indies in 1988 and the 1992 World Cup. India was hard because the tour was played there, with Indian umpires, with a Pakistan team on paper inferior to the Indians especially under home conditions; losing to India, as far as the people of Pakistan were concerned, was not an option. When the two play it ceases to be a game and turns into a highly pressurized contest, putting the sort of pressure on players that they don't feel in any other series. When we had lost in India in 1979, our captain was a broken man and retired from cricket. In the West Indies in 1988, we were facing one of the greatest teams in history; one sign of weakness and we would have collapsed. To go to their home ground, to play against them with home umpires, and to come away with a draw was my greatest triumph. No team had achieved that in the past decade. And the 1992 World Cup matches were completely about holding your nerve. Captaining the team developed in me the ability to take pressure, to hold my nerve in a crisis, and nowhere could I have had such training as on the cricket field. It was to prove immensely valuable to me later in my life.

(It was the same when I set up the political party, or took on building the cancer hospital; they needed leadership, the hospital project lurched from crisis to crisis, and the party has been in opposition for fifteen years – no other Pakistani party has done so and survived.)

I was under pressure from the British Pakistani community to tour England a month after the World Cup and they were promising to raise huge funds for the hospital. I was considering it, even though by this stage I had played twenty-one years of international cricket and was desperate to move on. Mercifully, the players' walkout in Shalimar Gardens made it easier for me to make the decision and I finally cut my links with the sport, closing that chapter of my life. I moved on quickly, plunging myself into my next great challenge. The hospital now needed all my time. I donated my entire prize money to the project and the win gave the fundraising efforts a huge boost. I was able to collect 140 million rupees during the six weeks after the World Cup, whereas in the first one and a half years of campaigning we had collected only 10 million rupees. It was not till 1994 that I had to worry about cash flow for the project again.

My cricket career might have been over, but politics was still beckoning. In the summer of 1993, I was asked to be a cabinet minister in the caretaker government of Moeen Qureshi that had been formed following the dismissal of Nawaz Sharif's government by President Ghulam Ishaq Khan. Qureshi himself called me. Again I declined. However, by now I was thinking about how I could make some kind of political contribution. At this point most Pakistanis were pretty concerned at the rapid downward slide of the country caused by the avarice and sheer incompetence of our politicians. Both Bhutto and Sharif had been in power once each and it had become blatantly obvious that their predominant interest was in amassing personal wealth and holding on to office by stifling opposition through any means. Neither had any vision for the country, as clearly manifested by their total lack of interest in investing in human capital. In real terms, spending on education and health nosedived during their eleven years of government despite the fact that, as the Asian Tiger economies have proved, both sectors always go hand in hand with development. At this stage, however, I felt that politics was not suited to either my introverted temperament or my very private way of life. Therefore rather than think of coming into politics myself I began to look for people I could support who would be an alternative to Sharif and Benazir. During this period I also started meeting a lot of politically minded people, and held endless discussions on the state of the nation. This was the first time in my life that I had met people outside my small circle of friends and cricketing circles.

Chapter Five

'Angels in Disguise': Building a Hospital, 1984–1995

SPORT IS RUTHLESS. BEFORE MY MOTHER'S DEATH, I WAS NEVER a compassionate person. In cricket, if you do not crush your opponent, he will crush you. I gave no quarter and asked for none. You cannot become one of the top sportsmen in your country without having a ruthless killer instinct. I had the same mindset when I dealt with the underprivileged in our society. Rather than having my pity, they had my contempt. They were poor because they were indolent and unwilling to work hard. Most of our elite classes have this attitude towards the poor, and Western governments have this attitude towards the developing world. My experience founding a hospital overturned these views, teaching me a great deal about both my fellow countrymen and myself. I saw the true potential of ordinary Pakistani people and overcame not just my own prejudices, but also some of my own insecurities. With this, I was drawing closer still to the idea of trying to help Pakistan politically. Besides, in challenging the status quo, and trying to fill a social security void left by a succession of Pakistani leaders, I found myself dragged into politics whether I liked it or not.

When, in 1984, my mother was suffering during the last few weeks of her life, I went to see a doctor in Lahore's Mayo hospital (where I was born) to seek his advice. I was sitting in his waiting room when an old man walked in with a desperate expression on his face. It was etched with pain that I immediately recognized as my own, and had seen on the faces of my father and my sisters for past few months. He was holding a piece of paper in one hand and some medicines in the other. Being unable to read, he gave it to the doctor's assistant and asked him if he had bought all the medication that was needed. The assistant told him there was one missing. 'How much will it cost?' asked the old man. When the assistant quoted the figure a despairing and hopeless expression spread across the man's face, and without another word, he turned and walked out. I asked the assistant what the problem was. He told me that this old Pashtun from Nowshera, a town in Khyber Pakhtunkhwa, had brought in his brother who was dying of cancer. Because there was no bed for the sick man he was lying in the corridor. This man would labour all day on a construction site nearby and look after his brother for the rest of the time. Although the government-run Mayo hospital is supposed to be free, patients have to buy their own medicines.

Having taken my mother for cancer treatment in London, I fully realized how expensive cancer drugs were. Even the cost of the morphine-based painkillers – if they were available at all – was exorbitant. Moreover, cancer treatment could last anything between six months to two years. Now it is possible to die of cancer pain-free, but at the time there was no concept of pain management in Pakistan. Here was I with all my resources and influence, yet I and my family were in such a desperate state – what must this poor man have been going through? I pondered over this during the rest of my mother's illness, and that old Pashtun's despairing face kept appearing before my eyes. One of the first things that had struck me when I took my mother for medical care in England was that she was suffering from what should have been a curable cancer – if it had been diagnosed and treated early enough. It pained me too that we had had to take her out of the country for treatment. Anyone who has been through this experience will understand what an ordeal this is for patients and their loved ones, irrespective of their wealth. Being abroad and far from your family support system – sometimes for months at a time – makes a hard situation harder still. It was then that I resolved to build a cancer hospital where anyone could walk in without having to worry about the cost of treatment and with the rich not having to seek treatment abroad.

However, at this stage I had no idea what it took to build a specialist cancer hospital, let alone in an underdeveloped country. As I began to make enquiries, I discovered that the government of Punjab had tried to build a cancer hospital in the 1980s. Despite all the money that was allocated to it, the plan was eventually abandoned because it was deemed un-feasible – too expensive to build and even more expensive to run. Besides, there were only two to three oncologists in the entire country and they would be reluctant to accept paltry government salaries. A cancer hospital also needed the most expensive equipment. Pakistan did not have enough qualified engineers to fix this equipment if anything went wrong.

For a while I was too busy with my cricket to give the idea any more attention. However, after 1987, I again began to ponder how to go about getting the project off the ground. The more people – especially doctors – that I spoke to, the more they discouraged me. I was having serious doubts at this stage and it is possible that I would have kept postponing the project, when in 1988 a cousin of mine, Qamar Khan, organized a fundraising dinner while I was playing a cricket tournament in Dubai. This was our first one and we collected about $20,000. After that there was no turning back. When I returned to Pakistan I gathered a few people together and formed a trust and a board of governors. Parvez Hassan, a lawyer with a strong background in working for charities, and entrepreneur Razzak Dawood joined the initiative and were to become completely involved. My friends Ashiq Qureshi and Azmat Ali Khan (who tragically later passed away from cancer in the hospital) also came on board. Babar Ali, a well-known businessman from an old Lahore family, lent his name to the project, as did the future finance minister of Pakistan, Shaukat Tarin. My father became chairman of the board.

Then we organized a meeting with twenty of the top doctors in Lahore to guide the board of governors of this trust on how to proceed further. All bar one of these doctors said the project was simply not feasible in Pakistan. One said that it was, but there was no way we would be able to treat the poor for free, the average cost of treating a cancer patient was too high. We were totally demoralized after the meeting. I had no idea how to deal with the situation. I could not get out of the project because not only had I publicly announced it but much more significantly I had already started to collect money. My cousin, the cricketer Javed Burki, suggested I just build a big dispensary in my mother's name and give up on the hospital ideal. My sisters, who were worried about me, suggested I should drop the plan or I would lose all the respect and credibility I had gained from my cricketing career. But it was too late. Even if I wanted to I could not. How could I return people's donations? Just as I was getting desperate, an encouraging meeting with the Pakistani Association of North American doctors spurred me on. Their promise of help encouraged me to cut down on my cricket commitments so I could concentrate on the project. I set up an office given to me for free by a friend, Omar Farooq, and hired our first employee.

Initially I did not work on the hospital out of the kind of passion I had once had for cricket. I had decided to build it for the poor, but my motivation was not out of any great feeling of responsibility towards society. It felt more like an obligation or a mission and stemmed from immense personal pain and the memory of that vulnerable moment seeing the old Pashtun in the doctor's waiting room. I was motivated too by the feeling that had there been a specialized cancer hospital in Pakistan, my mother could have been saved. My sense of charity was still limited though. My mother used to take a percentage of my cricket earnings each year to give zakat to the poor but after she died I stopped. I had lost a lot of money after putting all my savings in shares just before the world stock markets crashed in 1987. By this stage my spiritual journey had started and I could not help wondering if I had been punished in some way because I had not cleansed my money by giving zakat. I still did not give out of conviction, though; that was to come later, after I saw the generosity of the common man in Pakistan and my faith had developed to the point where I realized charity is not an option, it is a duty. The more people ridiculed the hospital project and told me it could never be done, the more determined I was to prove them wrong. This was one of the characteristics that had helped me in cricket. (I was dropped after my first test for Pakistan, and most of the players ridiculed my cricket, saying that I had made my first and last appearance for my country.) But it was a huge burden. I was told the hospital would be a white elephant. Others said I should focus on building a facility for primary care, saying a cancer hospital was too ambitious. But I was doing this because of the death of my mother, which had made me realize there was no cancer hospital in Pakistan. 'What will happen to poor people with cancer?' I would ask. 'They will die anyway,' was their reply.

One day, somebody from my social circle accused me in front of some friends of doing it all for publicity, just as celebrities endorse charities to get their names in the papers. I nearly hit him. His sneering was typical of certain sections of Pakistan's elite. They are completely decadent and utterly cynical. Desperately envious of anyone who has succeeded in the West, they are keen to drag you down to their level if you so much as aspire to help the country. The only other time I truly lost my cool in the face of detractors was in England. I met with a group of British Pakistani doctors at Shazan restaurant in Knightsbridge and they started to ask me a lot of technical questions about how the hospital would work. One of them in particular ridiculed the whole plan. He badgered me on technical points, as if to taunt me with my lack of medical knowledge. He told me this was not my field, that I would fail and ruin the great reputation I had made from my cricketing career. I almost left the dinner, so furious was I. The problem was that I was consulting all these doctors, but doctors, like most technocrats, are enslaved by logic. They are concerned with practicalities, whilst I was always a dreamer and my struggle in cricket had taught me to believe that nothing was impossible if one never gave up. They were realists whereas I was and always have been an idealist.

However, the concept of the hospital was still not clear at this stage. We had a volunteer doctor who was helping us but unfortunately she did not have the experience to undertake such a huge project. Our big break was still to come. I was in New York for a festival cricket match when I happened to meet a Pakistani cancer specialist called Dr Tauseef Ahmed at a dinner party. I told him of the project's difficulties. He responded by saying that there was only one Pakistani doctor he knew who had the capability of handling such a massive undertaking. The man in question happened to be none other than my first cousin Dr Nausherwan Burki – my mother's favourite nephew. It was Nausherwan who took on the entire medical side of the project, while I began to concentrate on the fundraising. A huge burden was lifted from my shoulders. Although there were a lot of people who played a heroic role in building the hospital, I have no doubt that Nausherwan was the most crucial. Had I not met him at that point in time, I would still be groping in the dark. At his first presentation to the board we all heaved a huge sigh of relief – here finally was somebody who really knew what they were doing. He gave us the confidence that this dream could one day become a reality. Nausherwan was no ordinary doctor. Not only is he an outstanding pulmonologist but his brilliant mind was always curious about every aspect of the health system. This was the perfect challenge for him. From the United States, where he was a professor at Kentucky University hospital, he planned every aspect of the project – from selecting the architects, hiring the medical staff and (using his contacts in Kentucky) getting the best-quality equipment at the best prices.

Although my quest for God had begun after my mother passed away, I was still leading a self-centred way of life. However, my faith and the hospital grew together. The hospital tested my belief in God to the limit and all the time kept strengthening it. In turn, my growing faith helped the hospital. It was a symbiotic relationship. The project removed all doubts within me that were it not for the will of God, it would have failed due to the many blunders made by me and my well-meaning but inexperienced team. So many times the situation appeared hopeless, yet somehow things would work out. When the hospital opened after a record construction time of three and a quarter years, rather than feel arrogant and brag about it, I felt totally humble.

Another great lesson in building the hospital was over-coming my pride and bringing my ego under control. Ever since I can remember I have always wanted to be self-contained, and hated to ask anyone for anything. I would feel a loss of dignity even asking my father for money (whereas Pakistanis often have no problem accepting money from their parents). When I announced the hospital project and the expected funds did not come, I was left with no option but to go out and ask for money. This was harder than anything I had ever done. I just cannot express how humiliating I found it to be kept waiting by certain businessmen who knew I had come to ask for funds. There were some who deliberately wanted to put me in my place, as they thought I was arrogant. As a sought-after cricket star I would pick and choose from the many invitations I received. I often turned down those from people who had made a lot of money and wanted to use their new-found wealth to rub shoulders with the famous. Now I had to turn to these people for donations. The media also tried to settle old scores. As a cricketer the press had needed me and I had been able to be selective about which journalists I talked to. If one wrote anything nasty about me, I would simply cut them off. Now I had to court them, so that they would highlight my project and help me raise funds. One bad article could mean the loss of huge amounts of donations. So I badly needed their goodwill. For the sake of the cause I really had to grovel to certain journalists and I found it simply excruciating.

I also changed towards children. Ever since I became a successful cricketer, my biggest followers were kids. There was, however, one problem – I just did not know how to behave with them. I was one of those adults who felt totally ill at ease with them. Whenever I was at home in Lahore, people would bring their children to meet me. Most of the time I would be so awkward about having to face yet another horde of them that I would tell my sisters to say I was not at home. My poor mother (who loved children) would be furious and force me to see them. All this changed. After one and a half years of fundraising, I ran out of steam in 1990. What

I have learned from running a charity is that if you have to raise a hundred rupees, the first ten are the hardest and the last ten are the easiest. I had kept going back to the same people for funds and they simply did not want to hear any more about the hospital. There was terrible donor fatigue and it seemed that I had reached a dead end. We could not start the construction of the hospital without substantial funds. At this juncture a friend suggested that since children were my greatest fans, I should go to the schools and ask them to collect funds for me, which horrified me. However, my sister Aleema, who had joined me in my mission, caught on to the idea. Within a month she had designed a whole fundraising campaign based on the children of Pakistan. It meant me going to schools all over the country, addressing them and inviting them to be in my fundraising team, which we named Imran's Tigers. Only those who were close to me would know how totally opposed to my nature this was. I worried that I would make a fool of myself and the children would make fun of me.

I can never forget my first day addressing a school assembly in Lahore. Tense when I set out, I almost came to blows with another driver in my worst case of road-rage. Drenched in sweat, I was so shy and awkward that a lot of the children began to giggle. We started campaigning at private schools but soon the state schools were also clamouring to join in. For two months I went to between five and six schools a day addressing their assemblies and explaining to them why it was important to have a cancer hospital in Pakistan. Each time before facing an assembly I had to muster all my courage to speak to them. Initially it was more terrifying than facing fast bowlers in front of a packed stadium. However, what happened as a result of my campaign was a sort of a mini-revolution in the country. The schoolchildren created history, never had there been such a successful fundraising campaign in the history of Pakistan. The children pestered their parents, uncles and aunts for money. They stopped motorists at traffic lights, and collected funds from door to door. Any child that collected over a certain amount of money would win a cricket bat signed by me. In a society like Pakistan where the family system is strong and children are adored I found we had hit upon the best possible way to collect money. I would be eating in a restaurant and the moment children spotted me, they would ask their parents for money and then hand me their donations. Unlike in the UK or the United States, in Pakistan children go everywhere – restaurants, functions, marriages – because all life revolves around the family. Not only was a huge amount of money collected, but more significantly the children themselves made everyone in the country aware of the fact that in a population of what was then 140 million people there was no cancer hospital. The campaign succeeded beyond my wildest imagination and enabled us to start construction. Today I meet Pakistani professionals all over the world who proudly tell me that they participated in my school fundraising campaign.

At the end of the campaign my inhibitions in dealing with children had disappeared and I felt really privileged that they looked up to me. Moreover I began to give more and more of what I had to the hospital. I had not been raised to be extravagant. My parents were always careful with their money and had brought me and my sisters up with an awareness that since there was so much poverty around we should never be wasteful and should give any extra money or food to the poor. My father had founded a charity called the Pakistan Educational Society, which funded the university education of underprivileged but talented children. He made me a member of the board when I was twenty-two. However, while previously I found it hard to give, and when I did give I felt I was doing the recipient a huge favour, now I gave out of a sense of duty and would feel satisfaction afterwards. From then on I would identify my needs, work out exactly what my expenses were for the year and whatever I made in excess of that I would give to the hospital. (Now, I also donate to the university I have founded in Mianwali.) I began to realize that once this exercise is done, it becomes fairly easy to start giving. Life became simpler and I ceased worrying about my earnings. I would never run out of money as an opportunity would always come up and I would make enough to keep me going. By the time the hospital opened in December 1994, I had given almost half of what I owned to the hospital.

The project lurched from one crisis to another. We had found a 20-acre plot outside Lahore and ground was broken in April 1991. With barely 10 million rupees in the bank we were embarking on a 700-million-rupee project. No wonder everyone was sceptical. You could never start a commercial project with that kind of financing. The problems were never-ending – hiring people, construction delays, equipment issues and a constant struggle to meet costs. Every time we feared we would have to halt the project because of a lack of funds somebody would always appear at the last minute with a donation. Even our first chief executive, an American by the name of David Wood, said our goal to provide 75–80 per cent free or financially assisted treatment was impossible. Backing up his argument with a Powerpoint presentation, he told the board that if we treated more than 5 per cent of the patients for free the hospital would close down within a few months. No other private cancer hospital in the world had managed what we were trying to achieve. But I had specifically promised people free treatment for the poor. And this was something many of our more impoverished donors held me to. 'Will it really be free for the poor?' they would ask, wary after a lifetime of being let down by the rulers and elite of Pakistan. The board and I refused to compromise on our objective. Not only was the hospital going to provide the proposed amount of free treatment, it had to be state of the art, and it had to be a research centre. I had no idea at this stage how to finance the free treatment. We overruled Wood.

The surge in donations and goodwill during the post-World Cup euphoria sustained us for a while but by 1994 the situation was coming to a head. It was a real uphill battle because we kept running out of funds and I had to constantly travel to tap overseas Pakistanis for help. In 1994 I toured New Zealand, Australia, Singapore, the UK, Norway, Germany, Denmark, Holland, the United States, Canada, the UAE, Bahrain and Saudi Arabia. Wherever in the world there was a Pakistani community, I was there asking them for money. By the summer of that year donor fatigue had got to the point where rich donors would hide if they saw me. This was when the real money was needed; construction had to be completed, staff had to be hired, down-payments for equipment had to be made. To make matters worse, I got unnecessarily involved in a ball-tampering controversy in June 1994, which made fund collection even more difficult. The two great Pakistani fast bowlers Wasim Akram and Wakar Younis, who had been nurtured and groomed by me and whose success I took great pride in, had decimated England back in 1992. Sadly, some English cricketers and British tabloids blamed their supreme ability in reverse swinging on ball tampering. I could not bear to see such unfair treatment of two great fast bowlers. I gave an interview to a biographer about reverse swing and ball tampering and got sucked into a controversy that ended up with me being taken to court a couple of years later by former English captain and all-rounder Ian Botham and batsman Allan Lamb. The controversy and the furore that followed inevitably hurt the fundraising campaign.

We had aimed to open in the summer of 1994 but by the spring the building contractor said we'd have to wait another year. The opening could be no later than December. It really had to open then because in 1995 Ramadan was in February and March; Ramadan is when Muslims make their biggest donations to charity and we needed that money in order to offer free treatment once the hospital opened. Not only that, but if we had to wait another year, till Ramadan 1996, we would have had to bear the cost of a medical and admin- istrative staff, all of which would have been on our payroll by then for over fourteen months. Relief arrived in yet another minor miracle: a new building contractor. T.M. Khan was an extraordinary man. He asked to have all the powers he needed and to be left alone to do the job. He succeeded against all odds.

But by October we still needed 4 million dollars to open the hospital and had run out of steam again. We were brainstorming one day when I pointed out that many ordinary Pakistanis often came up to me to give me small donations of 1,000 rupees or so. The will to give was there, but how could we harness it? Our adviser and my friend, Tahir Ali Khan, Pakistan's most brilliant marketing expert, suggested I should simply go round Pakistan with a donation box, appealing to the public for funds. Despite scepticism amongst the marketing team, he came up with a plan for a nationwide fundraising trip. First of all we had a trial run. On 5 October we set off with an open truck and a collecting box to the town of Daska, in central Punjab. We had put posters up around the town to advertise my arrival and within a couple of hours had collected about 500,000 rupees. On the back of that we prepared a whole campaign tour of twenty-nine cities, large and small, running from mid-November to 28 December. I would address school assemblies from seven in the morning up until about lunchtime, when I would hit the streets. Meanwhile, an advance team would go out and speak to the traders' organizations, groups that were to become my biggest fundraisers along with the school kids.

What followed was not just an eye-opener for me but a revelation to the people of Pakistan of their own potential. It was during this campaign that I started thinking more about going into politics. I was absolutely stunned by the generosity of ordinary Pakistanis. We did not have to provide entertainment for them as we did with our big fundraising dinners for the rich, but whatever people had, they gave me. Donors flooded to the open jeep where I sat next to the collection box, giving so generously that it left me bewildered. Men would hand over their watches and women throw down their necklaces and earrings from the windows of their houses. I would get back to where I was staying around midnight – usually after a fundraising dinner. At the hotel there would be more people waiting to hand me donations. Sometimes villages would call me urging me to come and collect the money they had raised. Before embarking on the tour, I had met the editors of all the main newspapers to tell them about the project and request their support. Bar one English-language daily, I must say all the papers were extremely cooperative, turning it into a competition by publicizing how much each town raised. After an exhausting six weeks we had collected 5 million dollars from the ordinary people of Pakistan.

I was quite perplexed to see poor people donating such a high proportion of their income to the project – especially given that it was a cancer hospital and was not going to be in their town. So I would ask them why they were giving. It was always the same reply, 'I am not doing you a favour. I am doing it to invest in my Hereafter.' This had a profound effect on me. I developed a love and respect for the people that I must confess I did not have before. One incident in particular touched and inspired me. I had just arrived home in Lahore, my whole body aching from a twelve-hour day of collecting cash, when some people arrived at the door. They said they had raised some money for the hospital and wanted me to come and collect it. I could see that they were poor and told them not to worry, that we could manage without their contributions. But they insisted and refused to leave, begging me to go with them. So I climbed into their Toyota, so battered it was barely capable of making the short journey to Shao ki Garhi, a neighbourhood near Zaman Park. There they led me down streets that reeked with the smell of open sewers, me cursing them under my breath, until we reached a small mosque. To my annoyance the money had not even been collected yet. A man used the mosque loudspeaker to announce my arrival and urged people to come and donate. I was so tired and angry I almost hit one of the men who had taken me there, but before I could storm off the locals started to come. The mosque was suddenly filled with people, the poorest of the poor, each offering me five rupees, ten rupees, fifteen rupees. My anger left me, I was genuinely moved and had to hold back my tears. I said I didn't want to take their money but they insisted, maintaining they had a right to participate in the campaign and saying they were doing it for the afterlife. Many told me their stories of pain and loss, of loved ones who had suffered and died for lack of medical help. One woman recounted how her son had passed away in a hospital waiting room. The only promise I had to make before I left was that hospital treament would be free for the poor.

It proved to me that generosity has a lot to do with faith and nothing at all to do with one's bank balance. There is all this debate amongst the media, the politicians and the intelligentsia in Pakistan about the extent to which the state should be based on Islam. And yet the common man in Pakistan lives by his religion, day in day out. It doesn't make him a saint but it produces certain qualities, one of which is a belief in the need to give now in order to receive in the afterlife. I started thinking that such people were capable of great sacrifices. Could these people not be mobilized to fight to save our ever-deteriorating country? Surely if there was a sincere government that genuinely wanted to eradicate poverty and injustice in our society, people would mobilize behind it – Pakistan would not then have to grovel in front of other countries and the IMF and World Bank for loans and alms every few months.

When I discussed this with the late Dr Ashfaq Ahmed, one of Pakistan's leading intellectuals, he told me about a meeting he once had with Chairman Mao in the 1960s. When Mao heard that Dr Ashfaq was from Pakistan, he said, 'Your people have tremendous potential.' Mao had been impressed by a story told to him by a Chinese ambassador to Pakistan. The diplomat had been playing chess with his Pakistani chess partner, who was fasting in the blistering heat of a Karachi summer. The poor Pakistani was suffering badly, and every few minutes he would pour some water on his head before making his move on the chessboard. When the Chinese ambassador asked him why he didn't just have a sip of water in private, his friend was indignant and replied, 'How can you fool God?' From that Mao decided that any people capable of such will-power and self-control must be capable of great things – it was just that the nation hadn't tapped that strength yet.

It was in building this hospital that, as well as discovering the generosity of the man in the street, I discovered how hard it was to achieve anything in Pakistan while also battling bureaucracy and corruption. The night before the official opening of the Shaukat Khanum Memorial Cancer Hospital & Research Centre on 29 December 1994, fifty thousand people came out in the cold to celebrate in Lahore's Fortress

Stadium. The next day ten-year-old cancer patient Sumera cut the ribbon in what was the most fulfilling moment of my life. Benazir and Zardari had not forgiven me, however, for snubbing their offer to do the honours. The state-controlled television and radio that up till then had given good support to the project suddenly blanked out both me and the hospital, making it harder to collect donations. Raising the 22 million dollars it took to build the hospital was the first hurdle, but we now needed additional funds for free treatment. The government-paid journalists launched a vicious campaign against me in the papers. Worse, barely a month after the hospital opened, I was hauled up in Lahore High Court and accused of embezzling people's donations. It was no coincidence that the court case coincided with the zakat campaign launched during the month of fasting to raise funds. The plan was quite obvious. If we treated the poor for free before we had enough money then the hospital would go bankrupt. If we did not do so then quite rightly I would be exposed by the government media as a fraud. In a country where the people have been taken for a ride so many times and are so cynical about everyone, they would have believed the worst about me.

Luckily, the case against me collapsed immediately. Our hospital had watertight financial controls and total transparency; our accounts were audited by one of the most prestigious firms in the country. Moreover, I happened to be the biggest donor to the hospital at the time. Benazir's government had not realized that. Also, fortunately for me, the people did not trust the government. They were aware that because it felt threatened by me it was trying to victimize me. Benazir's government was extremely unpopular by that point and lacked credibility. So here I was already in politics, without actually being in politics. I began to be treated as a political opponent, and a political opponent in Pakistan – whether in a democracy or military dictatorship – gets a rough deal. The entire state machinery turns against you. And in Pakistan, like in most of the developing world, the state is everywhere. My phones were tapped and wherever I went I was followed by a car. Everyone in the government was petrified to befriend me out of fear of losing their jobs. And since we have a big government, one has to deal with government officials all the time.

I was left with two choices: either I joined Nawaz Sharif and got the protection of his party or I had to go to Benazir's royal court in Islamabad and beg forgiveness for not inviting her to the hospital opening and convince her that I was not setting myself up as a political rival. My friend Yousaf Salahuddin, who was close to Benazir and Zardari, advised me to follow the latter course. He warned that otherwise Zardari would destroy the hospital. He offered to mediate. While Yousaf's suggestion was logical, it had the opposite effect. I went on an all-out attack in the press with both guns blazing at the governing couple's corruption. This had a far greater impact on the public than attacks from Sharif's party. Since Sharif was considered equally corrupt, his accusations against Benazir and her husband rang hollow. Especially since Benazir would immediately list the corruption charges against Sharif and his family. Now, for the first time, corruption became the number-one issue on the national agenda.

Despite the setbacks, we managed to treat 90 per cent of our patients for free that first year. We became pioneers in inventing and innovating fundraising techniques; today many charities have been inspired by and follow our fundraising model. There were other challenges to come though. Equipment would get stuck at customs, we would refuse to pay the bribes necessary to get it released and I would have to pull strings. The World Bank awarded us a $1 million grant for a waste-disposal incinerator but then withdrew the offer because Nawaz Sharif's government, which followed Benazir's, insisted it went to another hospital. A charity headed by the Argentinian president Carlos Menem offered to give the hospital a shipment of cancer drugs for free – all we needed was a letter from Rafik Tarar, Sharif's puppet president. He refused and the hospital lost the donation. Most shocking of all, though, was the bomb attack on the hospital in 1996, just a few weeks after I started to talk publicly about forming a political movement. Seven people died, including two child patients, thirty-five were injured and millions of rupees of damage caused. The device, planted under a chair in the waiting hall, destroyed the outpatient and endoscopy departments. If the building had not had such large windows the whole roof would have come down. I should have been there at the time to show the businessman Nasim Saigol around but he had cancelled just as I was about to leave home. I don't think I was the target of the bomb, but the innocent lives lost and the destruction caused both saddened and made me even more determined to succeed in my new endeavour. The pressure this incident brought was something I could deal with; I repeated the system that had worked for me in cricket, I blocked out thoughts of failure, and instead focused on what I had to do to succeed.

With so many obstacles, if it had been a commercial enter-prise it would have closed down, but instead it went from strength to strength to become the biggest charitable institu-tion in Pakistan. In the end, the hospital's success was its best protection. Its work has garnered so much goodwill. It contin-ues to treat a minimum of 65 per cent of patients for free with another 10 per cent paying a fraction of their costs. And it was still the only cancer hospital in the country – for rich or poor. Sooner or later even the opinion-makers would end up there, some for treatment, others to visit friends or relatives. So it became harder and harder for any propaganda against the institution to succeed. Everybody is treated equally, so that even the doctors do not know the difference between paying and non-paying patients. Rich and poor wait side by side in the waiting room and lie side by side in their sick beds. There is no special treatment, no queue barging, no taking prece-dence. All of this is rare in a country like Pakistan where the rich and powerful are accustomed to VIP treatment. Today the hospital generates enough money to more than cover its annual operating budget of 3.6 billion rupees. Over half its revenues are now earned through the sale of hospital services with the rest coming from donations from all over the world. Visits by international celebrities ranging from Bollywood heart-throb Aamir Khan to Princess Diana and Elizabeth Hurley have helped raise money too. In 2006 the hospital won the World Health Organization's UAE Foundation Prize for 'Outstanding work in health development'. It has treated more than 84,000 people, including myself. I had an emergency operation there in 2009 and my father spent the last two and a half months of his life there in 2008. Similar hospitals are planned for Karachi and Peshawar and we are already running outreach cancer-screening clinics in those two cities. Revenues from diagnostic centres in Lahore and Karachi and sixty-seven pathology collection centres all over Pakistan are helping the trust increase its self-sufficiency. As for the little girl who cut the opening ribbon back in 1994, Sumera is now one of the hospital's 1,500 staff and runs the gift-shop. Such is the reputation of the hospital today that politicians opposing me are petrified to attack it.

On a personal level, the hospital has taught me so much. Most importantly, I learned how to build and run an institution; crucially, if the leadership follow the rules, so does everyone else. I had learned this as a cricket captain; to discipline the team all I had to do was to ensure that the senior players didn't break the rules – the juniors automatically fell into line. Secondly, more important than the competence of the CEO was his integrity and passion. Integrity was indispensable, as no matter how competent, a dishonest person could destroy the institution; I'd seen in cricket how passion lifted a less-talented player's game so that he could contribute more than a passionless talented one.

I am proud to say that today the hospital is a model institution for the whole of Pakistan. Doctors and nurses come from hospitals all over the country to see how our systems work. Along with the Aga Khan hospital in Karachi, it has raised medical standards across the board in Pakistan.

I have also come to understand better the ordinary people of Pakistan, through the small miracles, the bigger tragedies and the simple faith of those I met in the hospital's wards. There I have seen how they deal with death, accepting it as the

171

will of God. Most moving of all was a young boy from Swat I spotted one day when I was visiting the intensive care unit. He was covered in tubes but his face radiated defiance. Impressed by his fight to stay alive, I became caught up in his case, meeting with his father and regularly checking with the doctors on his progress. By that time my son Sulaiman had been born and becoming a father wrought the biggest change on me in my life. It suddenly made me understand how vulnerable we are as parents. So I could feel the torment this man was going through seeing his son fight this life and death struggle. Then one day I went to check up on the boy and was told he had died. I sought out the father, expecting to find him a broken man. Instead he was resigned to his loss, saying it was the will of Allah. I was amazed at how quickly he had come to terms with it. I myself was overwhelmed by the boy's death and couldn't face work that day. I went home.

Mian Bashir became a regular visitor to my project office while we were building the hospital as it was near his house. He was a great source of help and encouragement – partially through his ability to occasionally foresee some pitfalls but mainly because of his great wisdom that never ceased to amaze me. One day we were having lunch in my office. I was feeling a little upset that the construction committee had not awarded the air-conditioning contract to the lowest bidder, who happened to be a friend of mine, Irshad Khan. During lunch Irshad called up furious, saying that there was something fishy going on as the contract had been awarded to a company that had left two projects unfinished and had a poor reputation in the industry. It made me feel even worse. Since he was my friend though I could not push his case as it would have been a conflict of interest. Without me telling him anything about the situation, Mian Bashir suddenly told me that the person who had been awarded the contract was in cahoots with one of the members of our construction committee and was not competent enough to finish the job. I was very concerned but Mian Bashir told me not to worry and that things would work out. Sure enough, a couple of months later that company was in financial trouble and the contract had to be re-awarded. It went to a highly competent competitor which thankfully finished the job on time.

Chapter Six

My Marriage, 1995–2004

WHEN I WAS LEAVING FOR ENGLAND FOR THE FIRST TIME AT the age of eighteen, my mother's last words to me were, 'Don't bring back an English wife.' She believed it would be impossible for a Western girl to adjust to our religion and culture. However, the decisions in my life have rarely been made through rationality and logic, more by impulse, to chase my dreams and my desires and passions. In both marriage, and my post-cricket career, I made somewhat unconventional choices for somebody of my background. Combining the outcome of those two decisions was to prove more difficult still. If marriage made me realize the happiness that comes from fatherhood and family life, politics taught me the price of taking on the status quo in Pakistan. This establishment is so venal that, unable to wield the usual weapon of corruption charges against me, they instead attacked me through my personal life, most particularly my wife. The thing to understand about Pakistani politics is that many politicians have so much to lose they will stop at nothing to gain or hold on to power. In terms of quality of life, political success is of no benefit to me, but for the likes of Zardari and Sharif, losing power might mean losing everything – their wealth, their homes, their status, their privileges and potentially their liberty – since many of them deserve to be in jail. Jemima and I were to discover how vicious this political mafia could be.

It was many years after my mother's warning before I even started to contemplate marriage. At a certain point, my deepening spiritual belief made me realize that I could not reconcile the life I had been leading as a bachelor with Islam. This was the most difficult part; everything else – fasting, praying, giving zakat – was relatively easy. The reason it was so difficult was because I had lost faith in the institution of marriage. Growing up in Zaman Park I used to think getting married was the most natural thing in the world and assumed that, like my sisters and cousins, I would one day have an arranged marriage. But the older I grew, the more disillusioned I became. Most of the cricketers who played with me in English county cricket and on the Pakistani team found it difficult to make a success of their married lives. For most of them it seemed like a burden. Quite a few of them found the temptations that existed in the life of an international sportsman irresistible. Besides, most married men used to look at my life with envy. So it was hardly surprising that I was disillusioned.

The only marriages I saw working were those of my sisters and cousins from my large extended family. Three of my four sisters were married and all had arranged marriages from within the large extended family. This was always the case with Pashtun tribes that had settled in Punjab or other parts of India. All three to varying degrees had their ups and downs with their husbands – especially in the early days when readjustment naturally takes place. Couples in arranged marriages face the same problems as those who have chosen their own partners, although expectations in arranged marriages tend to be somewhat lower. The crucial difference is that since it is a coming together of families, separation becomes difficult and divorce rare. The respective families – mainly the parents – act as marriage counsellors during the bad times. It is considered a good deed in Islam if someone can help a couple to sort out their troubled marriage.

In Pakistan most marriages are arranged. Parents choosing a husband for their daughter will look at the candidate's financial stability, his family's reputation and compatibility in terms of personality. In most cases a son or daughter can decline their parents' suggestions but it varies from region to region and class to class. In the north and north-west of Pakistan young people are not given a lot of choice, especially girls, whilst the children of the urban elite play a bigger role in choosing their own partners. In villages girls and boys grow up together and often know each other, so most of the matches are easy for parents to arrange. Problems arise when there is no eligible boy or girl in the village. Then a spouse will be found from further afield and it is quite possible that the couple will meet for the first time on their wedding day. Traditional families will most likely know a groom's entire background. Parents would not allow their daughters to marry someone who could not be pressurized through his family to keep the marriage going during rough patches. Marriage not only knits families together but the entire social life revolves around the extended family structure. The more powerful the family is, the harder it is to divorce a person belonging to that family. Some of the worst problems in arranged marriages arise where parents marry their children off to a certain family because of their financial status, regardless of whether the couple is compatible or not.

Whatever the problems, the underlying idea behind arranged marriage is that sacrifices must be made for the sake of the children. Over the years I have seen a lot of unhappy arranged marriages where couples have stuck it out for the sake of their offspring and their respective families. Women, who can be more vulnerable in our society, sometimes put up with mistreatment from their husbands just for the security of their children. However, there are of course lots of cases of men having to put up with difficult marriages too. Mian Bashir looked after his wife, who had fits of madness, for fourteen years. Doctors advised him to put her in an asylum but given the state of our mental health institutions he could not bear to do so. When she had her fits, she could be violent and his face bore the scars of that violence.

Whatever the ups and downs of their marriages, I could see that my sisters took great joy in their children. There was a time when they and their families lived with my father and me. Instead of being an imposition, it was wonderful – especially for my father. All their children grew up like one family in the same house and the three sisters treated all of them as if they were their own offspring. It was this that began to change my mind about marriage. I used to notice how their husbands would literally rush back home to be with their children. Even I began to spend more time at home so I could play with them. When any of my nephews and nieces did well at school, all of us, including the other children, considered it a family triumph. When two of my sisters moved into their own homes, the house felt empty. Fortunately they only moved a few hundred yards away and most evenings their children would still come round.

Making the decision to get married was one thing, but finding a Pakistani wife was another. I had already passed my mid-thirties but most eligible girls were married off in their early twenties. In Pakistan unmarried girls often live quite a sheltered existence. A woman under twenty-five would be too young for me, with too little experience of life. I also had to bear in mind that my extended family was quite conservative about the way to go about finding a wife. I had to make a choice after meeting the girl and her parents over a couple of brief meetings. Usually what happens is that the mothers, along with the sisters, survey their social scene and, after a careful process of elimination, pick a few eligible candidates. Then during marriage festivities amongst the community the potential spouse is pointed out. If the boy and girl in question are both interested then more intimate meetings, like a tea appointment, are organized. As for most Pakistani families, our weddings were segregated. It was too awkward for me, in my position and at my age, to go to the women's section to look at eligible girls. This would have been quite acceptable if I were in my mid-twenties, but in my mid-thirties it was a terrifying prospect. At one point my father got fed up (like the rest of my family) and decided to take matters into his own hands. He arranged tea at a friend's house so that I could meet his friend's daughter. I tried everything to get out of it but in the end, out of respect for my father and not wanting to embarrass him with a last-minute cancellation, I went along. The whole situation was horribly awkward for all concerned. When the girl came into the room I was so embarrassed I could not even look at her. Meanwhile her mother treated me as if I was a 25-year-old, rather than someone who was approaching middle age. I was even asked about my university days – again a question more apt for someone in their early to mid-twenties. The agony finally ended when my father and I begged to leave. On the way back he did not even bother to ask me what I thought of the girl. He realized how ridiculous the whole situation was – all he said was that since my mother had passed away he had simply tried to do his duty. We both laughed and I politely requested him not to make any more attempts to find me a bride.

I was still so busy playing cricket during this period that I was never in Lahore long enough to make a concerted attempt to find a wife. However, once I retired I made more of an effort. The girls I tended to meet were the westernized ones but I could not see them fitting into my conservative family. My sisters had strong characters and were not likely to be very tolerant of someone who flaunted family tradition. The last thing I wanted was that my marriage should isolate me from my family. As for the ones who would have been compatible with my background, educated girls from conservative families, it was too much of a lottery. How could I at my age marry someone after a few conversations? The idea of going to more tea appointments like the one I had been to with my father simply terrified me. In the end I had to accept the fact that I was too old for an arranged marriage.

I was still intent on marrying a Pakistani girl when by chance I met Jemima in London at a dinner organized by my Persian friend Sharia. I immediately found her attractive and intelligent and was particularly impressed by her strong value system and the fact that despite her young age she already had a spiritual curiosity. While I had previously met Jemima's siblings and cousins, I did not meet her parents till just before we got married. I had worried that it would be impossible to convince them – not only because of our age difference but also because of Jemima having to live in Pakistan. I was amazed at how firmly both Lady Annabel and Jimmy Goldsmith stood behind Jemima's decision. Of course there were warnings about the problems of a cross-cultural marriage – but neither was at all against Jemima's conversion to Islam. I was amazed at their tolerance, especially given the prejudice against Islam in the West. When the news of our marriage broke in mid-May 1995, the media in both Pakistan and the UK went berserk, particularly over Jemima's conversion. There was no shortage of advice for her in the English media about how dreadful life would be in Pakistan. The tabloids' prejudices about Islam and Pakistan were fully apparent. Jemima was told she would not be allowed to drive a car and would be veiled from head to toe.

The only positive aspect of this perplexing media coverage was that outraged Muslims put forward the Islamic point of view, something that was not often visible in the Western media. The gist of the advice given to her in the UK was that she was too young and innocent to realize that she was being lured away by an older man because of her wealth to a country where women were enslaved. I was not surprised that my motive for marriage was thought to be her money (that very accusation was put to Jinnah when he married his bride, twenty-four years younger than himself and a Parsi convert to Islam). After all, people with a materialistic mindset would think that. I felt this was extremely unfair to Jemima and failed to do justice to her intelligence and her attractive personality. It took great strength of character to cope with such unfriendly media exposure, all the more so because until then she had been almost entirely protected from this kind of intrusion. It was really tough on her and she coped most admirably. Though I did help Jemima by recommending books on Islam, I never tried to force my views on her. I remembered how hard my mother had tried to make me a practising Muslim; despite my great love for her, she had failed to convince me. It had been Mian Bashir who won me over with his gentle way of never asking me to do anything and allowing me to discover the truth myself.

In Pakistan Jemima received a warm and gracious welcome. As long as they adapt their behaviour to local customs, foreigners have always been received with great hospitality in Pakistan. It is only since 9/11 and the CIA drone attacks in Khyber Pakhtunkhwa that antagonism towards Americans – and inevitably other Westerners – has crept in. There was an initial frostiness amongst certain sections of the westernized elite but once they got to know Jemima they were friendly. This wariness would have been because Jemima, as a Westerner, made some of them feel insecure because their sense of superiority in Pakistan stemmed from their considering themselves to be westernized. However, what was hardest for Jemima were the politically inspired media attacks on her.

Even though I was not yet in politics, I was already regarded as a threat by the politicians because of great public appreciation for the cancer hospital. The government-sponsored media portrayed my marriage as an intricate plot by the Zionists to take over Pakistan through Jemima. It did not seem to matter that she was not actually Jewish. In fact she was baptized and confirmed as a Protestant. Her father Jimmy Goldsmith's father was Jewish and his mother was a French Catholic but he grew up in an atheist household. This campaign intensified when I announced my political party a year after our marriage.

When I married Jemima I had no intention of setting up my own political party. The country's rapid decline was alarming me, though, and I was already mulling over the idea of getting involved with some kind of political movement. I had been hoping that certain people I knew would form a political party I could support, but in the end they had neither the financial means nor the nationwide support to challenge the two established parties, the PPP (Pakistan People's Party) and the PML (Pakistan Muslim League). So that option was not available to me. I had also explored the possibility of support-ing one of the religious parties. I had assumed that their people must have the same understanding of faith that I did. Sadly I gradually realized that while some of the members of these parties had genuine faith, plenty of others had only a superficial understanding of Islam. Most of them were only using religion, as others used the ethnic or regional card, as a vehicle to get into power. They turned out to be just as corrupt as other politicians too. The more my understanding of political parties and specifically the religious parties deepened, the more I realized that faith without wisdom and knowledge could produce bigots completely lacking in compassion and tolerance. No wonder the Prophet (PBUH) considered the ink of a scholar to be holier than the blood of a martyr. No wonder either that the public usually rejects the religious parties at the polls. At no point in time have they garnered more than 19 per cent of the seats in the national assembly and their share of the vote is lower still. Hence the apparent paradox to the outsider, that while people in Pakistan will sacrifice their lives for Islam, they don't want religious parties running the country.

When the dust had settled after the furore over my marriage, I again started meeting politically minded people and having endless discussions about how to put up a challenge to the political mafia in Pakistan. I say mafia, because democracy is just a cover for the two parties that take turns in plundering our country. I was appalled at how the ruling class had squandered Pakistan's talent and resources, there seemed to be no limit to their greed. At the same time, I was struck by the generosity and fortitude of the Pakistani people that I had seen because of my work with the hospital, and the raw talent and resourcefulness of the Pakistani overseas community. So many of them, when given a level playing field, had succeeded in their chosen spheres. What, I asked, could Pakistan achieve if we had a system that actually rewarded rather than discouraged merit?

I came to the conclusion that the only way to change the system was to enter politics myself. However, whenever I thought about forming my own political party I could not work out how I would finance it. The reason why politics in Pakistan had been concentrated within a few families was because the vast majority of people had neither the time nor money to have the luxury of participating. True, Zulfikar Ali Bhutto in the 1970 elections created a movement that captured the masses' imagination so completely that he was able to defeat the established political houses with political nonentities. However, Bhutto was fortunate that money did not play as big a part in politics as it did after Zia's 1985 non-party elections. Bhutto also had three other advantages. One, he had been a cabinet minister for eight years in Ayub Khan's military dictatorship so already knew the political scene from within. Secondly, there was a huge political vacuum in Pakistan after Ayub Khan because he had crushed all the political parties in West Pakistan. Thirdly, in the Cold War politics of left and right, the entire highly organized left supported Bhutto. My dilemma was how to form a party of 'clean' people who had the time and money to work in politics.

I also had another issue to think of. I was a married man now and Jemima was trying to adjust to a completely alien environment and culture. If all my time was spent on politics and keeping the hospital going, how would I do justice to my marriage? We discussed the issue endlessly. It was clear by now that there was simply no way left but for decent Pakistanis to get involved in politics. Otherwise the country would be sunk by our politicians. Since Jinnah the quality of our leaders had been steadily deteriorating. All over the world career politicians are disliked, but in Pakistan, as in many developing countries, they are seen as crooks – and with a great deal of justification. What amazed me was that while almost every dinner-table conversation in the country condemned the politicians for destroying Pakistan's potential, no one was prepared to do anything about it. The affluent classes' response to the country's downward spiral was to get Canadian passports or US green cards. They just did not have the guts or the will to give up their comfortable lives and take on the corrupt political class. In Islamabad it was quite common to see members of the elite, who denigrated the politicians in private, grovelling at their feet at public functions.

When I announced my party, Tehreek-e-Insaf (Movement for Justice) on 25 April 1996, I had lost all fear of dying. This meant I knew exactly why I was going into politics, which was to take on the political mafia in Pakistan; they had always worked on the premise that anyone who threatened them should either be bought or eliminated. The other founding members and I presented it as a 'broad-based movement for change whose mission is to create a free society based on justice, with an independent judiciary as its bedrock'. At a news conference in Islamabad somebody asked me about my lack of experience in politics and I had to acknowledge that I had none. 'But then neither have I any experience in looting and plunder,' I added. I had big ideals but it was true that I was ill-equipped. My entry into this world was a bit like when I first saw people swimming. One summer holiday my cousins took me to the pool at Aitchison College. I was four years old and it was the first time I had ever seen a swimming pool. I could see that people seemed to be moving around near the surface of the water so I decided it must be quite shallow and promptly threw off my clothes and jumped straight in. I immediately sank to the bottom. After swallowing a lot of water, I was taught by my cousins to swim within a few days. Politics was a similar experience, though the learning process was much longer. I had nobody to teach me, no mentors and made many mistakes.

Neither Jemima nor I fully understood what I had got us into. Nor had we anticipated, despite all our discussions, how much strain it would put on our private lives. There was simply no time for family life; for the next month and a half I had to meet an endless stream of people, at all hours, and then I had to make frequent trips to the provinces to appoint party office bearers. We had a tremendous response, but no idea how to deal with it. My fellow founding members were as inexperienced in the political field as I was. Frankly, even if we had had some idea of what to do, we were simply not equipped to cope with it. We could not answer the mail or give proper attention to all of those who came to our Lahore office. One of the main problems I had was learning to judge people. So many people were coming to me, keen to get involved, but I could not tell if they were genuine or not. My sisters consider it one of my principal flaws that I always trust people too much. I would welcome volunteers on board only to then find out hours, weeks or sometimes months later that they were just opportunists and did not share my ideals at all. The political world was full of con men, whose only aim was to obtain power for their self-interest. It would take me almost a decade of meeting thousands and thousands of people before I could acquire the ability to distinguish between genuine and phoney people within minutes. There is no shortcut to learning this skill.

To make matters worse, the government-sponsored propaganda that I was part of a Jewish plot to take over Pakistan meant that we had a lot of people wanting to join us thinking they could make money out of the party. They reasoned that the Jews must have given us millions of dollars. After all, during the Cold War, socialist organizations in Pakistan received money from the Soviet embassy. So we had funny situations where people came looking for easy money, and were shocked when we asked them for donations instead. One day I found hundreds of cars parked outside my office. I had to fight through crowds of people to get into the office itself. It turned out that some local rag had written that Bill Clinton had given me the go-ahead. From that, these people had surmised that the Americans had decided to install me in power. Meanwhile, I had terrible relations with the Pakistani press. As a sportsman I had never felt the need to court journalists – as far as I was concerned, my performance said it all. But politics was different; in this arena the media could make or break you, just like in the hospital fundraising.

At the height of the chaos I had to go to England to defend myself in the libel case brought against me by Allan Lamb and Ian Botham. This stemmed from comments I had made about the issue of ball tampering back in 1994. The last thing I wanted was to waste my time with a court case but I was left with no choice. My formidable barrister, George Carman QC, felt the chances of winning in front of an English jury were minuscule (about 10 per cent) because Botham was a national hero. He advised me to settle out of court as the financial costs of losing were astronomical. At the start of the trial I felt fairly confident, since I knew I was innocent and that I had not made the alleged comments. But as it wore on proceedings seemed to be going against me. I started to worry. A loss would have meant bankruptcy and I was worried about how

I would support my family if I lost. There was nothing more humiliating than the idea of living off my wife or having to borrow money. Worse still would have been the blow to my two-month-old political party. In the middle of the case I called up Mian Bashir to ask him to pray for me. He sounded pessimistic and said, 'The judge is against you.' Sure enough, after the judge had done his summing up, George Carman asked the jury to leave and told the judge that for the first time in his forty-year career he had to make a complaint that the summing up was biased against his client. Despite the many stressful situations I had been in during my cricket career, the greatest tension I have ever felt was during the six hours or so while the jury deliberated. George Carman was already preparing me for defeat, and writing his appeal. As I was waiting, I got a message from a friend saying that Mian Bashir wanted to speak to me. I phoned him and found him in a cheerful mood. 'Allah is changing the jury's mind!' he said. It returned a 10–2 majority verdict in my favour.

When I got home a couple of months later, the fervour over my new party had subsided. Now at least we had a period of calm and could organize ourselves. I started touring various cities and towns to gather support and form our party's organization. The calm did not last long. On 5 November 1996, President Farooq Leghari dissolved Benazir Bhutto's government and announced elections in three months' time. When I met with Leghari, he told me that Sharif and Benazir had each siphoned off US$1.5 billion from the country and pledged to hold them accountable. My party was only six months old by then and I had lost two months in the UK because of the court case. Nonetheless we decided to participate in the election campaign. We felt it would be the perfect opportunity to organize ourselves as a national party. Plus I felt it was an ideal way to really get the issue of corruption debated publicly in the run-up to the polls. I realized that there was no way we could make much of an impact as far as votes were concerned as we had no organization at the grass-roots level. So it was already quite clear in my mind that we would campaign all over Pakistan and then withdraw a week before the polls. When I started our campaign everyone was amazed at the huge crowds that came to my rallies. The youth especially came to listen to me in droves, as this was the section of the population most hungry for change. When the Tehreek-e-Insaf's rallies, which were bigger than those for Sharif or Benazir, were shown on television, there was a rush of candidates keen to stand on our party ticket. We formed a board to select our prospective candidates. In our zeal to make sure that nobody who had any blemish on their character was given our party ticket, a lot of good people were lost. Anyone who had a political background was given extra vetting.

Seeing the potency of my attack, Sharif started making overtures to me. First he offered me the most senior position in his party after him, then he offered my party an electoral alliance with twenty seats in the national assembly. Everyone knew at this stage that Sharif was going to win the elections simply because there was no other national party apart from Benazir's now discredited PPP. For us it was a huge compliment that a party that was just a few months old should be considered enough of a threat to be made such an offer. However, I had no hesitation in rejecting him as I considered him just as corrupt as Benazir. An alliance with Sharif would have compromised my principles. I had only come into politics to oppose unscrupulous politicians like him so how could I align myself with his party? While I believe we all have to make compromises in life, they should be made to attain your vision, not on the vision itself. I was also fortunate in that, unlike professional politicians, I did not need power for its perks and privileges. I was very clear about the fact that unless I could implement my agenda of reform, there was no need to be in politics, as I already had everything I could possibly desire in life. I felt it would be much better to be in the opposition and be a check on the government than be part of the power structure and have my hands tied. Joining Sharif would not only have meant I became part of the status quo, but I would have also lost all my credibility.

The next development was that Benazir turned on Leghari, accusing him of being a traitor to the PPP. The ferocity of her attacks clearly rattled him and he threw his lot in with Sharif, forgetting his pledge to try him and Benazir for corruption before allowing them to contest elections. A month before the polls it became clear to everyone that Leghari's caretaker government had entered into an agreement with Sharif's PML (N), compromising what should have been a neutral administration. The entire establishment from then on began to bat for Sharif. Administrative officers chosen by him were posted in crucial positions in his political stronghold of Punjab.

It is almost impossible to beat whichever party is backed by the establishment in Pakistan. Once the establishment makes its party of choice clear, the powerful district administration comes into action and the local power brokers fall into line. Everyone wants to be on the winning side, because only the winner can gain the influence over the powerful bureaucracy needed to dole out patronage to his cronies.

Keen to align themselves with those looking most likely to take power, various other forces began to jostle for position: the big feudal families and the criminal world – the smugglers and the drug barons. In every district in the country there is an underworld element that controls anything from 500 to 2,000 votes. The criminal mafia has to be with the winning party as it needs its protection to operate. Even for the common man – be he bureaucrat, shopkeeper, police officer or cab driver – getting ahead in Pakistan revolves around his links with the incumbent rulers. I wrote an open letter exposing the points of the agreement between Leghari and Sharif. I decided the best thing to do next would be to pull out of the elections, as we had achieved the objectives we had set ourselves. However, by criticizing Leghari's government and calling him to account on his broken promises I had now opened myself up to attack on a third front.

A week before the polls I called a meeting of our senior party members and updated them on the situation. I told them that the maximum number of seats we might win was three but most likely we were not going to win any. I felt that our party was too young to take such a crushing defeat and that donations would dry up if we lost. How would we then finance the party? Moreover we simply did not have the resources or organizational capacity to participate. In Pakistan a political party needs to organize buses to take people to the polling stations and people to staff them, with polling agents for both men and women. It is a huge organizational and logistical undertaking. But the majority of our party hierarchy wanted to fight on; some had allowed themselves to be convinced by the size of the crowds at our rallies that we would win a lot of seats. This made me realize how people in politics delude themselves. They always underestimate the opposition's strength and exaggerate their own. In cricket it used to be the opposite. I had to constantly stress to my team not to overestimate the opposition's strength and be overawed. There were those in the party who felt that we would lose face if we backed out now. Another argument was that all the money spent by our candidates on elections would have been wasted. The person who swayed me in the end was Hamid Khan, a senior and much respected lawyer in our party. He felt that the experience we would gain from contesting the elections would be invaluable; having learned from our defeat we would be well prepared next time round, which is when our real chance would come.

In taking part in the elections we took the most difficult path. It really was the Charge of the Light Brigade but without the horses and without the arms. No party – however popular – can win an election without a grass-roots political organization. Our minuscule financial resources were nothing compared to those of the two main parties, both of whom had already made plenty of money from their time in power. We had major issues with media coverage too. At the time there was only one television channel and it was government-controlled. During the whole ninety-day campaign each party was only given a half-hour slot. This clearly did not give us enough air-time to mobilize and motivate people about our agenda and encourage them to get out there and vote. I had also had a problem getting my message across because of my inexperience and inability to deal with the press. I found my statements would come out completely distorted. I later discovered that there were journalists on politicians' payrolls who were experts at killing or distorting opposition statements. I came to realize that the freedom of the press was really a myth; the newspaper owners pursued their own agendas through their publications. The freedom of the press only stood as long as their interests were not threatened. In another indication of my inexperience, I made a media blunder just a few days before the elections. *Jang*, Pakistan's biggest-circulation paper, quoted me saying that while we hoped for the best, it was possible that we might not get even one seat. Of course no political leader should ever say that kind of thing, whether it is correct or not, because it completely demoralizes your workers.

Compounding our difficulties, the media campaign against us by the PML (N) had been highly effective. We were simply defenceless in the face of its onslaught. Their attack was focused entirely on my personal life. They even stooped so low as to keep calling up a female friend of mine, Sita White, and publishing lurid interviews with her. More damaging still was the conspiracy theory about a Zionist plot to take over Pakistan. They went to the extent of getting a newspaper to publish a photograph of a cheque for 40 million pounds supposedly given to me by Jemima's father for my election campaign. Then statements from political and religious figures were printed saying they would not allow the Jews to take over Pakistan. After the elections the paper involved printed a few lines on the inside pages, admitting that the cheque was a forgery. But the damage was done and it was too close to the elections for our struggling media office to change public perceptions.

Given our various weaknesses we had only one hope and that was for a heavy turnout. Unfortunately, on Election Day the polling booths were deserted, especially in the cities. Most Pakistanis obviously felt that voting would not change their lives for the better anyway. It was clear that Sharif would win and Benazir would be wiped out but no one had anticipated the margin of his victory. He ended up with a two-thirds majority in parliament although everyone looked at the number of votes cast with great suspicion. The president had announced a turnout of 25 per cent by the evening of the polls, while the BBC put it at less than 18 per cent. By the following morning the nation was told the turnout was 38 per cent.

It was only after Sharif's government was dismissed in 1999 that a senior member of the election commission explained to me how the polls had been rigged. Certain constituencies were selected for manipulation. Within those constituencies, polling stations where rigging was easily possible were earmarked as 'red polling booths'. The elections were held during Ramadan, so the moment the voting had finished at these booths, the election agents were taken to break their fast some distance away; in certain cases reluctant polling agents were ordered to go by the army personnel guarding the election stations. They were then kept away for forty-five minutes to an hour. In the meantime, a couple of members of the election commission stuffed the ballot boxes with votes for the PML (N) candidate. In order to avoid detection, they cleverly raised the amount of votes of the number-two candidate so that the gap between the winning candidate and the rest was not too glaring. There was, however, a huge gap between the top two candidates and everybody else. I have to say I felt sorry for Benazir, despite having been her biggest critic; all the cards were stacked against her. With the caretaker government and all its power firmly behind Sharif it was obvious that she did not stand a chance in hell. As expected, she was completely routed. As for Tehreek-e-Insaf, we failed to win a single seat.

(Following the 2008 elections, the Electoral Commission found that 37 million of the 80 million voters registered were 'bogus' – that is, duplicated, multiple, or bogus entries. In June 2011, on my petition to the Supreme Court, the 37 million bogus votes were annulled, and the court ordered 35 million youth votes to be registered.)

Luckily, over my twenty-one years of international cricket – which had included many a drubbing – I had developed a defence mechanism to protect myself and manage the more painful aspects of failure. One of my worst memories was losing to India in India on our 1979/80 tour. We had to sneak back into Pakistan in the dead of night and unannounced, so scared were we of being humiliated by the outraged public. The customs staff confiscated almost everything they possibly could off us, searching even our pockets and keeping us at the airport for two hours. For days afterwards we all avoided going out in public to escape the inevitable backlash. Yet seven years later we arrived at the same Lahore airport after beating India. We never even made it to customs. The airport staff carried us on their shoulders from the tarmac to the crowd of tens of thousands who had flooded the airport. For five miles from the airport into the city centre there were people lining the roads cheering us. The only other time I saw such jubilation and euphoria was when we landed in Lahore after winning the World Cup in 1992. So by the end of my career I had a pretty good idea about the dynamics of victory and defeat. I had learned not to lose my head when we won and to come to terms with and deal with the bad times, when you became the object of the general public's ire and even your close friends changed towards you.

The first thing to understand with failure is that there is no point in making excuses – there are no listeners. As they say, failure is an orphan, and you're alone. It is best to accept it graciously and congratulate the winner. Then you must have the ability to analyse where you went wrong; this is the hall-mark of successful people, that they are their own best critic. One of the reasons I succeeded in cricket, when compared to more talented cricketers than me, was because I could analyse my weaknesses accurately. In October 1984, when I started to bowl again after a two-year lay-off following a stress fracture in my left shin, I discovered I had developed a flaw in my bowling action. For three months I experimented and tried everything to remove the flaw, but nothing worked. Such was my concentration that I dreamed and saw myself bowling and worked out how to remove the flaw, all in my sleep. The next morning in the nets I corrected my action. Some cricketers' careers have been finished by analysing things wrongly, as there is a great danger that – demoralized by failure – you can actually make a wrong analysis and compound the failure. The best naturally gifted timer of the ball I ever saw was Zaheer Abbas: in 1978 he completely annihilated the touring Indian bowling attack in Pakistan. A year later, when we toured India, there was massive public expectation of him. I could see him crumbling under this weight but rather than blocking the fear of failure, and concentrating on managing his innings, he started looking elsewhere. First he started fiddling with his technique; one which, I reminded him, had enabled him to break records less than a year ago. A few days later he had his eyes tested, was there something wrong there? Two weeks after that, he was in such a state that he felt someone had cast a black magic spell on him, and he ended up being dropped from the team. Over the years, I found a lot of people being defeated by failure because of their inability to analyse their mistakes properly.

After the election disaster, I wanted to seek solitude, and make my own analysis of our disaster. Another part of my strategy is that it is useless reading any newspapers – why torture yourself by reading gloating articles by critics who were just waiting for you to fail? I cut down on public engagements too because the more people you meet the more suggestions you receive about where you went wrong. Suggestions being free, they are never in short supply, and all they end up doing is prolonging the bitter taste of failure. So I would always hunker down and keep myself to myself while I made my own analysis and prepared my strategy for how to bounce back. After the elections I grabbed the opportunity to have some time off and escaped to the Salt Range with my family, where we spent a blissful few days. I had hardly seen Jemima and Sulaiman for the previous few months. For all the pain of the political loss, the happiness I got spending precious time with my first-born more than compensated.

In fact this was the easiest defeat for me to accept, as I had already known that the best we could hope for was a mere three seats. We certainly were not ready and did not have the team to form a government and implement my vision. I felt too that these elections had at least been useful in providing us with an opportunity to put forward the issues of corruption and accountability. In addition, the campaign had helped us build up a national network. However, our loss had a devastating effect not only on my young party, but also on Jemima, my sisters and close friends. They had absolutely no idea how to handle the taunts and ridicule they faced when they went out in public or read the newspapers. Poor Jemima, as well as putting up with the whole Zionist plot story, had to see endless articles criticizing, mocking and ridiculing her husband. And I have to say I was roasted by the media. I was attacked by the right, the left and the powerful lobby of crooked politicians. The latter were particularly vindictive as I had advocated capital punishment for those whose corruption was proved beyond a certain amount. Since 1983, when I had broken my leg and had a bad year, I had had a series of successes – with both cricket and the hospital. The election defeat was the first big opportunity for those envious of that success and keen to see me fail. People love to see an icon fall – it is part of human nature. And we had been completely wiped out; it wasn't just a defeat, it was a decimation. It became clear to me that we could not beat the status quo politicians on their pitch; we could only win if we could create a movement like the 1970 Bhutto movement, where people vote for the party rather than the candidate.

A few weeks after the elections, Mian Bashir dropped in to commiserate. Jemima told him that she wished I had never gone into politics. She told him how much respect there was for me in Pakistan because of my cricket, and the cancer hospital, and that now I had become a figure of ridicule and the butt of jokes, my private life raked over in the media. She told him that she had always felt in her heart that I should only have done humanitarian work and stayed out of any controversy. He listened to her with a quiet smile before responding that the object of this life was not to be popular and that those who made that their purpose were condemned to live by fickle public opinion. Then he told her the story of this highly respectable and successful businessman who was happily married and leading a contented life. At the age of forty he was inspired by the Almighty to tell the people of his town that there was only one God. When he tried to convey this message, though, they became upset because it was against the beliefs of their forefathers, who worshipped many idols as gods. Besides, every year lots of people from all over the region visited the town to worship the idols and the townsfolk made a lot of money from these pilgrims. So their financial interests were also being threatened by the new message. When this man persisted he was subjected to all sorts of abuse and ridicule. Being honourable and sensitive, he was deeply hurt by people's attitudes. One day his uncle mocked and ridiculed him so much that he came home and cried in his wife's arms. Because his wife knew him so well, she knew he was telling the truth and totally believed in him. She stood by him and urged him on with his calling. That man was the Prophet Muhammad (PBUH) and he eventually succeeded in founding one of the greatest civilizations in human history. 'This is just a passing phase,' Mian Bashir said. 'Besides, if decent people do not come into politics, the country will continue to be plundered by crooked politicians and soon become unlivable in.' Jemima began to relax after that, though she would insist that I organized myself better so that I gave my family its fair share of time. I began to manage my time more efficiently, but my troubles were only just beginning.

The party was in severe financial difficulty. A lot of money had been wasted in the thick of the election campaign and we had incurred loans that had to be paid off. But who was going to fund a party that had suffered such a crushing loss? When I was captain, if we suffered a defeat I would avoid team meetings for a couple of days because they were counterproductive and would invariably turn into a blame-game that left the team divided and demoralized. The difference was that a cricket team had to rally itself for the next match, which gave them something to look forward to. In the case of my party, the next elections were five years away. Who was going to face the ruthless Sharif brothers all that time? Nawaz's brother Shahbaz was also a politician and the two of them were masters at victimizing their opponents. Just like a vanquished cricket team, my party started searching for scapegoats. Members who had urged us to contest the polls were crucified by the ones who had agreed with me that it was best to pull out. Others simply lost faith in my leadership. They had known me as someone who was successful in whatever field I entered. This political rout had shaken their confidence in me. These people did not realize that when I first played cricket I was not successful at all. In fact I was dropped after my first test match and it took me five years before I consolidated my position on the team; after my first tour a lot of newspapers called me 'Imran Khan't'. The hospital project too had plenty of early hiccups; the general opinion amongst our educated classes had initially been that it was a non-starter, and even once it was built, some sceptics never thought we would be able to run it.

Other differences between members of our party's central executive committee that had been simmering for a while now came out into the open. Some of my senior party members went into depression. A few just left the party, usually the ones who had felt that allying with me would provide a short-cut to power. Then there were those who could not think of hanging around till the next polls or were scared of political victimization. It is customary for the victor in Pakistani politics to use the police and bureaucracy to victimize his opponents. For example, income-tax officers can suddenly target your business or thugs will turn up on your doorstep to beat you up. My cousin Asad Jehangir joined the police force after graduating from Oxford in 1969. He once told me about an incident after the 1977 elections when he was posted to Sindh as a young and idealistic police officer. One of the local landlords came to see him after he had been elected. After exchanging formalities he politely requested the bewildered Asad to send a couple of policemen to his political opponent's house to give him a sound thrashing. In our feudal culture, it was almost as if it was the winner's prerogative to further humiliate the loser. The judiciary gives no protection to the opposition either, having always been subordinate to the executive. Because of this total lack of rule of law, some Pakistanis will vote for someone despite knowing he is totally crooked out of fear of retribution or the lure of patronage. Landless peasants are especially vulnerable because their land-lord can threaten to turf them out of their homes or beat them up if they don't vote for him or whichever party or candidate he is supporting.

Losing the elections not only made collecting money for the party difficult but it hit the cancer hospital. Each year it had a huge deficit because of treating the majority of its patients for free. At this point it only generated 30 per cent of its revenues and for the rest we relied on donations. During the elections my powerful political opponents had – as well as targeting my personal life – made allegations about the hospital in the press, claiming that it was not in fact treating the poor for free and that donations were being used on my election campaign. This inevitably caused some donors to doubt us and fundraising stalled. The two most important board members of the hospital, Razaak Dawood and Dr Parvez Hasan, asked me to give up politics as they feared it would destroy the great project. They told me to be realistic and that I had no chance of succeeding in our corrupt political culture. All my life I have been told to be pragmatic – I heard this again and again during the course of my cricket career and all through the early years of the hospital. But I resolutely remain an idealist. For me, pragmatism today in Pakistan means accepting a corrupt and oppressive status quo. At times like this in my life, when things seem hopeless, I always look back to similar occasions – in cricket or in the hospital – when persistence eventually led to success.

Nonetheless, even my idealism was tested in 1997, which was to prove an extremely difficult year. Aside from my political woes and the hospital funding problem, I had a personal financial crisis. The court case in England against Botham and Lamb had drained me financially, and since they

203

had appealed against the verdict against them, I could not get my costs back. Had the case gone to appeal there was no way I could have fought it as I had spent so much money during the elections. To top it all Jemima's father, Jimmy Goldsmith, was dying from cancer and she was totally distraught. He passed away in July 1997, leaving his family and friends bereft. A few weeks later Princess Diana died. Her visit to the hospital earlier in the year had brought fresh donations, giving us enough breathing space for me to organize some more fundraisers and stop it going under. She had offered to attend a fundraiser in Saudi Arabia later in the year to help further. Her death capped what was the worst twelve months of my life since 1985 when I lost my mother. Looking back, the only thing that made me happy that year was watching my son Sulaiman grow up. For me, nothing in my life gave me more joy than having children. Had I known how happy they would make me I would have got married when I was younger.

Aside from my faith and my family, what helped me during this period of my life were the lessons I had learned in cricket. They told me that there were no shortcuts in life. If you wanted something you had to work for it. And that hard work was never wasted. If one had a passion for what one wanted to achieve then hard work ceased to be drudgery. You only lose when you give up in your mind. In addition, I had learned that circumstances never remain the same; but never must one give up if one feels one is heading towards defeat. I used to find that at the start of a five-day test match one could never predict how the five days would pan out, as it was dependent on so many factors. The pessimists in the team would some-times conclude after the first day that we were going to lose and more or less accept defeat. Being an optimist I always used to look at it differently. I found unexpected situations would suddenly give you the opportunity to make a comeback in the game. For instance, the weather would change, or the way the pitch was playing. Or the other team could just make a mistake you could capitalize on. If you hadn't already given up you could make the most of these variables. I have kept this attitude in life. Besides, hopelessness is faithlessness. There were people within my party, as well as plenty of political commentators, who started predicting that after Sharif's heavy mandate no one would be able to dislodge him for the next decade. At this point my party was completely written off by everyone. Sharif's party itself was already planning for the next twenty years so carried away was it by its two-thirds majority. I thought differently and was to be proved right. With my usual dogged optimism, I set about dealing with the various issues on my plate. First was the hospital. On the back of Princess Diana's visit we had started a campaign to invite all opinion-makers, journalists, columnists and newspaper editors to the hospital to visit. By the beginning of 1998, all these efforts combined to lift the hospital's finances out of danger. By 1999 donations had gone back to the pre-election level. Meanwhile, my personal financial problems started easing up too. I began to write and commentate on cricket just enough to make my contributions to the party and pay the bills. In 1999 Botham and Lamb dropped their appeal, so I did not have to think of additional funds. With better organization I also began to have more time to enjoy family life. My greatest sacrifice for being in politics was not always being able to spend as much time as I wanted to with my family. In April 1999, the Almighty blessed us with our second son, Kasim.

Politics, however, was still a problem. I had managed to settle the party's debts within the year but raising money was almost impossible. Our office holders never had sufficient funds to do full-time politics. As the country's economic situation worsened, some of our office bearers went bankrupt; others had to work doubly hard to earn the same amount of income. A lot of my time was spent in settling disputes, usually when the workers of a particular area would refuse to acknowledge a senior office bearer because he was not giving enough time to the party. If the head of a district did not work, the whole district would become inactive. We were up against the feudal landlords and career politicians, people who had often inherited a constituency and had the infrastructure and resources to do politics full-time. I also had difficulty finding leadership for my party. This is in fact a general problem in Pakistan. During my cricketing career I always used to wonder why there was so much intrigue within the Pakistan cricket team. I played cricket in England for several first-class teams – Oxford, Worcester and Sussex. I also played for New South Wales in the Australian Sheffield Shield competition. I never saw any intrigue against captains in first-class teams I played for in England or Australia, even though some were pretty poor. Yet in Pakistan there were always groups within the team that were ready to undermine the captain whenever they lost. I was made captain in 1982 when the team rebelled and refused to play under the incumbent skipper. After I retired in 1992 there were multiple changes in the captaincy. Pakistan made close to thirty changes between

1992 and 2010 while in that same period Australia had only four different captains. I also had a problem of frequent infighting within the fundraising committees for the hospital that I had set up in various cities abroad. After a lot of research I realized that the reason for lack of leadership in Pakistan is partly because of our school system. Almost all of our test cricketers and political workers are state-school educated but sadly the public education system has deteriorated dramatically in the past forty years. Most schools just do not groom students in the art of leadership, failing to teach them how to handle responsibility. It was different at Aitchison, where there was a system of prefects, head boys and team captains. On top of that we had military training so that we were taught about teamwork and the qualities a leader needed to command respect. Unfortunately the vast majority of our private schools and almost all the government schools have neither any sports facilities nor any extracurricular activities. Students therefore do not have the opportunity to learn that authority brings with it responsibility and abusing that position loses one the respect of one's subordinates.

Despite my struggle to find the right people to work with and the sheer drudgery of the endless travelling, my crisscrossing of the country was highly educational and at times inspiring. This was especially so when I met people who, with no resources but lots of passion, were doing everything they could for Pakistan. I found the biggest hurdle in my way was cynicism. People had been led up the garden path so many times that they were sceptical about everyone. How could they be sure I was not like the previous politician offering change? The period of about four years after our failed election bid was one of great learning. Meeting so many people was an education in itself. I learned to judge people more effectively and gradually began to be able to make up my mind very quickly about the mindset of those I was dealing with. Sharif had corrupted politics so much that most people were looking to make money out of it. I found dealing with such types the worst aspect of politics. I learned to get to the point quickly. This ability to distinguish between the important and the trivial allowed me to manage my time better. Also, after dealing with our devastating electoral loss, and the subsequent stream of crises within the party, I had a good understanding of my team and knew which members I could depend on. I had discovered in cricket that you only know the real worth of your players when they are put under pressure.

As I had predicted, Sharif was not to last long. Between his economic mismanagement and growing disregard for the institutions of a modern state, antagonism towards him mounted. In September 1999 virtually the entire opposition formed the Grand Democratic Alliance (GDA) on a one-point agenda to campaign for his removal. That year he had railroaded the 15th Amendment – which would have given him dictatorial powers as the '*amir ul-momineen*', or leader of the faithful – through parliament with his brute majority. He was already behaving like a Mughal emperor after pushing through the 13th Amendment (which made the presidency impotent) and the 14th Amendment (which made the parliament a rubber-stamping body and meant that no member of his party could disobey the chairman or they would lose their seat). After the 15th Amendment there would have been no check to his already unprecedented powers. We feared that once the senate election took place in March 2000, Sharif would then command a majority there too, enabling him to make the 15th Amendment law. Sharif and his party had already done something that remains one of the most disgraceful events in our country's history: senior members of his party, along with party workers, physically attacked the Supreme Court of Pakistan in 1997, and the chief justice – who had dared to start contempt proceedings against Sharif – had to flee from the court.

The Grand Democratic Alliance held rallies in all the major cities. It was clear that public opinion had turned against Sharif; though the ordinary people of Pakistan were not concerned about the 15th Amendment, they were being crushed by growing unemployment and a faltering economy on one side and constant price rises (especially utility bills) on the other.

Further weakening Sharif's position was growing tension with the army chief, General Musharraf, after the ill-conceived and disastrous Kargil operation. In May 1999, New Delhi discovered that Pakistani soldiers and Kashmiri freedom fighters had occupied the Kargil heights, in Indian-occupied Kashmir. Ironically this came just three months after Sharif had hosted the Indian prime minister Atal Behari Vajpayee on his historic peace-making visit to Lahore – the first time, since the Indian involvement in the conflict in East Pakistan that had led to the establishment of Bangladesh, that the two heads of government had met formally and issued a declaration (and a memorandum of understanding which committed both parties to peace) as a result. According to Sharif's version of events, the then commander-in-chief of the army, Musharraf, had launched the operation without consulting him; however, Musharraf insisted that the prime minister had been on board. Whatever the truth of the matter, Sharif found himself in a difficult situation. Pakistan was slammed by the international community and the Indians retaliated. Seeing the Pakistani position was untenable, Sharif was forced to beg Bill Clinton for help in brokering a peace deal with New Delhi. Sharif ordered the troops to withdraw, confusing a humiliated Pakistani public who had been fed the official line that only Kashmiri freedom fighters had occupied the Kargil heights and that Pakistan had no control over them. There then followed a cold war between Musharraf and Sharif. Any genuine leader would have hauled the army chief in front of him and court-martialled him for what turned out to be one of Pakistan's biggest debacles – not just in terms of lives, money and international reputation but also damage to the Kashmiri cause. Instead Sharif dithered for months before eventually attempting to remove Musharraf in the most bizarre way. On 12 October 1999, the army chief was mid-air on his way home from a trip to Sri Lanka when Sharif sacked him and appointed Ziauddin Butt as his replacement. He diverted Musharraf's plane in order to buy himself more time and a chaotic few hours ensued before army officials loyal to Musharraf rebelled and launched a full-scale military takeover. The victorious Musharraf had the prime minister and his cronies arrested. Military rule was back.

The amazing thing was that the same GDA members who had been virtually pleading with the army to remove Sharif (there was no constitutional way of getting rid of him) were later to club together with him and form another alliance against Musharraf. Benazir's PPP began to make overtures to Sharif when she realized that the army was not going to ask her to join the government and was instead bent on pursuing corruption charges against her. When I found out, I could not believe what contempt these opportunistic politicians had for the people of Pakistan. Just a few months previously they were telling the public that Sharif was the greatest threat to democracy in the country and now they had to ally with him 'in order to save Pakistan's democracy'. Benazir and Sharif had been trying to expose each other's corruption to the public for eleven years. Indeed the Sharif government had spent a fortune in taxpayers' money trying to get Benazir convicted of graft and had put Zardari in jail; yet when they realized that Musharraf was intent on charging them both, they clung to each other. That sums up Pakistan's politics from 1988 to 1999. No wonder that according to a Gallup survey, 80 per cent of the population supported the military takeover. As for Sharif, he was later tried and convicted on charges of hijacking and terrorism. He took a plea bargain to avoid life imprisonment and was exiled to Saudi Arabia in 2000.

While I welcomed what seemed like an end to the Benazir–Sharif merry-go-round, I was also thankful for Musharraf's coup for personal reasons. Since our marriage Jemima had been doing her best to get involved in life in Pakistan. Not only had she converted to Islam and adapted to Pakistani culture, but she had learned to speak Urdu quite well. In the elections she had campaigned for me, giving speeches in Urdu. She had also helped me with the hospital fundraising. We could sell our fundraising dinners much better if she was guaranteed to be there. She also started a clothing business, having clothes embroidered in Pakistan and selling them in the West. All the profits went to the hospital and her business gave employment to hundreds of women. I was particularly proud of her when she decided to help Afghan refugees in Jalozai camp living in sub-human conditions. She had read an article about how some children had died of cold at the camp, home to thousands of refugees since the Soviet invasion of Afghanistan. Being a mother herself, this affected her deeply and so she launched a charity and raised millions of rupees for tents, provisions and medical clinics for the refugees.

However, just as we were working to make our cross-cultural marriage succeed, external forces were attempting to sabotage our family life. We discovered how truly vicious the political mafia in Pakistan could be. In December 1998, just to embarrass me politically, an antique-smuggling accusation was slapped on Jemima by Sharif's government. It alleged that tiles Jemima had sent to her mother as a Christmas present were antique, despite the fact that they were bought from a shop that never even claimed they were of historical interest. Pakistan's laws are very strict about the exporting of antiques. After the case was registered, Jemima had one of the tiles examined by three museums in England and had a thermo-luminescence test done to date it. All confirmed the tiles were modern. So keen was the government to implicate Jemima in the case, though, that it did not even follow the customs department's own laws. A nine-member committee comprising members of the archaeological department, the customs department and the person accused have to deliberate before an object is declared an antique. Instead, one government employee in the archaeological department declared them to be antique. The case should have immediately been thrown out of court but was pending for months and the judge kept giving the government time to improve its case. Since smuggling is a non-bailable offence in Pakistan and potentially carried a sentence of up to seven years in jail, I decided that Jemima should stay in England until the case was over. This again meant a disruption to our family life. Neither of us could take a risk with a government-controlled judiciary, especially with a two-year-old and another baby on the way. After the military coup, the case against Jemima was immediately thrown out, but she had been forced to stay out of the country for eleven months in total.

Sadly, even after this major respite, politics was to cause further disruption to our family life. If the 1997 elections had been hard on our marriage, the 2002 polls were even tougher. At least in 1997 Jemima had been able to participate in my campaign; this time she had to stay out. Instead of being able to be the asset she should have been, my political opponents had turned her into a liability. Because they couldn't hurl the usual accusations of sleaze at me, they attacked me through her. It was especially hard for her not to be actively involved because she is basically a very political person. This was a great blow for our marriage. A cross-cultural marriage can work if your passions and objectives are the same but Jemima had to be sidelined. And even then she was not spared; spurious stories about her continued to emerge in the Pakistani press. A comment about having read a book by Salman Rushdie for her university dissertation on post-colonial literature turned into a story saying she had chosen him as her guide. There were demonstrations calling for her citizenship to be revoked. Hard for anyone, this kind of treatment was particularly distressing for somebody like Jemima, who was naturally shy and sensitive. Compounding our difficulties, during the campaign I was away touring the country for about five months. I was campaigning almost single-handedly, my best candidate having withdrawn. I barely saw my wife and children. In the end, the party won one seat – my own in Mianwali, which given the lack of freedom the elections were conducted under, with the whole state machinery helping my opponent, was a great achievement.

It came at a heavy personal cost. When I returned home to Islamabad I found Jemima demoralized and for the first time realized that she was losing the battle and giving up. I had already started to harbour guilt about her being so unhappy. She had tried incredibly hard, but my political career and the constant attacks on her were very difficult. I felt guilty because as the older partner I was more responsible for our marriage. She was so young when we married and when we made the decision to launch my party – how could she have known what such a life would entail in a foreign land? But I should have thought about all the possible consequences. For the first time I began to think that maybe I had been irresponsible; just because I was battle-hardened after years of struggle did not mean that my wife should have been thrown at such a tender age into the turbulent world of Pakistani politics. Adapting to a completely alien culture was already challenge enough. Personal attacks on people's families, especially their wives, are rare in Pakistani culture. It had never occurred to me that people could stoop so low as to attack a young foreign woman because of her husband's political work.

So when Jemima said she wanted to return to England to study for a one-year masters degree in Modern Trends in Islam at London's School of Oriental and African Studies and take the boys with her, as devastating as the news was, I didn't resist. As always, I believed that somehow circumstances might change. I hoped that if the political climate improved I could lure her back, or that she would come to realize that the life we had created together in Pakistan was worth staying for. But in my heart I knew it was the beginning of the end. Above all, a marriage cannot work with two people living on different continents. Within a year I could see that she was absorbed by her life back in London with her family and friends and was happy there. The six months leading up to our divorce and the six months after made up the hardest year of my life. The children's obvious distress exacerbated the misery; they are always the ones who suffer the most in divorce. Sulaiman, being older, felt it more and seeing his pain doubled my pain. I missed them terribly. Nothing filled the void. I loved fatherhood more than anything I had ever experienced in life. Having had children after my cricket career I had been at home to watch every phase of their growing up and was a hands-on parent, an experience so many fathers miss out on because of their work. My life had been work and family; I hardly ever saw my friends or went to dinner parties. Now not having them around was the hardest thing to come to terms with. For the first time I began to understand how people could lose the will to live. Usually someone who wakes up every morning with optimism and joy at facing a new day, I suddenly found it hard to get out of bed.

Once again, faith got me through these difficult times. Once I had come to terms with the divorce I picked myself up and threw myself back into pursuing my political and humanitarian work. The optimist in me cannot help but see the brighter side of a situation and I felt that in many ways I was luckier than most in my divorce. There was no acrimony, none of the bitterness caused when one partner has been unfaithful to the other, no financial disputes and no lawyers involved. Jemima is very generous in giving me time with the boys. They come to stay with me during their school holidays and I then devote myself entirely to them. Whenever I'm in England, I stay with my ex-mother-in-law, Lady Annabel, who still treats me as part of the family. Her sons Ben and Zac are like younger brothers to me. The rest of the time I am free to focus on my work. Moreover, the burden of Jemima's unhappiness was lifted from me and if there's one thing worse than seeing a loved one leave, it's seeing a loved one unhappy. As the Quran says: 'After every hardship there is ease' (Quran 65: 7 and 7: 42); and I consoled myself with the Quranic verse that sometimes Allah doesn't answer our prayers because he knows what's best for us.

It is hard to say that with hindsight I would have done things differently anyway. My married friends always envied me my life when I was a bachelor but the greatest happiness and contentment in my life came from my marriage. I always was a risk-taker so I was willing to take the lows with the highs. Whenever I looked back and thought about what else I could have done I felt that, given the circumstances, I had worked harder at making my marriage work than at anything else in my life. So there were no regrets. If anything could have prevented me from marrying Jemima, it was the realization that she was maybe too young and inexperienced to be presented with such a challenge. It pained me that she had to endure all the suffering that divorce entails. She gained two beautiful sons, though, and a second home in Pakistan, where she was much loved. She is still very attached to the country and always the first to rally round when disaster befalls us – be it floods or earthquakes. People often ask me why I didn't go to London to save our relationship but it was never an option. I could never imagine living in London, just making a living out of cricket journalism. For me that would have been a purposeless existence. I cannot even imagine life without a passion and a purpose; once I had cricket, now I have my political struggle – which was to become all the more urgent after the turmoil in Pakistan unleashed by the 9/11 attacks. And Jemima knew that. She did not marry a lounge lizard; my drive was one of the things that had attracted her to me. I think I would have been diminished in her eyes if I had lost that drive.

Chapter Seven

The General, 1999–2001

AFTER MUSHARRAF HAD COME TO POWER IN A MILITARY COUP in 1999, many of us in Pakistan hoped he might bring a new lease of life to our country, following years of unstable and corrupt civilian governments. Nawaz Sharif's plans to award himself dictatorial powers under the 15th Amendment were a genuine threat to any hope of establishing a proper democracy in Pakistan. Thank God we are saved, I thought at the time, as Musharraf promised to hold fresh elections, introduce genuine democracy and clean up corruption. Initially sincerity oozed out of him.

Yet even at my first encounter with him, in a secret meeting a few months after the coup, the alarm bells should have rung. I should have realized then and there that the general had no vision and no understanding of the importance of the rule of law. He had already issued his first Provisional Constitutional Order (PCO) and thrown a few judges out but he had left two of the most corrupt judges in place. So I took the opportunity to ask him why he hadn't cleaned up the judiciary properly:

surely, I said, if his main concern was good governance and curbing corruption this was the first thing he had to do because only a strong, independent judicial system can act as a check and balance on an executive. All of the worst instances of corruption in developing countries come from politicians having too much power. The reason they get away with it is because the judiciary is always subservient to the executive, or is in fact an extension of the executive. 'Imran,' Musharraf said, 'if we touch the judiciary we'll become pariahs for the international community.' Of course he'd already done this himself; as it was, he should have worried about fixing Pakistan first, and then worried about the rest of the world. If the people of Pakistan had been behind him, he could have handled the world. As he was to find out seven years later, when he did remove the chief justice, even the backing of the world's only superpower could not keep him in power when the people of Pakistan turned against him. The same thing happened to the Shah of Iran (and more recently Hosni Mubarak in Egypt and Zine El Abidine Ben Ali in Tunisia); when the Iranian people turned against him there was nothing the Americans could do to save him.

At first, many of us overlooked Musharraf's early errors, thinking he was being badly advised, or that he did not understand politics. And we had been so disillusioned by the corrupt governments of Nawaz Sharif and Benazir Bhutto that had ruled Pakistan for the previous eleven years that we were full of hope. In the end, though, it became apparent that his only vision was how to keep himself in power. Every compromise he made was to strengthen his own position. Just as an earlier dictator, General Zia ul-Haq, had seized on the

Soviet invasion of Afghanistan in 1979 to make himself indispensable to the Americans, so too did Musharraf use the 9/11 attacks on New York and Washington to bolster his position.

On 11 September 2001, I was speaking at a political rally near Peshawar, the capital of Khyber Pakhtunkhwa, when I heard about the attacks on New York and Washington. As we watched the second plane fly into the tower live on television I felt a sense of foreboding. Like many, I was shocked and appalled by the sight of people so desperate to escape the inferno inside that they threw themselves out of the building. Never had I seen such a horrific tragedy live on television. It had a huge impact on everyone I knew. My first thought was to hope the hijackers weren't Muslim, my second was to hope they weren't Pakistani. When it emerged they were Arab I knew that nothing would ever be the same for the Muslim world again. As far as Pakistan was concerned, though, the fact that none of its nationals were involved made little difference. A media circus descended on Islamabad within a week and we suddenly found ourselves on the frontline of the 'war on terror'. Musharraf, previously viewed with suspicion by the Americans, suddenly became a key US partner. When US president Bill Clinton had come to Pakistan in 2000 he had refused to have a photograph taken of them shaking hands, so wary was he of being seen to endorse a military dictator. But all concern for Pakistani democracy evaporated after 9/11, as Musharraf became Washington's greatest ally against 'Islamic extremism'.

US dollars poured into the country, just as they had in Zia's time, as Musharraf helped the Americans against Pakistan's former Afghan Taliban allies. After 9/11 he rounded up hundreds of people and handed them over to Washington for bounty; according to the charity Reprieve, 95 per cent of the people handed over by Pakistan were innocent. In his memoir Musharraf declared that he had transferred over seven hundred al-Qaeda suspects to the United States, yet in doing so he had violated article 4A of the constitution, which states that any person on Pakistani soil cannot be given over to another authority unless he is taken to a court of law and provided with the chance to prove his innocence. Musharraf violated the law of the land to prove to the Americans that he was a 'bulwark against Islamic extremism', just as many Arab dictators have done over the years. The United States in turn used Musharraf; its commitment to democracy, so loudly proclaimed during its later invasion of Iraq, abandoned in favour of the 'war on terror'. It cared only that the Pakistan army should be used as cheap mercenaries in America's war. Just as the Americans had done with Zia, they preferred one strong military ruler to a chaotic and demanding democracy.

General Ehtisham Zamir headed the political wing of the Inter-Services Intelligence (ISI) agency, and was tasked with bringing together General Musharraf's 'coalition of reform'. He was looking for my party's support for the General, to give him ' the strength to take on the crooked politicians'. After the referendum, in spring 2002, designed to give legitimacy to Musharraf's presidency, we met again and he told me of the 'Grand National Alliance', and that's when the alarm bells started ringing. Zamir gave me the ISI's assessment of how many seats each party could get in the autumn elections; I asked about the plans to get rid of the corrupt politicians, and he told me about the reality – that it was unfortunate but the people of Pakistan voted for crooks. I realized we'd been led up the garden path and, for short-term gains, the long-term interests of Pakistan were going to be crucified. Sadly this has been a legacy of intelligence agencies in Pakistan who, without a proper broad-based analysis, have made decisions which have proved disastrous for our country. (Other secret agencies have done tremendous harm in the world, especially the CIA, which for short-term goals has created so much chaos in so many countries.) This was my first experience of dealing with the ISI. After that, I resolved never to let the agencies influence our decision-making in the future.

I met Musharraf for the fifth and final time on 23 July 2002, when he invited me to President House in Islamabad; I was hoping to change his mind about making this coalition of crooks. It was then I realized how much those of us who had supported him initially had been fooled by his promises to clean up the political system. Also present were Musharraf's spokesman and national security adviser, along with the head of the ISI, and Zamir. The meeting was friendly enough at the start, as he told me he wanted me to join his coalition. He claimed that he had always thought that I was the only clean politician in the country. When he told me who the politicians were in his 'coalition of reform', I was shocked. Some of these politicians were considered the epitome of corruption in the country, and I told Musharraf that joining them would lose me all credibility, since my main platform was anti-corruption. Musharraf said that if I didn't join him I would lose. I told him I would rather lose than discredit myself. Benazir and Sharif had been personal friends before they joined politics; the only reason I opposed them was because of their corruption. They did at least have a vote bank, though, whereas some of the politicians in Musharraf's so-called coalition of reform that he wanted me to join were both crooked and without a vote bank. I warned him that if he insisted on associating himself with these corrupt politicians then Benazir and Sharif would benefit. People by this point were sick of their corruption but if Musharraf went ahead with his coalition of the crooked the voters would reason that all the main parties were corrupt anyway, levelling the field again for Benazir and Sharif. 'Unfortunately, people in Pakistan vote for crooks,' he said, repeating the phrase I'd heard before, telling me that I was too idealistic and to be pragmatic.

I told him that he should have put in place a strong judiciary, an independent election commission, a credible national accountability bureau and then held free and fair polls. 'If you had done all that,' I said, 'you'd be the biggest name in Pakistan after Jinnah.' He said there was a risk involved. It was then that it occurred to me he meant a risk for himself, as opposed to for Pakistan. He could not comprehend the potential damage to the country from his alliance with corrupt politicians. It dawned on me that he had a naive belief that as long as he was in power he could control anything. He had no idea about the mess he was creating. Up till then I had assumed Musharraf was being misadvised by his close aide Tariq Aziz, but now I realized that rather than helping him form some kind of political vision, advisers like Aziz were simply counselling him on how to stay in power. That was my last meeting with Musharraf and from then onwards our paths diverged.

By not joining Musharraf my party fell between two stools. Because we had previously been seen to be close to him we were not considered an opposition party. But now we were firmly out of the establishment-backed coalition. Consequently a lot of potentially good candidates abandoned us. The ones that were left were turned on by the ISI; its agents either threatened the Tehreek-e-Insaf candidates or cajoled or lured them into Musharraf's PML (Q) (the Pakistan Muslim League – a breakaway from Sharif's party, distinguished by the 'Q' for *Quaid*, short for *Quaid-e-Azam*, or Great Leader, the title given to Jinnah). Some candidates gave up altogether, telling me they could not fight the ISI. They said they would be wasting their money. Cash is essential for political candidates in Pakistan, who can spend a minimum of 10 million rupees in rural constituencies. No politician in the country's history up till then had ever beaten the establishment.

From October 2002 onwards, my party went through the most difficult period of its existence. Although following the 1997 election rout things had been extremely tough, it was after the elections in 2002 that we went through our toughest phase. Having just one seat and with the entire party in disarray, it became a question of survival, just keeping our heads above water. I have no doubt that had I not won my seat – against all odds, because the entire government machinery was working against me – it would have been all over for my party. (I won with a 5,000-vote margin, a record to that point for the constituency.) Having that one seat meant I could just keep the party alive; but it was hard, as barely twenty of the top leadership were active, and even they were difficult to keep motivated. Others either left the party or became dormant. One positive of this difficult period was that I realized who were my real team – it's only in a crisis that you know the worth of those around you. The one man who resolutely stood beside me through thick and thin was Saifullah Niazi. The other who was a great support through these tough times was Rashid Khan.

It took me a year to clear the debts the party had incurred during the elections; we moved out of our big central office in Islamabad and shifted the office into my parliamentary lodge, given to me as member of parliament. I cleared our last remaining debts in an unusual way; I was with my family in England, and my brother-in-law, Ben Goldsmith, kept asking me about what would happen in an England versus South Africa test match. I discovered his interest came from his 'spread-betting' on the game. I decided to watch the match, and learned he'd already lost about £10,000 on the game, so I told him that in order to give him tips I would have to watch the match, and that every pound he made after recovering the £10,000 he'd lost would go towards clearing my party's debt. I have never gambled in my life and have never understood its attraction, but now for the sake of clearing my party's debts I watched the test match with Ben for the next two days, telling him what to do and when. Not only did he clear his debt, but we made enough money to clear my party's debt as well. At one point the bookie asked, 'Mr Goldsmith, you don't happen to be sitting with your brother-in-law, do you?'

For the next few months, the party had to be run on a shoe-string budget; no one donates to losers. For the next three and a half years, the party fought for its life. The one thing that saved us was independent television; from 2004 onwards, I had access to the TV current affairs programmes, and I took clear stands on various issues – especially on the 'war on terror', which I always felt was a disaster for Pakistan while it enriched the elite; and from March 2007 onwards, standing with the chief justice in his struggle against the president.

In my view, Musharraf really started to go downhill after the 2002 elections. He had tried to split the opposition to guarantee victory for his own party, the PML (Q), by encouraging the Muttahida Majlis-e-Amal (MMA), a coalition of religious parties. But his plans backfired when almost the entire Pashtun belt voted for the MMA in protest against the US bombardment of Afghanistan. Since I had been canvassing in two constituencies in Khyber Pakhtunkhwa, I knew that all the Pashtun would vote for the MMA in sympathy for the Taliban, who were now considered fellow Pashtuns fighting the American Goliath on the other side of the border. But the intelligence agencies, who were orchestrating the elections for Musharraf from behind the scenes, had never expected them to do so well, and the MMA's success upset his carefully laid plans to rig the outcome. After the polls Musharraf struggled to pull together enough politicians to obtain a clear majority. Despite his commitment to fight corruption, he was forced to bribe and blackmail some corrupt politicians, who accepted promises of posts as ministers in return for cases against them being dropped.

But even dictators have limits on their authority and in Musharraf's case the challenge came from the judiciary – the very judiciary whose importance he had overlooked when he first came to power. In late 2006, Chief Justice Iftikhar Chaudhry had embarrassed the government by reversing a high-profile decision to privatize Pakistan Steel Mills and Musharraf began to think he was becoming too independent. The chief justice had also initiated investigations into the 'forced disappearances' of people believed to have been detained without due process by the Pakistani military and intelligence services as part of their contribution to the 'war on terror'. Worried that Chaudhry would refuse to allow him to flout the constitution by contesting presidential elections due that year while remaining head of the army, Musharraf suspended him on 9 March 2007 on allegations of abuse of office and nepotism. He had not, however, anticipated the strength of the popular reaction. A move that might have been carried out quietly in Zia's day, when the only TV channel was the government-owned one, was now loudly broadcast by the independent television media. Ironically, Musharraf had during his regime encouraged the boom in commercial television channels. And initially he was the chief beneficiary as he came across well on television compared to the discredited politicians. A more active media was not to his advantage, though, once his popularity started to wane.

Developing countries persist because the governments are not held to account by a judicial system – corrupt politicians cannot afford to allow an independent judiciary. In Pakistan, every military dictator has subjugated the judiciary. Sadly, even the democratic governments have never allowed an independent judiciary to flourish – from Bhutto, through his daughter Benazir, to Sharif whose senior party members physically attacked the Supreme Court. (There are currently fifteen injunctions from the Supreme Court, including those dealing with corruption, being defied by Zardari's government.)

Musharraf now tried to crack down on the judiciary as protests against his treatment of Chaudhry spread like wildfire. The chief justice refused to stand down and the media and opposition parties, my party being in the forefront, leapt to his defence as our country's lawyers took to the streets for the first time. A constitutional crisis threatened as the wave of public sympathy for the lawyers' movement stoked calls for an end to Musharraf's seven-and-a-half-year military rule. This was a defining moment. The chief justice was supposed to uphold not only the rights of individual Pakistanis but also those of the country's institutions and the constitution. If the state could not even protect his rights, how could it protect the rights of the most vulnerable sections of society?

The lawyers' movement was a significant development for Pakistan, offering hope of a plank of civil society activism that did not represent any particular religious or political group. The way in which the surge in independent media had sharpened political consciousness in Pakistan was consistently underestimated by Musharraf, and later by Sharif and Benazir. After years of only state television, PTV, there was now a plethora of current affairs programmes and chat shows to fuel debate about the state of the nation. My party was the greatest beneficiary, enjoying an upsurge in popularity thanks to the greater visibility the media provided and the way in which it was highlighting some of the issues we stood for. One of my party's main demands when I had founded it in 1996 was for an independent judicial system, and for years ours was a cry in the wilderness. Finally it was an idea whose time had come.

The one most powerful name behind the entire lawyers' movement backing the chief justice was a founder member of

Tehreek-e-Insaf, Hamid Khan. While he controlled the lawyers' movement from behind the scenes, I was able to mobilize my party and the politicians behind the chief justice. The first press conference was held in conjunction with Qazi Hussain Ahmad, then the head of Jamaat-e-Islami.

Chaudhry set off on a tour of courts and lawyers' associations around the country, drawing huge crowds of people who tossed rose petals at his cavalcade and called out anti-Musharraf slogans. On 8 May, along with my party members, I spent a night outside Lahore's Data Darbar shrine, built in the eleventh century, waiting to welcome Chaudhry to the city. He was supposed to have arrived by early evening but had been waylaid on the Grand Trunk Road from Islamabad by crowds of well-wishers waiting at the roadside to greet him. So he did not make it to Lahore till about 7 a.m. All night streams of people from Lahore's Old City kept coming up to me to talk about what was happening. It was then that I realized something quite incredible was taking place in Pakistan. There was a general awakening of the public for the first time since I had entered politics. As the sun came up a man shouted from the distance, 'Imran, Sahib, a new dawn is rising.' I'll never forget that. Pakistan had changed.

The strength of support for Chaudhry panicked Musharraf, which showed a few days later in his handling of the chief justice's trip to Karachi. Chaudhry was due to address the lawyers of the Sindh High Court Bar Association, but his visit turned ugly. At least thirty-nine people died and more than a hundred were injured after the Muttahida Qaumi Movement (MQM), allies of Musharraf, attacked Chaudhry's supporters. The MQM, initially founded to represent the interests of the descendants of the Mohajirs, immigrants who came from India in the bloody tumult of Partition, now essentially operates like a terrorist organization. Karachi is their stronghold. MQM gunmen fired straight into a procession of political parties heading to the airport to receive the chief justice. At the time, I was participating in a live television programme called *Capital Talk*. In the studio we watched real-time footage of people bearing MQM flags and firing into the crowds with Kalashnikovs. But the television anchors were so petrified of stating the obvious – that these were MQM supporters – that they kept referring to them as 'militants'. The secretary general of my party, Arif Alvi, called me on my mobile to tell me that he and other party members – who were there to demonstrate in support of Chaudhry – were under attack by the MQM gunmen. He said the police and the paramilitary Pakistan Rangers just stood by and watched the mayhem. Amongst those injured were ten of my party members. Luckily all survived. While once upon a time in Pakistan the public would have been shielded from an event like this, now it was all broadcast on television. Human Rights Watch slammed the government for arresting opposition activists in the run-up to Chaudhry's visit. It suggested it had 'deliberately sought to foment violence in Karachi' and failed to rein in the unrest, whether through incompetence or complicity. Musharraf's liberal credentials were in tatters. Furious, I decided to try and get the MQM leader Altaf Hussain charged in London, where he has lived in self-imposed exile since 1992 because of assassination threats. It was impossible to have him tried in Pakistan; people are too terrified of the party to testify. When there was a hearing into the violence in Karachi, proceedings were disrupted by crowds of MQM supporters and it was postponed indefinitely. I gave Scotland Yard a file on Hussain but witnesses were too cowed to come forward even in London. Then Musharraf, and later his successor Asif Ali Zardari, denied the British police permission to come to Pakistan to interview witnesses.

By 16 July, Musharraf was forced by public pressure to reinstate Chaudhry. But the general was now badly weakened. He tried to recover some ground by reaching a deal – brokered by George W. Bush's administration – with Benazir Bhutto. Having fled the country in 1999 to avoid corruption charges she was allowed to return to Pakistan to contest elections. In return for her agreeing to share power with Musharraf – with her as prime minister and him as president – he introduced the National Reconciliation Ordinance (NRO). This meant all corruption cases against her and her husband, Asif Ali Zardari, were dropped. This was made out to be something like South Africa's Truth and Reconciliation initiative, but it was in a completely different context to post-apartheid South Africa, where it had been a question of bringing two communities together. More importantly, there was no Truth. None of those people ever admitted to corruption, including Zardari. They thought by using the word 'reconciliation' they'd be exonerated, as if this was all about political victimization. All the billions lost to corruption were waved aside by this ordinance – which later was annulled by the Supreme Court as being against the law of the land. This ordinance would come to have disastrous consequences for Pakistan; now we have many criminals sitting in many key positions today. Corruption would turn to plunder. Yet still Musharraf remained weak; and still he remained threatened by the judiciary, who could potentially wreck his plans to get himself re-elected as president. The deal signed with Benazir – at the time one of the country's most popular politicians – gave him the political space to make his next move. In October he won the presidential polls but controversy over his eligibility to stand rumbled on. On 3 November, he sacked the chief justice, purged the Supreme Court, declared a state of emergency and muzzled the media. That's when my arrest warrants were issued.

As I warned in an article I wrote for the Pakistani newspaper *The News* while I was in prison, Musharraf was in the process of implementing the first phase of his plan to gain power for another five years with a 'massive crackdown on the genuine opposition, lawyers, human rights activists and the civil society. He is hoping that the police brutality will induce enough fear in the people for him to crush all dissent within a couple of weeks, before he takes the next step of getting himself endorsed by his pocket judges.' He was already planning to hold parliamentary and provincial elections on 8 January 2008. I was worried the issue of the judiciary would soon be forgotten. Even the other politicians did not really want an independent justice system at that point – they changed their tune later when they realized it was a popular issue. Musharraf had hoped to use the cover of the US 'war on terror' to justify the need for extreme measures to crack down on domestic dissent. Sure enough, a few weeks after the declaration of the state of emergency, the new judges he put in place removed the final legal challenge to his re-election, clearing the way for him to resign as army chief as he had promised, and be sworn in as a civilian president. As it turned out, though, the general had overreached himself, and in the end even the Americans could not save him.

Chapter Eight

Pakistan Since 9/11

TEN YEARS AFTER AL-QAEDA'S ATTACK ON THE UNITED STATES killed almost three thousand people, the Muslim world is still paying the price. The US response has led to death and destruction on a far greater scale than anything seen in Washington and New York. The vast majority of those who have died as a result of the 'war on terror' were innocent and had absolutely nothing to do with 9/11. Estimates for the number killed in the invasion and occupation of Iraq range from around 100,000 to over a million. Tens of thousands of innocent Afghan civilians have likewise lost their lives – 80 per cent of Afghanis had not even heard of 9/11, yet they have been in the middle of death and destruction for the last ten years. In Pakistan the analyst Farrukh Saleem estimates that 33,467 Pakistanis died in terrorism-related violence between 2003 and 2010. How many more Muslims will have to pay the price? The insane 'war on terror' has decimated two countries, Iraq and Afghanistan, and brought a third one, Pakistan, almost to the verge of collapse. The three countries, despite all the US aid pumped into them, were all in *Foreign Policy* magazine's list of top-ten failed states for 2010. Nor has the 'war on terror' done the United States public any favours. Apart from actually making them less safe by increasing extremists' antagonism towards America, it has helped contribute to their economic downturn. Joseph E. Stiglitz and Linda J. Bilmes in 2008 put the total cost to the United States of the Iraq war alone at $3 trillion, although by 2010 they were saying this had proved to be conservative. The campaign against terrorism has also done tremendous damage to the reputation of the world's only superpower. A measure of a country's civilization is how it responds to pressure. When tested, the United States failed to rise to the occasion, trampling on its own principles and standards – principles and standards that had once inspired generations across the world, who saw in US history an example of the triumph of freedom and equality over colonial rule. I, like many in the developing world, grew up impressed by the United States and its ideals of democracy and human rights. Yet we saw them all violated in the name of the 'war on terror'.

For me, the high point of US moral authority was after the Second World War, when the Nazis, who were responsible for the deaths of over 30 million, were given a fair trial. Churchill wanted them summarily executed but Roosevelt insisted on a trial. In the words of Justice Robert Jackson, the chief United States prosecutor at the Nuremberg Trials: 'If certain acts of violation of treaties are crimes, they are crimes whether the United States does them or whether Germany does them, and we are not prepared to lay down a rule of criminal conduct against others which we would not be willing to have invoked against us.' This was a show of clemency and moral universalism not accorded Muslims since 9/11. Trying terrorism suspects like conventional criminals, rather than classifying them as 'enemy combatants' and throwing them in Guantanamo, would have given the United States a moral authority that would have helped win hearts and minds in the Muslim world at this vital juncture in history.

Instead, the wars in Iraq and Afghanistan, the drone attacks in Pakistan's north-west, Abu Ghraib prison, Guantanamo Bay, extraordinary rendition, the use of torture – as well as terms like 'enemy non-combatants' and 'collateral damage' – have blackened America's name. Muslims were appalled by the hypocrisy and dishonesty when America attempted to hide its imperialist designs on Iraq behind the smokescreen of allegations of weapons of mass destruction and a spurious link between Saddam Hussein's government and al-Qaeda. Saddam's secular Iraq had nothing to do with Osama bin Laden and his fundamentalist version of Islam. Besides, the United States had previously backed Saddam in the Iran–Iraq war. Nor did it escape people's attention that while it proclaimed its desire for democracy in Iraq, Washington had for decades backed authoritarian strongmen in the Middle East in order to protect its own interests. During the Cold War, the threat of communism was the excuse for supporting autocrats in the third world; now the bogeyman is radical Islam.

After 9/11, governments from Russia to Israel and India have stepped up brutality against insurgents in their own countries under the cover of the 'war on terror'. Their vicious suppression of any kind of dissent has further fuelled extremism. With revolt spreading across the Arab world in early 2011, they have been wrong-footed, caught on the wrong side of history. For years dictators like Mubarak have used the threat of Islamism to keep the United States on their side – just as Musharraf did. Even during his last days in power Mubarak tried to spook the Americans into saving him by claiming radical Islamists would take over Egypt. At the same time, Muammar Gaddafi was also blaming Libya's uprising on extremists, most notably al-Qaeda. But now the ordinary people of countries like Egypt and Tunisia have been revealed to desire nothing more sinister than democracy, rule of law, freedom, jobs and equality. The myth that the Muslim world is made up of a small section of westernized 'moderates' and a mass of ignorant conservatives ripe for exploitation by radical Islam has been fully exposed. The US-backed dictators and monarchs do not represent the aspirations of the people, who simply want the same rights taken for granted in the West.

The irony is that these dictators or puppet rulers, as illustrated by the Shah of Iran, Afghanistan's Hamid Karzai and our own Musharraf and Zardari, can achieve very little for the United States. The policy is usually counterproductive in the end because by toeing Washington's line the ruler loses all credibility and the respect of his people. As Michael Scheuer says about American foreign policy in his book *Imperial Hubris*, particularly in regards to Afghanistan and Pakistan: 'The lesson is not only that others will not do our dirty work, but that others will stop us from doing our dirty work as completely as possible. So committed are we to finding others to do hard and bloody things for us that we misread reality and enlist allies who cannot or will not do the job.'

In Muslim countries there is immense suspicion about certain lobbies taking advantage of the attacks on Washington and New York to pursue their interests. In the forefront was the lobby described by President Dwight D. Eisenhower in 1961 as the industrial-military complex, along with the neo-cons and their 'Project for the New American Century', a Washington think-tank aimed at promoting American principles around the world. The 9/11 attacks provided the neo-cons with the perfect excuse to overthrow Saddam Hussein since they had been pushing for the idea of regime change in Iraq since 1997. (The United States' own inquiries subsequently found there was no connection between Iraq and 9/11.) Aligned with them were the Israelis, who felt threatened by Iraq, and of course the oil industry. Ismael Hossein-Zadeh, an economics teacher at Drake University in Des Moines, Iowa, and author of *The Political Economy of US Militarism*, goes so far as to suggest that the United States has been taken over by a 'military-industrial-security-financial cabal' aiming for 'full-spectrum dominance' of the world. By dividing the globe into 'friends' and 'foes', 'powerful beneficiaries of war and militarism compel both groups to embark on a path of militarization, which leads inevitably to militarism and authoritarian rule'. The war profiteers behind this US militarization of the world, apart from draining national resources and adding to national debt in the various countries affected, also stoke fear and suspicion amongst different peoples and therefore provoke more conflicts.

Much of Washington's reaction to 9/11, however, has been self-defeating and it has made many mistakes. A major one was failing to distinguish between the Taliban, a medieval militia focused on domestic power, and al-Qaeda, an international organization aiming to attack American interests across the globe. The Taliban were part of the mujahideen forces that fought the Soviets. They only took power because of the failure of the post-Soviet governments to impose law and order and start rehabilitating the devastated country. Mullah Zaeef, the former Taliban ambassador to Pakistan, describes in his book *Living With the Taliban* the chaotic conditions that prevailed when the warlords ran Afghanistan. It was those conditions that led to the Taliban taking over. In over 1,400 years of Islamic history, it was the only time there had been any Taliban-type theocracy; Zaeef says that Taliban leader Mullah Omar asked him for help as they had no idea how to run a state – these were boys who'd grown up in war, they'd known nothing else for sixteen years. Afghanistan had descended into chaos, with mujahideen leaders carving out their own territories. Zaeef was asked to take on different ministries because they could hardly find any educated Taliban who knew anything about statecraft. The United States accused the Taliban of harbouring al-Qaeda, but the Taliban inherited Osama bin Laden and his organization, which was already in Afghanistan when they took over. Furthermore, several times the Taliban offered the Americans compromises that they declined. According to Mullah Zaeef, when the Americans were pushing for Afghanistan to hand bin Laden over after the bombings of US embassies in Kenya and Tanzania in 1998, the Afghans offered to have him tried either in the Supreme Court of Afghanistan or in a court formed and chaired by three Islamic countries and held in a fourth Islamic country. Washington refused, demanding that he be handed over unconditionally. He claims they would not even consider dealing with bin Laden in The Hague. He also says Mullah Omar made the Americans another offer a few days after the 9/11 attacks, agreeing to have bin Laden tried by an Islamic court – if not in Afghanistan then in another Muslim country. The Taliban leader stressed the need for the United States to produce evidence of his involvement in the attacks, as for any trial. To me this seems like a perfectly reasonable condition. When the Russians tried to extradite Chechen rebel commander Akhmed Zakayev from the UK on terrorism charges in 2003, London insisted that Moscow prove their case in a court of law. A British court then rejected the request because of lack of evidence. Bush was determined to invade Afghanistan, though, and war, instead of being a last resort, became the first option after 9/11. Right from the start, Washington showed it was not prepared to use due process in dealing with whoever it considered as terrorists.

This disregard for various international conventions meant the United States failed to mobilize support from the Muslim world – which would have been more than willing to help bring all those involved in the 9/11 attacks to justice. I can say that in Pakistan at the time I heard nothing but deep sympathy for the United States because of those terrible images of innocent people jumping to their deaths from the burning Twin Towers. Instead Bush declared a war against terrorism as if the United States was fighting a conventional army. Most significantly, rather than simply treating those terrorists as criminals, war was declared against radical Islam. It was as if this was another ideological enemy for the West to rally against after fascism and communism. Lies and distortions by the United States and various European governments have been used to get the Western public behind the wars in both Iraq and Afghanistan.

Inevitably, this fanned the perception that all Muslims were on trial. The first phone call I received from a journalist after 9/11 was from ITN's Martin Bashir. 'As a Muslim, aren't you embarrassed by the attacks?' was his immediate question. I was shocked, then realized this was what others would be thinking too. Implying all the world's 1.3 billion Muslims should feel in some way responsible for an act of a handful of criminals is a bit like asking a Christian to feel responsible for Hitler or Stalin and their atrocities, or asking a Catholic in Rome if they supported the IRA blowing up children and tourists in Omagh in 1998. By putting a whole religion in the dock the United States and its allies alienated many 'normal' Muslims. Bush's response also served to further the terrorists' cause. They were elevated from mere criminals to holy warriors acting in the name of Islam. This meant that there was obviously going to be a minority of Muslims who viewed them as martyrs and approved of what they did. This was only to get worse over the course of the decade. The death of many innocent Muslim civilians serves as a rallying call for al-Qaeda in its recruitment drive. This 'war on terror' actually manufactures terrorists. Even if they are not prepared to go to the extremes of the late bin Laden and his cohorts, the resentments bin Laden listed are felt by many Muslims. The 'war on terror' simply added to the list of grievances by causing the death of more innocent Muslim civilians. Many more terrorist attacks since 9/11, including the 7/7 bombings in

London, the failed Times Square bombing, and recently the shooting of two American soldiers by a Muslim at Frankfurt airport in Germany, were all in reaction to the wars in Afghanistan and Iraq.

I was dismayed by the West's refusal to try and understand the root causes of the religious fanaticism that had been growing for years in the Muslim world, fuelled by injustices against Muslims in Kashmir, Chechnya, Bosnia, Palestine and other places. The 9/11 attacks were undoubtedly acts of terrorism, but much of the fighting going on in many of these places is a question of ordinary Muslims reacting to what is perceived as foreign invasion or occupation. When a Muslim insurgent fights he does so in the name of Islam because to fight against injustice is jihad. Moreover, people signing up to fight alongside their Muslim brothers from other countries is simply like British or American Jews wanting to do national service in Israel. It is a question of identifying with the struggle of your co-religionists. To the Islamic world, it seems that the international community is always ready to leap to the defence of Christians but that it turns a blind eye when it comes to Muslims' right to self-determination. The UN agreed to a referendum on Christian-majority East Timor's independence from Indonesia but a UN resolution to hold a referendum on Kashmiri independence was never implemented, nor were various UN resolutions against Israel.

There are many conspiracy theories surrounding 9/11, but for me the biggest conspiracy of all was the way in which genuine political concerns in the Muslim world over the Palestinian–Israeli issue were portrayed as religious war-mongering. When Saudi Prince Alwaleed bin Talal bin Abdul

Aziz Al-Saud suggested that US policy in the Middle East, and on the Palestine question in particular, might have contributed to the 9/11 attacks, New York Mayor Rudolph W. Giuliani promptly rejected the prince's offer of 10 million dollars for the Twin Towers Fund. 'I am telling Americans what America is beginning to know already,' the prince told the *New York Times* at the time. 'America has to understand that if it wants to extract the roots of this ridiculous and terrible act, this issue [of the Palestinians] has to be solved.'

Bush claimed al-Qaeda 'hate our freedoms – our freedom of religion, our freedom of speech, our freedom to vote and assemble and disagree with each other'. Yet the British journalist Robert Fisk, one of the few Westerners to have interviewed Osama bin Laden, has written that the al-Qaeda leader listed three main reasons for his hatred of the United States: its support for Israel against the Palestinians, its support of the Saudi monarchy and the presence of US troops in Muslim lands. This is backed up by bin Laden's twelve-page treatise 'Declaration of War Against the United States', which states his intention to fight the United States and lays out his political reasons for doing so. Again, his grievances involve US backing for Arab police states and Israel, US presence on the Arabian Peninsula, US troops being stationed in Islamic nations and US support for other countries that oppress Muslims, especially Russia, China and India. He made no mention of hating the West's way of life or democracy.

Instead of addressing the Muslim world's primary source of grievance against the United States – the Israel–Palestine situation – Washington blamed rising Islamic extremism. Bush's suggestion that there was some kind of cultural battle going on between the West and Islam risks becoming a self-fulfilling prophecy. The Western media often portrays Islam as being incompatible with Western values, in the way that communism and fascism were. But if you are going to make one religion your foe, how do you define that religion? Islam is different in every country – it varies across the world. Moroccan Islam is different to Indonesian Islam which is different to Pakistani Islam. Even within the four provinces of Pakistan there are differences in the way the religion is practised. Within every religious community there are a variety of cultures and views and every human community and every religion has a minority of radicals. To many Muslims, US interference in internal politics, its disregard for other countries' sovereignty, its backing of corrupt dictators, and most of all its invasion of Iraq and Afghanistan are just the latest examples of colonial injustices in a long list that started with Napoleon's invasion of Egypt in 1798. Young Muslims today are horrified to see the independence their forefathers battled so hard for compromised by corrupt rulers who have bartered the freedom and sovereignty of their country to get US backing. Of course, the white Western man has been imposing his version of events on the world for centuries. When I was growing up we used to read comic books in which the Red Indians were the baddies and the cowboys the goodies. When I got older I discovered that actually the Red Indians were decimated, wiped off their own land, like the Aborigines in Australia. Then we had decades of governments – and with them popular culture – invoking fear over the threat of communism. Now when I watch films with my sons, the baddies are often Muslims.

245

I expected a backlash after 9/11, but had not anticipated its ferocity. The campaign to instil fear amongst Western populations about the threat from what has at times been hysterically referred to as 'Islamofascism' has given way to rising Islamophobia. The ascent of right-wing, anti-immigration parties in Europe, the misleading and sometimes downright sensationalist reporting against Muslims in the right-wing Western media, France's ban on the burka, Switzerland's ban on minarets and the furore over the Muslim community centre near New York's Ground Zero have helped the radicals' cause and alienated ordinary Muslims. Bush's attitude of 'you are either with us or against us' has hardened attitudes towards the United States – and by extension the West. Bush and Blair claimed this was a war against radical Islam; but how was the man in the street, in the West, going to differentiate between a moderate and a radical Muslim? I saw these developments from both sides, as I was in the unique position of knowing how the people in the West viewed this whole 'war on terror' and, at the same time, as a politician in Pakistan I saw how the 'man in the Pakistani street' perceived this as a war against Islam. And I watched helplessly as ignorance played a big part in this 'war on terror', exacerbating the divide with the Muslim world.

Yet while the 'war on terror' perpetrated the myths equating Islam with radicalism and violence, a Gallup survey published in 2008 revealed that the vast majority of Muslims worldwide condemned the 9/11 attacks. It seemed that actually most of them aspired to the West's standards on freedom of speech and politics, fair judicial systems and democracy. Like most non-Muslims, their priorities and dreams involved better jobs and security, not holy war or bloodshed. The survey's findings are clearly borne out by the 2011 uprisings in the Middle East. According to the poll, only 7 per cent of respondents around the world thought that the 9/11 attacks were 'completely' justified and viewed the United States unfavourably. But they were motivated more by fears of US occupation and domination, rather than cultural differences. What most Muslims surveyed and most admired about the West was its technology and its democracy – the same two answers given by Americans when asked the same question.

Furthermore, research by University of Chicago political scientist Robert Pape dispels many of the misconceptions surrounding suicide bombing and Islamic fundamentalism. After studying every suicide terrorist attack in the world from 1980 till 2003 he concluded that the world's leading practitioners of suicide terrorism are Sri Lanka's Tamil Tigers – a secular, Marxist-Leninist group of Hindu background. He also found that 95 per cent of suicide terrorist attacks are part of coherent campaigns organized by large militant organizations and have secular and political rather than religious goals. They are in response to military occupation of territory considered by the terrorists to be their homeland. It's also worth noting that the study revealed suicide bombers are often well educated, middle-class and politically motivated, not the poor and uneducated or religious fanatics which our dollar-addicted ruling elite would have the West believe.

Terrorism has nothing to do with Islam, and everything to do with politics. But many Muslim leaders, eager to ingratiate themselves with the United States, had neither the guts, nor frankly the understanding, to explain this to the West. So instead of underlining the urgency of dealing with the reasons behind the jihadis' rage, the vast majority of Muslim leaders, petrified of US power and desperate for its support, all presented themselves as 'moderate' Muslims and staunch allies against extremism. I blame the westernized elite of the Muslim world too. They also hid behind moderate Islam, perpetuating the idea that an ideology, not political injustice, lay behind terrorism. This idea that one has to distinguish between a moderate and a radical Muslim is extremely dangerous. The 9/11 attackers did not look or behave like bearded fundamentalists, nor did Faisal Shahzad, the Pakistan-born US citizen convicted of an attempted car-bomb attack in New York's Times Square in 2010. The collective failure of the Muslim world's elite to fight back was a sorry indictment of our intellectual firepower. Anyone who tried to point out the causes behind terrorism or suggest political rather than military solutions was ridiculed or labelled a sympathizer, and often reference to Chamberlain's appeasement of Hitler was made. All debate was stifled. This was reminiscent of the kind of propaganda used by Joseph Goebbels, the Nazis' minister of propaganda, who manipulated the masses by scaring them with potential threats, and if anybody objected, accusing them of being unpatriotic, even treasonous. Meanwhile, Western intellectuals just did not have the knowledge of Islam to counter the rising tide of Islamophobia. Our best defence came from the left-wing media in the UK, such as the *Guardian* and the *Independent*. Unlike real liberals such as the British-Pakistani journalist Tariq Ali, the left-wing media and intelligentsia in Pakistan failed to take a stand against the many human rights abuses of the 'war on terror'. The main reason behind this was that they genuinely believed there was a threat of Talibanization of Pakistan, and they felt this perceived threat was greater than the human rights abuses caused by the drone attacks and operations by Pakistani forces in the tribal areas. Journalists and columnists who had previously presented themselves as anti-imperialist liberals suddenly backed our surrender to the US 'war on terror', and their silence on the threat to Pakistani sovereignty and to their countrymen being bombarded was deafening. Most shockingly, some of those who call themselves liberals have backed the bombing of villages, whether by drones, the Pakistan air force helicopter gunships or artillery, and have accepted the deaths of innocent civilians, women and children, as 'collateral damage'. The NGOs did nothing, as most were funded by Western donors, and the mainstream parties were likewise silent because they were so scared of losing Washington's backing. That left only my party and the religious parties to take a stand.

Much of my politics since 9/11 has been based around opposing corruption and Washington's 'war on terror', and highlighting the many devastating and long-term consequences both have had for Pakistan and for the West. Because of this I have been accused by the so-called liberals in Pakistan's English-language press of being a right-wing hardliner and even pro-Taliban. I always maintained there was never going to be a military solution, either in Afghanistan or in Pakistan's tribal areas. In fact, the war has led to a growing radicalization of our society and the creation of terrorists. According to the WikiLeaks cables released in 2010, the former US ambassador to Pakistan, Anne Patterson, also considered the drone attacks and military operations 'counterproductive'. For someone who grew up being told by my parents how lucky I was to live in an independent country after centuries of colonial rule, I found Musharraf and Zardari's total subjugation of Pakistan's sovereignty to the US as the ultimate humiliation.

First to go in Musharraf's string of abandoned principles was our relationship with Afghanistan. Soon after the 9/11 attacks, Washington gave him a list of seven demands. These involved clamping down on al-Qaeda operations on the Pakistani border, handing over intelligence information, granting US access to Pakistan's naval and air bases, breaking off diplomatic relations with the Taliban regime in Afghanistan and cutting off their fuel supply. Musharraf immediately agreed to all seven demands. A good relationship with Afghanistan had been key to Pakistan's strategy of 'strategic depth' towards India. That meant ensuring a pro-Islamabad regime in Kabul to counter any potential aggression from the east. Pakistan had recognized the Taliban regime since 1996; the alacrity with which Musharraf capitulated amazed even Washington, dismayed the Pakistani military and shocked the public. He took us into the 'war on terror' when no Pakistani had been involved in the 9/11 attacks and al-Qaeda was a CIA-trained militant group based in Afghanistan, and there were no militant Taliban in Pakistan. He also gave US intelligence agencies a free hand to pick up any Pakistani citizen or foreigner suspected of terrorism. After being strong-armed by the Americans, Pakistan's political elite shamefully accepted dollars in exchange for turning on its own people.

The problem with Musharraf was that he had no road map and therefore no idea about when to compromise and when not to. There was no parliament or cabinet for important decisions to be debated, and therefore they were made out of short-term expediency and opportunism. Of course he should have offered to help the United States apprehend the perpetrators of the 9/11 attacks. After all, he was in a prime position to explain to the Americans the best way of dealing with al-Qaeda. But as the leader of Pakistan he should also have made sure that Pakistanis' interests were protected. He tried to rally public opinion behind him by using exactly the same weapon that Bush and Blair used to galvanize their public – fear. He maintained that cooperation with Washington was vital for safeguarding Pakistan's nuclear assets and its policy on Kashmir. In an all-party conference not long after 9/11 he told us that the United States was like 'a wounded bear', lashing out all over the place. We had to go along with whatever it wanted otherwise we could be destroyed – General Musharraf wrote later that the US Deputy Secretary of State, Richard Armitage, told his intelligence director that we had to help the US or Pakistan will be bombed 'back to the stone age'. He told us India was willing to take our place as the US's ally against the Taliban and that the United States could use India to destroy us just as they had used the Northern Alliance in Afghanistan to destroy the Taliban.

I have never seen Pakistanis so petrified of US anger as during this period. This is a typical example of how fear can be used as a weapon by the ruling elite to make the people fall in line; at the same time, it shows that policies based on fear always end up in disaster. (A decade later, Pakistan would realize the full impact of these fear-based policies, when its very existence would be at stake.)

Yet by continually capitulating to Washington's demands, Pakistan is in a worse situation than it was before 9/11. Contrary to Musharraf's line that Pakistan had to stand alongside Bush in the campaign against terrorism or India's hand would be strengthened, the invasion of Afghanistan succeeded in replacing a pro-Islamabad regime with a pro-New Delhi government in Kabul. Pakistan's main geopolitical concern has always been – and still is – India. It now feels encircled, with India building up its influence across Afghanistan in the form of aid, consulates, trade and even the soft power of Indian culture through television and films. Nor have our efforts given us any kind of special status in Washington. Despite all our sacrifices, if any attack was to take place against the United States by a person with any links to Pakistan, we could still be bombed by our so-called allies. According to the eminent journalist Bob Woodward in his book *Obama's Wars*, if Faisal Shahzad's attempt to detonate a bomb in New York had succeeded, the United States would have bombed 'up to 150 known terrorist safe havens' in Pakistan.

Meanwhile, as has been made evident in the material made available by WikiLeaks, the US embassy in Pakistan operates more or less like the viceroy's office in the days of the British Raj. And it would brook no criticism. While the Pakistan government was treated as an ally, the people of Pakistan were treated as potential enemies. There were so many examples of Pakistanis being maltreated in Europe and the US. In Macedonia, six Pakistanis were shot dead as terrorists; only later did it emerge that they were businessmen. In Greece, five Pakistani businessmen were jailed, interrogated and tortured – only they were innocent. In Britain, there were many cases of Pakistanis being picked up by the security services; the worst case was one where seven Pakistani students were suspected of terrorism and locked up for six months in high-security jails before being found innocent and then deported. Two of them came to see me at my office in Islamabad; they were boys from ordinary families, whose parents had sacrificed so much to send them to England for their education, and here they were deported when it was clear they were innocent and had their careers ruined. I met a couple of Pakistanis on a plane who told me horrendous tales of their being picked up in the US, maltreated in jail and then deported.

Because of my frequent and vocal objections to the 'war on terror', many of its victims have come to me for help over the years. Following 9/11, non-Pakistani Muslims, particularly Arabs, were very vulnerable in Pakistan. The disgraceful way Muslim foreigners were treated during this period is a shameful part of our history. They all became potential terrorists and many were denied any opportunity to prove their innocence. People were picked up and just disappeared. Some were killed without any independent investigation into whether they were guilty or not. This is where, in seeking to protect its own against terrorism, Washington contributed to the abuse of human rights in other countries. In the UK when London's Metropolitan Police shot dead an innocent Brazilian man after the 7/7 attacks there was national outrage, leading to a proper inquiry and compensation for the family. But in Pakistan it was – and still is – as if human life is worthless. I started to receive a succession of visits or calls to my office from people whose loved ones had disappeared, picked up by the Pakistani army or intelligence agencies. They wanted to know what their husbands or sons or nephews had been accused of and where they were. But nobody would help them, such was the fear of associating with anyone even linked to accusations of terrorism. In 2003, I led the first demonstrations with the families of the missing persons outside Parliament. A year earlier, in 2002, Dr Amir Aziz was picked up and 'disappeared'. He was an orthopaedic surgeon who would take a team of doctors to Afghanistan every summer for voluntary medical work. I knew Dr Aziz as he had also done volunteer work in my cancer hospital. According to news reports at the time, Aziz was picked up by police working with FBI agents and accused of supplying anthrax to al-Qaeda and Taliban militants. I called up a few opposition politicians and one of the religious parties, suggesting we organize a press conference to highlight the doctor's arrest. They were all too scared to do anything so I did the press conference alone. Soon the Pakistani Medical Association in Lahore protested against his detention. Then the other political parties started to raise objections. The man was released without charge after being kept in the American embassy for a month. He told me he believed that were it not for the public protests, he would have ended up in Guantanamo Bay.

The family of Dr Aafia Siddiqui also came to me. The Americans have claimed the Pakistani neuroscientist and mother of three was an al-Qaeda member, although she has never been charged with terrorism-related offences. Her family believe that Siddiqui disappeared in 2003 for five years because she was imprisoned and tortured by the Americans. Washington denies this. However, an audiotape released by Siddiqui's lawyers in February 2011 appeared to back up the family's story, containing an apparent confirmation by a man named Imran Shaukat, identified as a senior Pakistani counter-terrorism official, that the Pakistani police arrested her in 2003 and handed her over to the ISI. British journalist Yvonne Ridley believes Siddiqui was the mysterious prisoner 650, the woman whose screams and crying tormented her fellow prisoners at Bagram airbase in Afghanistan. When Siddiqui first disappeared her uncle rang me and told me that the last her family had heard from her she was about to take a train from Karachi to Islamabad with her three young children and that she had been too scared to travel by plane because she had heard she was on some FBI list. Aafia's mother then called me asking for help. I agreed to do a press conference with her. But the following day she backed out after receiving a phone call from one of the Pakistani intelligence agencies warning her that if she went ahead with the press conference she would never see her daughter or three grandchildren again. Initially, the PPP and PML (N) did not dare touch Siddiqui's case. Many Western-financed NGOs swallowed their supposed concern for human rights and also steered clear of it. In 2008 I agreed to hold a press conference with Yvonne Ridley in Islamabad calling for Siddiqui's release. While previously the press had avoided the story, now it got extensive coverage. Siddiqui was to become a national cause célèbre. Soon after the press conference, she was apparently arrested by the Americans in Afghanistan. They claimed that while in custody she grabbed a gun and fired on US army officers and FBI agents, without hitting any of them. She was whisked to New York, charged with attempted murder and in 2010 handed down an 86-year jail term. Siddiqui's conviction had an inflammatory reaction over US double standards and set off rallies in the streets of Pakistani cities; US soldiers implicated in the deaths of innocent civilians in Iraq and Afghanistan are unlikely to ever receive such a sentence, and when CIA operative Raymond Davis cold-bloodedly murdered two teenagers he was whisked out of Pakistan by the US in early 2011.

In 2008, a member of my party from Waziristan who lived in Karachi, Jehanzeb Burki, suddenly disappeared. He had been picked up by soldiers of the frontier force, and taken to the Bala Hisar fort in Peshawar. My party staged demonstrations in Karachi, and I spoke to the senior police official, demanding to know what had happened to him. He was released a few days later, and told me he'd been interrogated not just by officers of the frontier force but also by some Americans. They wanted to know why he had given 500,000 rupees to the Taliban when he was visiting his home in Waziristan. Jehanzeb admitted to giving the Taliban the money, but added, 'Would you have saved me if I'd refused the Taliban?' According to him, others in his situation had not been that lucky; had there not been demonstrations for him in Karachi, this could have been a death sentence. Jehanzeb's story typifies what is happening in the tribal areas, squeezed between the Taliban on one side and the security forces on the other; as there is no law there, summary executions on both sides take place all the time.

One of the most shameful events in our history took place in Quetta only this year, 2011: five unarmed Chechens, three women and two men, were gunned down at a security checkpoint, by the police. The police claimed they were terrorists, but a photograph was released of one of the women, who it turned out was seven months pregnant, showing her putting her hand up to beg for mercy – or pointing to God. I found that so awful. God knows how many such incidents have taken place that have not been caught on camera.

Another scandal illustrating the Musharraf government's appalling record on due process was the treatment of Mullah Zaeef. The Taliban government's ambassador to Pakistan was – with total disregard for diplomatic immunity as outlined by the Geneva Convention – seized by the Pakistani authorities a few months after the 9/11 attacks and handed over to the Americans. I had met Zaeef in 2000 while he was working in Islamabad to talk about the build-up in tension at the time between Iran and Afghanistan and found him to be a very civilized, cultured and softly spoken gentleman. In his book *My Life with the Taliban*, he describes what happened when the Pakistanis handed him over to the Americans:

They ripped the black cloth from my face and for the first time I could see where I was. Pakistani and American soldiers stood around me ... The Pakistani soldiers were all staring as the Americans hit me and tore the remaining clothes off from my body. Eventually I was completely naked, and the Pakistani soldiers – the defenders of the Holy Quran – shamelessly watched me with smiles on their faces, saluting this disgraceful action of the Americans. They held a handover ceremony with the Americans right in front of my eyes. That moment is written in my memory like a stain on my soul. Even if Pakistan was unable to stand up to the godless Americans I would at least have expected them to insist that treatment like this would never take place under their eyes or on their own sovereign territory.

There were so many cases like this. Anyone having anything to do with the Taliban was considered a terrorist. Yet up till 9/11 Pakistan had been one of only three countries to recognize the Islamic Emirate of Afghanistan (Saudi Arabia and the United Arab Emirates were the others), so of course there were people with links to institutions and people there. In Pakistan, the Taliban were considered fundamentalists, but not terrorists. As for al-Qaeda, few Pakistanis had ever heard of them. If they had, they considered them to be like the Afghan mujahideen, a jihadi organization that had originally been formed to fight the Soviets.

Regardless of what any of these terrorism suspects are believed to have done, the most important point is that due process should have been followed. That is the mark of a civilized country. Pakistan's fragile democratic institutions were under attack, though, as Musharraf's government chipped away at rule of law across the board. The general had to take increasingly unconstitutional steps to shore up his power as his alliance with the United States dented his popularity. One compromise followed another. On coming to power he made an immediate show of cracking down on graft. Zardari had been jailed for corruption while Benazir had already left the country to escape charges levelled at her under Sharif's regime. Sharif himself was sentenced to life imprisonment on hijacking and terrorism charges the year after the coup, but in another one of Musharraf's compromises, he was soon pardoned and went into exile in Saudi Arabia.

I was still holding out hope for Musharraf in 2002, when he announced a referendum to extend his term as president. His assumption of power had been challenged by several court petitions so he had introduced the Oath of Judges Order in early 2000, which required judges to take a fresh oath of office, swearing allegiance to military rule. A few refused and resigned in protest and others were dismissed by Musharraf. The Supreme Court was insisting that he hold national elections by 12 October 2002. So he needed a referendum to bolster his legitimacy as president after the return to democracy. My party's central executive debated for a day and a half whether to support this highly unconstitutional proposal. After all, the general had promised a return to democracy within three years of his coup. In the end, we could not decide, so I rang Musharraf, who invited us all to go and discuss it with him in person. He persuaded us that he needed the guarantee of another five years in office in order to implement his anti-corruption campaign. He succeeded in charming everyone, even the few sceptics on our central executive committee. He succeeded because we were still wary of Benazir and Sharrif making a comeback, amid memories of their incompetence and corruption.

Nonetheless, the referendum turned out to be a disaster, drawing widespread allegations of ballot rigging. Musharraf claimed 50 per cent of the voting population turned out, and that 98 per cent voted 'yes' to five more years of him. It was so obviously not true it was a national embarrassment. The government had been able to deploy all its resources to encourage turnout while banning political parties from holding rallies against the referendum. My party was deeply embarrassed about supporting this fraudulent referendum, and I had to go on television eventually and apologize to the nation for supporting it. This made my party and me realize that in future never again would we support anything unconstitutional.

The United States conveniently turned a blind eye. 'I am not going to indulge in the specific dynamics of politics in Pakistan,' Deputy Assistant Secretary of State Donald Camp told the *New York Times* when asked about the upcoming referendum. Washington's indifference to the state of internal Pakistani politics continued throughout most of the decade, even as Musharraf's government became mired in corruption. Having allowed the country's crooked political mafia to infiltrate his government, Musharraf became increasingly compromised. At one point he had about eighty federal ministers – most of the positions doled out as political bribes. The National Accountability Bureau became simply a weapon with which to intimidate the opposition. With each desperate effort to retain power, Musharraf succeeded in taking us back to the old days of Benazir and Sharif – exactly the kind of climate of sleaze he had first pledged to eradicate.

Musharraf's final and greatest compromise was the National Reconciliation Ordinance (NRO), a power-sharing deal he concocted in 2007 to enable him to run for re-election as president and bring back Benazir Bhutto as prime minister.

Under the agreement brokered by the Americans and the British – despite the implications for the country's governance – more than 8,000 bureaucrats, government officials, bankers and politicians charged with corruption offences between 1986 and 1999 were given an amnesty, including Benazir and Zardari. According to documents given by the National Accountability Bureau to the Supreme Court, these people were suspected of robbing Pakistan of 1,060 billion rupees, with Benazir and Zardari together accounting for 140 billion of that total. Add to that the 2 billion rupees of Pakistani taxpayers' money previously spent pursuing corruption cases against Benazir and Zardari in Swiss courts. The NRO also annulled thousands of cases of murder and assassination believed to have been committed by the MQM. This was something neither the Americans nor the British would ever have allowed in their own countries, but of course the priority was the 'war on terror', and the US needed a puppet government in Islamabad which had no qualms about the bombing of villages in our tribal areas, and wasn't squeamish about 'collateral damage'. As Hilary Synnott, British High Commissioner to Islamabad from 2001 to 2003, put it in his book *Transforming Pakistan: Ways out of Instability*:

The dilemma for the Bush administration was that it judged that, despite his double-dealing over militant groups, Musharraf's leadership was needed to help in the fight against terrorism. At the same time, it also advocated elections and progress towards democracy. Yet the outcome of truly open and democratic elections seemed unlikely to deliver an effective system of governance for Pakistan or to provide sufficient support for the

US military campaign. The only answer seemed to be for some kind of deal to be made between Musharraf and a potential elected leadership, the outcome of which, it was hoped, would do the least damage, either to Pakistan or to US interests.

Of course it has damaged both – but most of all Pakistan.

In brokering the NRO and giving Pakistanis the impression that Benazir Bhutto was being rehabilitated in order to do Washington's bidding, the Americans had given her the kiss of death. Much later, WikiLeaks revealed Asif Zardari had told the US Ambassador that Benazir was only returning to Pakistan after 'getting a green light from the Americans'. A few weeks before Benazir's death, I was at a conference in Delhi and talking to Mehbooba Mufti, the Kashmiri politician, when Jeb Bush – George W. Bush's brother – joined us. He asked me, were people excited about Benazir coming back? She is a dead woman walking, I said; a target to the militants on one side, because she had adopted Washington's policies on al-Qaeda and the Taliban, and on the other side a target to politicians threatened by her, scared they would lose power. They could have her assassinated and blame the Taliban.

Poor Benazir didn't have a chance. She might have escaped when Musharraf declared a state of emergency on 3 November 2007; she boycotted the election and flew to Dubai. She had seen the low turnout at her rallies; her popularity had plunged as she was perceived as a US stooge and had aligned herself with Musharraf. Sadly for her, Washington forced her to change her decision and within forty-eight hours she was back in Pakistan.

Musharraf, after finally resigning from his army post, succeeded in his plan of being sworn in for a second term as president, but poor Benazir was assassinated in a suicide bombing at an election campaign rally in Rawalpindi in December. Zardari has vowed to hunt down those responsible but there has been little progress in the investigation and her death remains one of the most speculated upon mysteries in Pakistani history. The government spokesman immediately blamed Taliban leader Baitullah Mehsud. It was the reaction of the People's Party that was hard to understand; after making various accusations, at the establishment, at the Taliban, and at the Q league, they called for a UN inquiry. People asked, why would a party sitting in government ask the UN to conduct an inquiry when all the intelligence agencies were controlled by that party now in power? The UN inquiry took three years and, in April 2010, dismissed allegations against Zardari, blamed Musharraf for failing to protect Bhutto and accused police and intelligence officials of hindering the probe into her death. Everyone knew it was a cover-up and whoever had with undue haste hosed down the crime scene did 'irreparable damage' to investigations. We didn't need three years of UN inquiry to tell us this obvious fact. In February 2011 an arrest warrant was issued for Musharraf in connection with Bhutto's assassination.

When I came out of jail in 2007, I felt there was so much opposition to Musharraf he was unlikely to win even if he rigged the polls, and felt the APDM (All Parties Democratic Movement) should contest the elections. However, other opposition parties and members of the lawyers' movement were less confident. Musharraf had only given us five weeks' notice for the elections. Emergency rule was still in place, there was a clampdown on the media and Musharraf controlled the caretaker government, the local administration, the intelligence agencies, the election commission and the Supreme Court. They felt it was impossible to have free and fair elections. If he won he would declare the polls a referendum against the chief justice, and the puppet judges he had already started to fill the judiciary with would be legitimized. That would put an end to any hope of having an independent judicial system for Pakistan. The Americans didn't seem to care. The State Department kept talking about free and fair elections and reversing the state of emergency, but failed to mention the reinstatement of the judges – especially the chief justice of the Supreme Court (WikiLeaks, in 2011, would reveal that US ambassador Anne Patterson was not in favour of having the chief justice reinstated). If the judges were not reinstalled, how could there be free and fair elections? Was Musharraf going to be left to decide what was free and fair?

So the APDM, the alliance of parties opposed to Musharraf, announced an election boycott on 24 November. Then things started happening fast. Nawaz Sharif was suddenly and mysteriously allowed to return to Pakistan despite a ten-year ban on him re-entering politics, raising suspicions of foreign forces behind the scenes. There was considerable pressure from the Americans and the British for everyone to run in the elections and legitimize the anticipated win for the so-called 'liberal alliance'. Having led the move to boycott the elections, Sharif then started to waver before finally betraying us all by succumbing to a combination of American, British and Saudi

Above left: After Friday prayers at the Badshahi Mosque, Lahore, 2003.

Above right: Praying in the mosque at the Cancer Hospital built in my mother's name, Lahore, 1994.

Right and below: Campaigning in the elections in 1996 and 1997 as my party gets off the ground.

Above left: Addressing an election rally in 2002. Over the years my party has grown in Pakistan; in 2009 a rally was held (*right*) when I was banned from flying into Karachi from Lahore.

Right: Press conference after coming out of jail in 2007. In England (*above*) my wife Jemima and her mother Lady Annabel Goldsmith, along with my son Kasim, had campaigned for my release.

Above: My party was at the forefront of the movement to restore the Chief Justice, who was sacked by President Musharraf on 9 March 2007.

Right: In England I led protesters to Number 10, Downing Street, opposing Musharraf's visit to Britain in 2008.

Below: Later that year, my party was part of the All Parties Democratic Movement (APDM), of which ex-prime minister Nawaz Sharif's party was also a member.

Left: The Shaukat Khanum Memorial Hospital and Research Centre in Lahore, founded on 29 December 1994, named after my mother. The hospital provides free treatment to those who can't pay, and first-class facilities to everyone.

Below: The hospital was bombed in 1996. Jemima and I inspect the damage.

Bottom: Princess Diana's visit to the hospital in 1997 helped enormously with our fundraising campaign. Her heartfelt sympathy for the patients has never been forgotten.

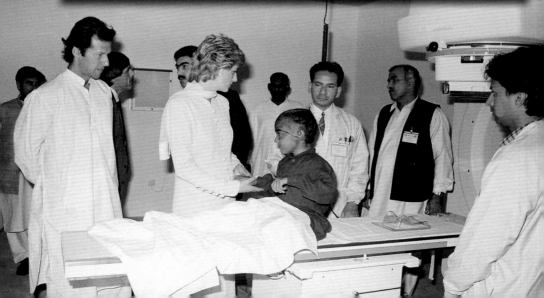

Fundraising for the hospital took me all over Pakistan, to mosques and schools as well as to businesses and homes. Thousands of people made donations and their generosity overwhelmed me. (*Below*) At St Joseph's School, Karachi, fundraising in 1994.

Below: Namal University in Mianwali. Inaugurated in 2008, it awards degrees from the University of Bradford in England, where I am Chancellor.

Left and above: Jemima and I married in June 1995 in England. Here, Jemima is with my sisters Rani and Uzma in Zaman Park, Lahore.

Right and below: Jemima with our first-born son Sulaiman, in 1996. My home in the hills above Islamabad.

Above left and right: Arriving with Jemima at the High Court in England in 1996, where I am being sued for libel by Ian Botham and Allan Lamb. Holding the award for Sportsman of the Millennium at the Pakistan TV awards of April 2000.

Right and below: I don't play cricket any more but I love to watch it: with Shane Warne and my brother-in-law Zac Goldsmith at a charity match in 2007, and with Sulaiman and Kasim watching the test match between Pakistan and England in Rawalpindi in 2005.

My party's name means 'Movement for Justice' and here we are campaigning for just that.
Above: Against corruption, in 2010.

Above right: Against the drone attacks in the tribal areas in May 2011. In July 2011 (*right*) I addressed a public rally in Faisalabad, and later (*below*) the Faisalabad lawyers at the District Bar Association. I truly feel my party's time has come.

pressure. I remember him disappearing for about forty minutes during an APDM meeting to take a phone call from then British Foreign Secretary David Miliband. Most of the rest of the APDM, a combination of religious, regional and secular parties as well as my own, went ahead with the boycott. Later, we discovered that Asfandyar Wali, leader of the Awami National Party (ANP), the main Pashtun party, had been somehow lured into also running during a trip to Washington. The 2008 elections were never meant to bring democracy to Pakistan, which the lawyers' movement, along with my party and backed by the civil society groups, had struggled so hard to get. Instead we were betrayed by self-serving politicians in cahoots with the Bush administration.

By 2004 anger had been growing over the wars in Iraq and Afghanistan, rampant human rights abuses and Pakistan's loss of sovereignty. For the Muslim masses, and especially the jihadi groups, the invasion of Iraq was the last straw, confirming their belief that the United States was at war against Islam. Their anger at Pakistan's alliance with Washington deepened. As we'll see later, the crucial turning point was when Musharraf launched military operations in Waziristan – sparking a revolt against the army by tribal Pashtuns. It was also the year that the CIA also launched its highly controversial covert campaign to target militants with drone attacks in the tribal areas. It was also the time when the jihadi groups that had been nurtured by both the ISI and the CIA during the Soviet war in Afghanistan turned against the Pakistan army. The ideological element within these groups went and joined what became the Pakistani Taliban. One of them was Ilyas Kashmiri, a former decorated 'asset' of the ISI, who had joined a jihadi group to fight in Kashmir. After 2004 he turned against the army and was responsible for many daring attacks until he was killed by a drone attack in Waziristan in June 2011.

Attacks against security forces, particularly the army and the police, shot up after 2004; there were assaults on offices belonging to the ISI and FIA, the Federal Investigation Agency, as well as against Pakistan air force employees. Musharraf himself became a target with at least four attempts on his life. In 2009 six soldiers died in an audacious assault on the army headquarters in Rawalpindi.

Another decisive factor in this growing hostility towards the security forces was the Lal Masjid affair in 2007 when the army stormed Islamabad's Red Mosque, killing scores of religious students holed up inside the mosque and its madrassa compound. For several months beforehand tension had been rising between the mosque's students and the authorities but Musharraf failed to take any effective action over what should have been simply a police matter. The mosque students were fundamentalists, not terrorists, and should just have been punished for the specific crimes they had committed. They were stoking opposition to him and making vigilante-style attempts to curb what they saw as immoral activities in Islamabad – threatening DVD shops and even kidnapping some Chinese women alleged to be working as prostitutes. They were infuriated by Musharraf's campaign of reform for madrassas, his demolition of mosques built illegally on state ground and his attempts to impose western-ization as part of his so-called 'Enlightened Moderation'. In their eyes, he was a Western stooge out to destroy true Islam.

(This is an example of how Western puppets actually fuel extremism in the Muslim world.) Musharraf came under increasing pressure from the westernized elite to crack down on them. His popularity, already on the wane since 2004, had taken a further hit with the lawyers' movement that year. Seeing an opportunity to prove himself to his Western backers too, Musharraf took a typically heavy-handed approach. He could have turned off the utility supplies and waited for the students to cave in (it was summer and they would not have lasted long without water and electricity). Instead he sent in the army, despite the fact that there were also women and children within the complex. There are various versions of what exactly happened. A delegation of religious leaders had tried to negotiate a peaceful solution and – according to the newspapers – the students had been prepared to surrender if certain conditions were met. One of the two Ghazi brothers who ran the mosque told the media before the army launched its final full-scale assault that there were only fourteen guns in the mosque complex at the time. Chaudhary Shujaat, head of the PML (Q) party, was the last to go inside the Red Mosque before the operation started. According to him, he had managed to work out a deal with those left inside the mosque, which meant they would lay down their arms and come out. When he found out that Musharraf refused to accept any compromise he was appalled and called Prime Minister Shaukat Aziz, only to find he was out eating ice cream with his family. Even now Chaudhary becomes emotional, because he can still see the faces of the students who were incinerated inside. Nobody really knows how many died in the carnage that followed. The government claimed at least a hundred militants and students were killed but Qazi Hussain Ahmad, leader of the religious party Jamaat-e-Islami, has put the number at over seven hundred. There has never been an investigation. The site was sealed up and the bodies removed, to be thrown in an unmarked grave. This whole debacle coincided with the APDM's first conference, which took place in London, conveniently wiping the massacre off the news.

However, Musharraf's zeal was counterproductive. First of all, the Lal Masjid assault turned the Pakistani masses against him. They saw it as an issue of class rather than religion. They felt that the authorities dealt with the matter so violently because the madrassa students were from poor families, and that therefore they could get away with it. Had the students come from English-medium schools, would they have been treated like that? One of the biggest reasons Musharraf was to do so badly in the 2008 elections was resentment over Lal Masjid. Even one of his strongest candidates, Sheikh Rasheed, afterwards blamed the affair for his own defeat. It also had tremendous repercussions for national security. Many of the mosque students were from Khyber Pakhtunkhwa's Swat area and militants there launched a campaign of retribution, attacking convoys and police stations and setting off bombs throughout the valley. Lal Masjid basically created the Swat Taliban, as it threw up Maulana Fazlullah, who became known as the 'Radio Mullah'; more on him later.

Musharraf was just as heavy-handed in his dealings with an insurgency in the province of Baluchistan. Since Pakistan's creation, the Baluchis have waged a succession of revolts to demand greater autonomy and a greater share of the profits from the province's rich supply of natural resources. Almost half Baluchistan's five million people live below the poverty line. When insurgents escalated their attacks on the army in 2005, Musharraf retaliated with a major offensive. The killing of the 79-year-old rebel tribal leader Nawab Akbar Khan Bugti provoked violent unrest in Baluchistan. It cemented Baluchi hatred of the army and turned what had been a rights movement into an armed struggle for liberation from Pakistan. This gave India the opportunity to exploit the situation, just as Pakistan had exploited the grievances of the people of Kashmir after the rigged elections in the valley by the Indian government in 1989. Today the unrest in Baluchistan is costing the country a fortune in security to try to prevent regular terrorist assaults and sabotage attacks on gas pipelines. Non-Baluchi settlers, particularly professionals like teachers and doctors, are being assassinated and hounded out of the province. Over 100,000 settlers have been forced out.

The February 2008 elections were a disaster for Musharraf. Benazir's return to Pakistan was not warmly received, and, by associating herself with Musharraf through the NRO deal, she had damaged her reputation. However, her tragic assassination sparked anger against Musharraf; it became the last straw and set off a wave of sympathy for the PPP, which gained the most seats, but no clear majority. Sharif's PML (N) did surprisingly well given their lack of preparation, cashing in on the popularity of the lawyers' movement. The two main opposition parties formed a coalition. It was the first time in our history that a pro-establishment party had lost the polls.

Musharraf had made many mistakes in the run-up to the elections, mistakes that were both military and cultural. His campaign of 'Enlightened Moderation' helped further alienate sections of Pakistani society, making them more likely to sympathize with extremists. According to an article he wrote for the *Washington Post* in 2004, this two-pronged strategy of his urged the Muslim world 'to shun militancy and extremism and adopt the path of socioeconomic uplift' while calling for the West, and the United States in particular, 'to seek to resolve all political disputes with justice and to aid in the socioeconomic betterment of the deprived Muslim world'. What this probably would have meant was Muslims giving up their armed struggles against what they perceived to be foreign occupation, without any guarantee that the West would resolve conflicts in places like Palestine, Kashmir and Chechnya or withdraw from Iraq and Afghanistan. Musharraf modelled himself on two other military men – Iran's Reza Shah and Turkey's Mustafa Kemal Ataturk. They too believed that by imposing the outward manifestations of westerniza-tion they could catapult their countries forward by decades. For Musharraf westernization was modernization, but he used westernization selectively. The West's success lay in genuine democracy, strong institutions, education, an inde-pendent judiciary, a free media and free speech, whereas Musharraf was doing the opposite. This is the solution for the Muslim world: a genuine democracy, freedom of speech that allows open debate, an evolution of our culture, and above all rule of law. What it does not need is pseudo-westernization with Muslim westernized elites aping superficial aspects of the Western society, in reaction to which we have seen the growth of fundamentalism, which in turn stunts the growth of our culture.

Musharraf took the Pakistani elite's obsession with being Western clones to new heights. There were fashion shows put on for foreign dignitaries in the houses of the president and the prime minister. (I can remember a politician's wife complaining to me about how embarrassing she always found this.) Female television presenters on some channels were told to wear Western dress. The use of English in the media was encouraged. Musharraf often spoke in English himself at press conferences and Shaukat Aziz, then finance minister, delivered the national budget in English, a language spoken by only a tiny minority of the country. On TV, programmes like the Pakistani version of *Blind Date* started appearing; in the past they would never have been seen on our screens due to the sensitivities of the culture of the masses. For ordinary Pakistanis, this came across as Western vulgarity and bred fear and resentment. In my constituency, Mianwali, locals told me about their dislike of it, complaining that it had become difficult for families to watch television together.

And so, thanks to Musharraf and America's 'war on terror', Pakistan finds itself in its sorry predicament today. We now have our worst ever government – that of Zardari. A man perceived by most Pakistanis to be our most corrupt politician inherited the leadership of the PPP party following Benazir's death and became president by producing a piece of paper that he said willed the party to him and his son – which no one has been able to authenticate. On the basis of that, he has become our president. My party was the only one to protest, organizing a demonstration on Islamabad's Constitutional Avenue, where we declared we were protesting to let later generations know we were not part of this crime – where someone with a criminal record could become our president. The other parties were too afraid of Zardari, knowing he had the ability to ruthlessly exploit any weakness in a corrupt politician. The most bizarre behaviour came from Sharif. Not only had he jailed Zardari for corruption during both his terms as prime minister, but he had spent millions of rupees of taxpayers' money on pursuing cases against him. Now he became Zardari's biggest supporter and in the presidential election did not even challenge his nomination papers. Of course the reason was not that Sharif suddenly had a change of heart; through Zardari he wanted to get rid of Musharraf, and he was scared that Zardari as president would open up corruption cases against him. However, one good thing that came out of the elections was that there was a lull in terrorism, as both the PPP and the PML (N) had spoken out in favour of a political solution to the 'war on terror' and said they were against military action in Khyber Pakhtunkhwa. The lull lasted till May 2008 when, under pressure from the Americans, Zardari launched a military operation in Bajaur, in the tribal areas. The bombing of the Marriott Hotel in Islamabad in 2008, when over fifty people died, was widely believed to be in response to the Bajaur operation.

Not only has terrorism broken all records under Zardari, but so has corruption. In 2010 Transparency International ranked Pakistan the thirty-fourth most corrupt country in the world with about 70 per cent of respondents perceiving Zardari's government to be more corrupt than that of Musharraf. And graft, together with incompetence, cronyism and tax evasion, is destroying the country's economy. Major state corporations such as the railways, Pakistan International

Airlines, Pakistan Steel Mills and the Water and Power Development Authority have become bloated white elephants, costing the national exchequer a total of 250 billion rupees a year. These organizations are plundered – only for the tax-payer to pick up the bill for the losses due to corruption and inefficiencies. Most controversially, Pakistan has one of the lowest tax collection rates in the world with a tax-to-GDP ratio of about 9 per cent – only about 2.5 million are regis-tered to pay tax, representing less than 2 per cent of the population. The country relies instead on sales tax, which of course everybody pays at the same rate, regardless of income. The poor effectively subsidize the rich, and the powerful do everything they can to maintain this injustice. Our politicians are some of the worst culprits. A survey found 61 per cent of Pakistani parliamentarians pay no tax at all. According to his 2009/2010 tax returns, the billionaire Nawaz Sharif paid income tax of 5,000 rupees (about US$60), while Zardari paid nothing at all. Rich landowners also participate in this ruthless exploitation of the poor; agriculture is untaxed, despite the industry employing almost half the population. Five per cent of the farmers own 37 per cent of the land, yet they pay no income tax.

So the United States, by giving the Pakistani government aid in return for its contribution to the 'war on terror', is simply propping up this appalling system. Why should the Pakistani rich bother to pay taxes when foreign loans and aid money are always there to cover up their incompetence and corruption and pay for their lavish lifestyle? And why should politicians bother to fix the economy when they can artificially maintain it with American dollars? This also begs the question – do

American taxpayers really want to be subsidizing Pakistan's elite at a time of domestic economic woes and rising un-employment? Pakistan's economy is sinking fast; it is ill-equipped to deal with the enormous cost of bearing the brunt of America's 'war on terror'. Zardari, speaking recently in Turkey, put the cumulative cost of the 'war on terror' for Pakistan in the nine years since 9/11 at US$68 billion while the total aid that has come to Pakistan is U$20 billion. US aid money for the military doesn't help the economy and non-military aid seems to disappear into the bank accounts of the political leadership and their cronies.

Another crutch holding up our ailing economy, and there-fore the government, is World Bank and IMF loans that everybody knows Pakistan will never be able to repay. These loans, along with US and European aid money, are like bribes to the Pakistani political elite to keep fighting America's war for them. This was painfully evident when in October 2010 Pakistan's foreign minister Shah Mehmood Qureshi told the European parliament: 'If you want to help us fight extremism and terrorism, one way of doing that is making Pakistan economically stable.' Pakistan's ruling elite threatens the West with fears about Islamic militancy to extract more money out of them. Even more blatant is a quote from Zardari in Bob Woodward's *Obama's Wars*. He told the Americans: 'You know this country is awash with anti-Americanism, and they are going to hate me for being an American stooge. You have to give me economic resources so that I can win over the people, so that there's something in it for them.' Meanwhile, the inefficiencies and distortions in the economy mean higher prices for ordinary people, who are already struggling under unprecedented inflation. That in turn fuels corruption amongst the police and government officials.

In return for total subservience to the United States, the ordinary people of Pakistan have suffered immensely. The corrupt politicians have dug in deeper, the elite have got richer and the militants are more numerous and more determined. The ordinary people of this country are facing economic hardship and bloodshed in the streets. Every day the newspapers are filled with reports of people killing themselves and sometimes their families because of desperation over how to make ends meet. Thirty-four thousand innocent people have been killed since 2003, millions have been displaced by fighting and we are facing civil war in the tribal areas and a rising insurgency in Baluchistan. The country today faces unprecedented unemployment, inflation, breakdowns in infrastructure, shortages of gas and power, and lawlessness. The war has been a disaster for the people but made the powerful richer. Our capital is like a city under siege, its people subject to routine security checks as if every Pakistani is a potential terrorist, a situation the police often make use of to extract bribes. Capital is pouring out of the country. A fortune is spent on the security of politicians, to the detriment of the rest of the population. In Punjab, almost half of a 900-strong elite police force is deployed to protect the Sharif family, while 64 per cent of all police in the capital are on VIP duty.

Cleverly, Zardari has made sure to co-opt the opposition by giving the main parties a stake to uphold this corrupt system. The PPP controls the centre and Sindh. Sharif, meant to be the main opposition leader, had his party in a shaky alliance with the PPP in the Punjab until recently. The MQM has

Karachi, and the ANP (Awami National Party) has Khyber Pakhtunkhwa. Even the MMA (Muttahida Majlis-e-Amal, the religious coalition) leader Maulana Fazl ur-Rahman, who is perceived to be very pro-Taliban, became part of his cabinet at one point. As a result of the NRO, men with criminal records are occupying key ministries in the government and corruption has turned into plunder. With so many vested interests keen to maintain the status quo, how are we to transform our country?

Chapter Nine

The Tribal Areas: Civil War?
My Solution

Wo farebkhurda 'shaheen', jo pulla ho kargussoan mein
Ussay kiya khubbur kay kiya hey, ruh-o-rusm-e-baadshahi
That befuddled falcon, who was raised among vultures
What does he know about the ways of his kind?

Allama Muhammad Iqbal

IN 1990 I TOURED WAZIRISTAN, THE TRIBAL AREAS OF PAKISTAN along the border with Afghanistan, for the first time, on the invitation of the Burki tribe, to which my mother belonged (both my mother and father were from Pashtun tribes, the Niazi and the Burki). This was the only region in Pakistan that had remained untouched by colonialism, its people proud warrior folk who have never been subdued by any invader despite the long list of legendary conquerors and adventurers who have passed through their lands – including Alexander the Great (356–323 BC), Mahmud of Ghazni (971–1030), Tamburlaine (1336–1405), the Mughal Emperor Barbar

(1483–1531), Nadir Shah, the Persian Napoleon (1698–1747), and the more recent superpowers, the British and the Russians. According to Sir Olaf Caroe, the last British governor of what was then the North-West Frontier Province (NWFP), in his book on the Pashtuns, 'The lands which are now Afghanistan and the North-West Frontier of Pakistan have seen perhaps more invasions in the course of history than any other country in Asia, or indeed the world.' As early as 1898, Winston Churchill – then a war correspondent – reported back from the North-West Frontier, 'The frontier tribes will never accept foreign occupation.'

I had initially been reluctant to make my first visit to the tribal areas, but was persuaded by my cousin Sohail Khan, who was in the Frontier Force (originally formed from regiments within the British Indian Army, and selected purely from the Pashtun tribes). We went to Kaniguram, in South Waziristan, where my mother's family originally hailed from. The Burki tribe still lives there and gave me a royal welcome with drumming and dancing and a hail of fire into the air from anti-aircraft guns and Kalashnikovs – the sound was deafening.

These people fascinated me; it was like going back in time to the Wild West, an uncultivated terrain of desolate mountain ranges where every man openly carried a gun and was a warrior, making it the most unique place in the world. If the young men saw me, they would come up and challenge me to a shooting contest, targets would be set up and I would have to prove myself against them. Even the very young boys had heard I was a good shot and wanted to test themselves against me. It seemed everyone knew how to fire a weapon.

Despite this fierceness, one of the tenets of the Pashtun code is *melmastia* (hospitality). It is not just a matter of giving the guest the very best your household can provide, it also extends to defending your guest's safety with your life – *nanawati*. *Badal* (avenging blood) is the bedrock of the Pashtun code of honour. One of the theories about my mother's branch of the Burki tribe was that they broke away nearly three hundred and fifty years ago and settled in Jalandhar in India to escape a blood feud (Pashtuns, either escaping vendettas or searching for an easier living, made settlements all the way to Delhi and beyond). The Pashtuns are known for being fiercely protective of their women. However, Pashtun women in the tribal areas are not kept in as strict purdah as they are in the cities. In the countryside in FATA (the Federally Administered Tribal Areas), you can see women working in the fields. But when they move to a town or city they wear the burka outside the home, or are confined within four walls by their male relatives for fear that they will come into contact with men from outside the family.

The Pashtuns maintain this extremely strong family system in some form or other even amongst their communities that have migrated to other areas. The Pashtun homeland stretches from Afghanistan, where they are the largest ethnic group, across Pakistan's tribal areas and the province of Khyber Pakhtunkhwa, but the largest Pashtun city is Karachi, in Sindh province. Waves of Pashtun migration to the commercial capital of Pakistan since the 1950s mean that it is now home to several million of them. Dr Akhtar Hameed Khan, the founder of the Orangi Pilot Project, a social initiative in a squatter quarter in Karachi, found that because of their powerful family system the tribal Pashtuns always forged ahead of the other two ethnic communities living in Orangi.

The social structure of the tribal areas that I observed, and their culture, is very different to that in the rest of Pakistan. Far from being the lawless savages of popular myth, the people have lived by an ancient democratic system which allowed them to carry themselves with self-respect and dignity. The concept of honour in South Asian culture has received a bad press because of the deeply offensive honour killings, but by upholding one's honour impoverished people living hard lives can maintain a sense of dignity and command respect. In the tribal area this highly decentralized form of democracy is based on the *jirga* system – local councils of village elders, similar to the Athenian democracy of the city-states of ancient Greece. Every household has a voice in the running of their lives and every man is considered an equal. Because people fully participate in decision-making, it has created self-governing communities of responsible individuals with no bureaucracy and no centralized government. In terms of dealing with crime, the Pashtun jirga system acts as a jury that dispenses free and quick justice. A culprit will usually be known to everyone in the village and will be hauled in front of the jury; there is no question of false witnesses as everybody knows everybody else's credibility. So successful is the system that the tribal areas – until the upheavals of the past few years – have typically been almost crime-free compared to the rest of Pakistan, and this despite every man being armed. The right to carry arms is, for them, a guarantee of freedom, just as early American jurists allowed their citizens this right. As I mentioned earlier, revenge is part of their code of honour;

when someone in a family is killed, the whole family are bound to seek revenge. This code of honour is simple, and it pre-dates Islam – it is embedded in their genes. In 1872 a Pashtun, Sher Ali Afridi, imprisoned on the Andaman Islands where he was serving his sentence, killed the visiting viceroy Lord Mayo. He felt his imprisonment was an affront to his code of honour and had thus vowed to kill a leading British official. (When someone attacks them, either the US with drone aircraft bombing villages or the Pakistani army on operations, both of these are doing more than causing casualties; they are also creating enemies.) Caroe wrote that in the 1930s there was as much crime in a week in Peshawar as there was in a year in the whole of the tribal area. This system of equality and justice was a big contrast to what I had seen growing up in Punjab, where might was right and landlords could get away with all kinds of abuses towards poor people.

The British created the North-West Frontier Province in 1901 and divided the region into settled and tribal areas. In terms of the Great Game (the phrase coined to describe British–Russian rivalry in the region), the province was a vital buffer zone between the British Raj and Russian expansionism in Central Asia. But the British had struggled to impose direct rule on the tribal area, eventually coming up with the solution of the Frontier Crimes Regulation (FCR) in the 1870s. Based on tribal law, this system still applies in FATA. It seeks to appease the aggrieved party rather than punish the guilty. The government representative, known as the political agent, handles disputes but has to accept the verdict and punishment decided by the jirga. Tribes are encouraged to keep the peace through subsidies. Most controversially, the FCR also imposes a system of collective punishment on the entire tribe for crimes. At independence in 1947, the NWFP voted to join Pakistan but its tribal areas became a part of the new nation in 1948 only on condition that they be allowed to continue to live by their own laws. So while Khyber Pakhtunkhwa is a fully integrated province of Pakistan, FATA is semi-autonomous and still ruled by the colonial-era system; the Pakistani government governs through a combination of political agents, who are federal civil bureaucrats, and tribal elders, with only forty-four of Pakistan's laws agreed to prevail there, leaving their way of life intact. There is no Pakistani police or judiciary in the tribal areas although the roads are subject to federal law. I was particularly lucky to have been able to travel within FATA, because you need special permission and an armed escort from the government to visit.

These tribal people are in many ways inspiring; the Powindahs were especially fascinating to me. These are the Pashtun nomad tribes who for centuries have migrated between the highlands of Waziristan and Afghanistan in the summer and the plains of Khyber Pakhtunkhwa and Punjab in the winter. On our way to Kaniguram we saw the Powindahs on the move. Once, about half an hour before sunset, we came across a small encampment by the side of a stream. One of the beautiful sheepdogs the Powindahs keep, known as Kuchi or Gadi, stood guard. I desperately wanted to buy one of these animals; my parents always kept Kuchi and they make intelligent watchdogs. So I approached the tents and a young man came up and greeted me. He recognized me, saying he had seen me on television playing cricket once during a trip to Dera Ismail Khan, a town in Khyber Pakhtunkhwa. He invited me to where his father and uncle were sitting and introduced me. Unfortunately they did not have any pups but we got talking. As we sat there I became aware of this incredible scene all around me. The Powindahs had pitched their tents just a short while before after a long day's walk. The children were playing amongst the dogs, sheep and goats. A grandmother was chasing the smaller kids, some women were preparing food, a father was washing his children in the stream. There was laughter and complete harmony all around me. Here were people living the toughest life imaginable, with virtually no material possessions, and yet I never heard one complaint during my conversation. For these resilient people, the existence of God and life after death were as obvious as the sun and the moon. On another trip I came across a different group of Powindahs, and I met a tribal elder whose son had recently been killed fighting the Soviets in Afghanistan. The son's photo had been garlanded with flowers and depicted a young, strapping, handsome man. He had, the Powindahs told me, been the life and soul of their community. 'I'm sorry,' I said to the father. He simply looked at me and said, 'You should congratulate me, my son has embraced martyrdom for a higher cause.'

One of the main things that struck me during a series of trips to the tribal areas that I undertook between 1990 and 1992 to research my book about the Pashtuns, *Warrior Race*, was the total lack of education. So fiercely did they defend their culture that the tribesmen never allowed the British to build schools during the Raj. Yet when I visited them I found they craved education. Everywhere I went they wanted schools but successive Pakistani governments have given them precious few educational facilities. Without education, the tribal areas' culture cannot evolve. This is particularly sad because it is a society that would respond well to education.

The Pashtuns have clung fiercely to their way of life throughout the centuries. They have no fear of authority, unlike people in the rest of Pakistan, especially in Punjab and Sindh, where centuries of feudalism have made the masses bow before power. It is the confidence derived from their democratic system that has enabled the tribal people to become great generals, officers and even rulers all over India for centuries. Unlike the poor living under the feudal system, who do not aspire to leadership, the tribal Pashtuns are brought up as natural leaders. It is this difference in mentality that made the Pashtun areas harder to conquer than much of the Indian subcontinent. Throughout history even warring Pashtun tribes will cast aside their differences and stand up to an invader. This is how, in going after a few hundred al-Qaeda fighters for America's 'war on terror', the government has raised a rebellion amongst tribes with the potential fighting power of a million armed men. In succumbing to Washington's pressure to send the Pakistani army into the tribal areas, we have a conflict that could lead to the collapse of the Pakistani state.

In addition, the people of the tribal areas remain marginalized from mainstream politics. Pakistan only gave them the right to vote in 1997 (previously only the *maliks*, or tribal leaders, could vote or contest elections). Most of the country's main political parties have chapters and representatives in FATA, but candidates can participate in polls only on a nonparty basis. It also remains the most underdeveloped area of Pakistan, neglected by the state and isolated by its mountainous terrain, which makes the delivery of services and infrastructure challenging. About 60 per cent of the population lives below the national poverty line and per capita income is half the national average. Per capita public development expenditure is said to be a third of the national average. Eking a living out of the land in many areas is tough, and opportunities to earn a wage limited. The Community Appraisal and Motivation Programme (CAMP), an NGO that operates in FATA, has conducted a series of surveys in the area. When asked to name a living national politician they admired, 50 per cent or more of respondents said they could not name one or did not admire any of them. In the 2010 survey I got the highest rating at 13.1 per cent; Zardari was the nearest contender at 4.4 per cent. Similarly, a 2010 poll in FATA by the New America Foundation and Terror Free Tomorrow found that Tehreek-e-Insaf was the most popular party with just over 28 per cent of the vote. The next most popular was PML (N) with 10 per cent.

In neighbouring Baluchistan the tribes are also known for their ferocity and strength. However, thanks to a succession of rulers, from the British to the current Pakistani government, using the Baluchi *sardars* (leaders) to control the people, the system of leadership has degenerated from an egalitarian one into an almost feudal-like subservience, as aptly described in his book, *A Journey to Disillusionment*, by the Baluchi sardar Sherbaz Khan Mazari. In contrast, the Pashtuns have often rebelled against any malik seen as an agent for the British or the central government. Because of the jirga system, they are also used to a tradition of debate and are more receptive to intellectual discussion. The university I have built in Mianwali, which is on the edge of Khyber Pakhtunkhwa, has drawn great interest, not just from locals but also from people from Waziristan looking to educate both sons and daughters. Female literacy in the tribal areas is woefully low, estimated at 3 per cent compared with a national average for women of almost a third (male literacy in FATA is 29.5 per cent). In conservative areas of Pakistan it is not that people are against female education per se, they just want to know their women-folk will not have to travel far and that they will be safe. They are also suspicious of education for women being used by for-eigners to chip away at their traditions. One of their greatest fears is that a westernized education will detach women from their religion and their culture, hence the suspicion of foreign-ers and westernized Pakistanis in parts of the countryside. At Namal University we have made sure that cultural norms are respected. It helps too that people there know and trust me. We have actually managed to engineer a mini-revolution, with conservative families sending their daughters to study along-side men.

It cannot be emphasized enough how isolated some of these communities are. In parts of the tribal areas, some of the villages have been left alone for years. In these border areas with Afghanistan, where the Pashtuns move freely from one side to the other, they remain untouched by any form of authority. On the Afghan side, it is much the same.

Ignorant of the history and character of these people, and fired by 'imperial hubris', in October 2001 the United States and its allies invaded Afghanistan expecting to succeed where the British in the nineteenth century and the Russians in the twentieth century had failed. This war was ill-fated from the start. A military campaign defined as a battle against

Islamic extremism soon became in Afghanistan a liberation struggle against foreign invaders. And the battle of Afghanistan's 15 million Pashtuns has incensed Pakistan's 25 million Pashtuns. In a repeat of what happened with Vietnam and Cambodia, the Americans have allowed the war to spill into a neighbouring country. Musharraf and then Zardari have forced the Pakistani army to launch military operations in the tribal areas, but since our soldiers are seen as proxies for the Americans they have run into fierce resistance as the militants have declared jihad against them. We now find ourselves fighting what has become an undeclared and bloody civil war.

The Americans complain that Pakistan, whether officially or unofficially, helps insurgents fighting the allied forces in Afghanistan. But they have failed to understand the Pashtun mentality (as, sadly, did Musharraf). Many Pakistanis – in the army, the government and the general public – were against the invasion of Afghanistan from the start. But for the Pashtun, their loyalty is clear-cut. Anyone with even a basic knowledge of the history of the region knows that for reasons of religious, cultural and social affinity, the Pashtuns feel a deep-rooted duty to help their brethren on either side of the Durand Line. For them, the international frontier is irrelevant. So no government, Pakistani or foreign, will ever be entirely successful in stopping them crossing over the 1,500-mile border to support their people or feeling obliged to offer them shelter if they venture into their territory.

Soon after the invasion of Afghanistan, the Americans bombed the Tora Bora cave complex in the White Mountains, believed to be Osama bin Laden's headquarters. A few hundred al-Qaeda militants crossed the border into Pakistan's tribal areas; they were probably initially welcomed as guests by the Pashtun tribes, in accordance with their ancient traditions. The Americans claim that these militants set up bases from which to wage battle against US and NATO troops in Afghanistan.

In addition, the Americans believed that al-Qaeda's leaders, including Osama bin Laden and Ayman al-Zawahiri, were hiding in the region. Washington, failing to understand that the Pakistani government only has indirect control over the tribal areas, threatened to use force if Islamabad did not prevent the tribes from harbouring militants. Those who knew the region warned the government against provoking an uprising but Musharraf was unable to stand up to Washington and in March 2004 the Pakistan army launched its first major operation to root out al-Qaeda – sending helicopter gunships and thousands of troops into South Waziristan. According to Lieutenant General Aurakzai, suspicions that recent assassination attempts against Musharraf had been planned in South Waziristan also spurred him into sending in the troops. At this point, Musharraf put the number of foreign militants in the province at five to six hundred. Yet according to Lieutenant General Aurakzai, when he took the army into the tribal areas and worked with the tribes, the tribes handed over around 250 al-Qaeda militants to the army. Thanks to pressure from Washington, Pashtun officers in the army were weeded out before the operation and Aurakzai himself, who hails from the Orakzai Agency (an area of FATA), was forced into retiring one month early. Major General Safdar Hussain, a Punjabi, replaced him. The operation was a disaster, with many casualties on both sides. After several weeks of fighting, the operation ended in the Shakai agreement, in which the tribesmen agreed to encourage foreign militants to register with the authorities in exchange for a kind of amnesty. The accord soon broke down when the Americans killed Nek Muhammad in June 2004 through a drone attack.

This pattern of military operations in Waziristan followed by truces continued for the next couple of years. American pressure mounted convinced that the area was a safe haven for militants. Aurakzai, who was governor of Khyber Pakhtunkhwa between 2006 and 2008, told me that most of these agreements fell apart under US pressure and were never broken by the militants, including the Miranshah accord he negotiated in North Waziristan in September 2006. Some analysts and media commentators have complained that this agreement was instrumental in allowing the militants to increase their power and infrastructure and combine the various local militant groups and factions into a cohesive Pakistani Taliban – the Tehrik-e-Taliban (TTP). However, Aurakzai says the army's actions in the tribal areas were counterproductive, because 'collateral damage' through bombing villages added to the ranks of the militants, unifying opposition and intensifying hatred towards the Pakistani government and its American backers. 'I advocated using good intelligence then targeted operations against the militants that did not hurt local people. If the locals side with the Taliban, there is no way you can catch someone in the tribal areas,' he told me. Once he was trying to explain to a US army delegation the advantages of having a peace agreement with the Taliban: we were taking too many casualties, he said, and military operations cause collateral damage which in turn increases militancy. One of the Americans bluntly replied, 'We are paying you to fight, not to draw up peace agreements.'

Hence the US pressure for Pakistan 'to do more' in the tribal area had a very heavy price for Pakistan. Our subservient leaders kept buckling under American pressure, engaging in military operations, bombing villages in the tribal areas, leading to a backlash of terrorist attacks in Pakistani cities. We Pakistanis became used to this whenever a high-powered delegation came from Washington; either the tribal areas would be bombed, or some high-value al-Qaeda member would be picked up to coincide with the visit. Once a government minister told me on the eve of Condoleezza Rice's visit to Pakistan that the next day she would receive five presents; sure enough, the following morning it was reported that five al-Qaeda had been killed 'in a shoot-out', conveniently hitting the headlines the day she arrived. When George W. Bush visited Pakistan, the headlines read: '40 foreign militants killed in North Waziristan.' Later the truth emerged; family and friends in Saidgai village in North Waziristan had gathered to welcome a businessman returning from the Gulf, and it was these innocent civilians who had been bombed.

(Sir Olaf Caroe also documented the time-honoured pattern of Pashtun vengeance – every time the British launched an operation against the tribes these would retreat into the mountains; there would be a lull in violence and then the insurgents would regroup and return, numbers boosted by the relatives of the dead now duty-bound to exact retribution. As a result, before bombing a village, the British would drop leaflets in the area so the people would leave and the attack would cause only material damage.)

I have heard so many stories of innocent people suffering because of this campaign, including from one of my own party workers. Khalil ur Rehman, Tehreek-e-Insaf district party head in Bajaur, was travelling in the tribal areas with his family when a Pakistani army helicopter appeared overhead. As per the army's instructions for locals in FATA, they got out of the car and put their hands up. But the helicopter fired on them anyway. Khalil's six-year-old son lost his legs and his brother and nephew both died. I took Khalil to tell his story on one of Pakistan's most watched talk shows, *Capital Talk*. 'We would die for Pakistan but after this how can I stop members of my family joining the Taliban?' Khalil told the interviewer.

Another side effect of the army's action is that it has stoked rivalries and created frictions between tribes. One has turned against the other as some side with the Taliban and others side with the army. The government encouraged tribes willing to help to form *lashkars* (informal militias) to fight the insurgency but they were just decimated by the militants, who viewed them as American lackeys. Even once there is peace these vendettas will continue to take their toll for years to come as families try to avenge the death of loved ones. A Waziri tribal elder and former senator I knew, Faridullah Khan, was killed in 2005 because he was considered to be pro-government. This is exactly what used to happen under the British; any malik perceived to be collaborating with the colonial rulers was killed, particularly in Waziristan, which is known as the wildest part of the tribal areas. I have a picture of Faridullah standing with Jimmy Goldsmith (Jemima's father) from when we visited the tribal belt in 1995. The death of respected elders like him has had serious repercussions for FATA, undermining the tribal structure and creating a power vacuum – a vacuum that has been in part filled by the Pakistani Taliban. For the sake of flushing out what they said were a few hundred foreign fighters, Islamabad effectively created thousands of pro-Taliban fighters and killed many innocent civilians. But it was too embarrassing for the government to admit that it had set the army on its own people; twenty-six Pakistani journalists have been killed so far in FATA, and there is a strong suspicion that they were targeted because the government didn't want independent reporting of the situation there. As happened with East Pakistan, propaganda, lies and deception have been used to try to shield the public from what was really happening.

Still more damaging than these army operations has been the covert use by the CIA of unmanned drone aircraft in the tribal belt. Shamefully this is done with the connivance of the Islamabad government. As Zahid Hussain points out in *The Scorpion's Tail*, it is the first time in history that 'an intelligence agency of one country has been using robots to target individuals for killing in another country with which it is not officially at war'.

When the issue of military operations was debated in the National Assembly in 2004, I was one of the few voices speaking out for people I'd travelled amongst. Almost all of the parliamentarians were ignorant of the tribal areas and were clueless about the mess that was being created. I said, if you had read the history of the area, you would not have found yourself in this quicksand; I was attacked for romanticizing them, and later accused of being a Taliban sympathizer. It was obvious to anyone who understood the region that this attack on the people in the tribal areas will be a disaster for Pakistan; and sure enough, in two drone attacks on consecutive days in South Waziristan, over 100 people were killed in September 2004, which sparked off the beginning of the Masud tribe's rebellion against the government. To make matters worse, the government tried to claim that those being killed in these attacks were all 'foreign militants', a lie designed to make people swallow the awful truth – that in return for dollars we were bombing our own people. It's sad that the government are repeating the actions that befell the country during the 1971 East Pakistan crisis, using propaganda to cover the fact they were fighting their own people: for 'foreign militants' now, it was 'Indian-backed' then.

Numbers of casualties are hard to verify, given the vastly different accounts that come from the army and the Taliban. Reporters are not allowed into the tribal areas and media reports often cite locals as saying the corpses of those killed are burned beyond recognition, making it even harder to establish who has been slain. After a drone attack, no one dares go to help the wounded as there is always a fear that the site could be bombed again. So for hours people can hear the cries of the wounded. Major-General Ghayur Mehmood claimed in early 2011 that almost all those killed in drone strikes were terrorists, showing how low our government had sunk, blatantly lying to cover up these immoral drone strikes. At a Pakistani Ex-Servicemen Association meeting I attended, a tribal elder from North Waziristan, Khulabat Khan, challenged this, arguing that if an attack killed twenty people then at least eighteen of them were civilians. He questioned how the government could verify the identity of the dead when drone attacks are typically in areas where the Pakistani military does not operate. Based on their drones database, Peter Bergen and Katherine Tiedemann at the New America Foundation estimate that between 1,492 and 2,328 people have died in 244 drone strikes between 2004 and May 2011. They put the civilian fatality rate over this period at approximately 20 per cent. However, analysis by Pakistani newspaper *The News* found that in 2010 about 59 per cent of those killed were civilians. Furthermore, *The News* estimates that – despite this appalling record – the attacks only killed a fifth of the hundred-plus high-value targets on the CIA's hit list in 2010. This campaign, initiated by Bush, has been ramped up under Obama's remit. *The News* estimates that unmanned aircraft strikes hit an annual record of 124 in 2010, more than doubling from 2009. One also has to imagine the number of innocent people maimed and injured in these incidents. This campaign of terror from the skies has provoked immense anger and outrage in Pakistan. Kareem Khan from North Waziristan tried to sue the head of the CIA (who was whisked away from Pakistan) for the death of his son and brother in a drone strike in Waziristan, seeking US$500 million in compensation.

To justify this rampant violation of Pakistani sovereignty, the Americans have run a consistent campaign of demonization against our country. A succession of US officials and analysts have branded Pakistan 'the most dangerous country in the world for everyone' and a 'nuclear-armed crucible of jihadi culture, exporting terrorists and destabilizing its neighbours', accused us of hosting 'the most dangerous component' of al-Qaeda, being 'the most anti-US country in the world' and the most likely source of the next terrorist attack against America. Everybody from Senator Bob Graham to Bruce Riedel, former national security adviser to President Clinton, as well as Vice President Joe Biden, has participated in this chorus of condemnation. What Washington fails to understand is that the existence of a small minority of hard-core militants in certain areas of the country does not mean Pakistan is on the verge of being taken over by religious fundamentalists. The 'war on terror' is certainly pushing people towards extremes of opinion, but those who know Pakistan know that there will never be Talibanization in Pakistan. In Afghanistan, the Taliban succeeded not because of their ideology but because they promised people rule of law after years of war and the atrocities and corruption of the warlords. There is some misconception in the West that the Afghan Taliban replaced a secular government. In fact, they took over from warring mujahideen that included people like Gulbuddin Hekmatyar, initially supported by the CIA when he fought the Soviets, and who was considered a religious fanatic by the Russians.

In every country where Islam has spread, the character of the people has shaped the religion. Often, the underlying culture remains with only those customs repugnant to Islam filtered out. Because of the hostility of their territory, the Pashtun culture has always been austere and conservative. Islam is an intrinsic part of life for Pashtuns, as for most Pakistanis. If there is support for sharia law it is because they believe it offers a fairer system of justice and a more equal society than the Pakistani state has hitherto given them. They are also strongly against the way the United States has handled Islamic terrorism since 9/11 and see the fighting in Afghanistan as a battle for freedom against foreign occupiers; thirty years before, the men fighting in Afghanistan against foreign occupation were hailed by US President Ronald Reagan as the 'moral equivalent of America's founding fathers'. In the 2002 elections there was a sweeping and unprecedented victory for the Muttahida Majlis-e-Amal (MMA) – mainly headed by the two religious parties Jamiat Ulema-e-Islam (JUI) and Jamaat-e-Islami (JI) – because of their opposition to the invasion of Afghanistan. But that does not mean there is wide support for the Taliban ideology. The militants' attacks on girls' schools and the desecration of saints' shrines are particularly resented. In its 2009 'Understanding FATA' poll, the NGO CAMP found that respondents ranked democracy, the independence of the judiciary and women's rights as the biggest human rights issues in Pakistan.

Besides, as the Pak Institute for Peace Studies (PIPS) concluded in a report on attitudes towards militancy and extremism, local culture has proved resilient. 'Even in the areas where culture or traditions had been subdued by radicalization,' as the militants tried to impose their version of Islam on local people, 'the culture reasserted itself once this militant influence faded.' It uses the example of Swat, where following a major military operation to oust the Taliban in 2009, local traditions and customs resumed. Even in the nineteenth century during the twilight days of India's Mughal Empire, when Syed Ahmed Barelvi founded a revolutionary Islamic movement it failed to take hold. Barelvi preached jihad against non-Muslim influences and tried to rally the

Pashtun tribes to his cause but they disliked his rigid brand of Islam and abandoned him, leaving him to be slain by the Sikhs who had at that time conquered the settled Pashtun areas. There is a strong Sufi influence in Pakistan, which will always be at odds with the strict literal Islam of Wahhabi ideology that influences many militant groups. This tension is represented by the two main schools of thought for Sunni Muslims in Pakistan. Barelvis typically lean towards South Asia's traditional brand of Sufi Islam with its saints and shrines and message of tolerance. Deobandis, on the other hand, are more ideologically aligned with the Wahhabis and are therefore more sympathetic to the Taliban's version of Islam.

Pakistan could have suggested far more effective methods of rooting out al-Qaeda. To those of us who know the tribes, the obvious solution was to work with them, to cajole them and to encourage them to collaborate. After all, they have been known to contribute to Pakistan's national interests in the past. The tribal Pashtuns sent their lashkars to fight in Kashmir in 1948 and supplied volunteers to the Pakistan army in the 1965 war. But one government after the other has failed to defend Pakistan's own interests. Bob Woodward's *Obama's Wars* cites Zardari, in a discussion with then CIA director Mike Hayden about drone attacks, saying the chilling words: 'Collateral damage worries you Americans. It does not worry me.' He might as well have said that, to him, US dollars are worth more than Pakistani lives. The WikiLeaks cables exposed the true extent of the Pakistani government's collaboration in these unlawful extrajudicial killings. One quoted Prime Minister Yousaf Raza Gilani as saying about the drone strikes: 'I don't care if they do it as long as they get the right people. We'll protest in the National Assembly and then ignore it.' But of course the strikes often *don't* get the right people. How can an exploding bomb in villages differentiate between innocent civilians and militants? The cables also revealed that small teams of US special forces soldiers have been secretly deployed alongside Pakistani military forces in the tribal areas, helping to track down militants and co-ordinate drone strikes, something that Islamabad has never publicly acknowledged. Furthermore, the cables record Pakistani officials telling US counterparts that locals don't mind the attacks, belying the survey by the New America Foundation and Terror Free Tomorrow that found more than three-quarters of FATA residents opposed them. In fact, it revealed only 16 per cent thought these strikes accurately targeted militants. It also showed that, with thousands of mer-cenaries from companies like Blackwater inside our borders, such is the suspicion of these agents who live in high-walled villas in the cities, and travel in convoy in their four-by-fours with tinted glass, that the majority of Pakistanis believe these contractors are themselves involved in terrorism – especially after the Raymond Davis affair.

Within Pakistan, both Musharraf and Zardari have found willing support from the country's elite, ever fearful of the supposed advance of Talibanization. There is a Chinese saying that one should know one's enemy, but Bob Woodward's *Obama's Wars* demonstrates the Americans' frightening ignorance of the Pashtun character and its emphasis on hospitality and revenge. They think Islamabad has control over the tribal areas, but not only does the federal government have little sway over them, most shockingly the ruling elite is as clueless as the Americans about this area. That is why I have told visiting US politicians again and again that Washington must seek alternative points of views about what is happening in the tribal areas. I have recommended they speak to people who come from the region and have first-hand knowledge of what is really going on there. As revelations from WikiLeaks show, it is becoming clear that our dollar-addicted elite has a vested interest in prolonging this war to keep US aid flowing in.

The US puppets have tried to use the same scare tactics on Pakistanis in an effort to rally public opinion around their policies. Most Pakistanis have seen through the propaganda, and insisted it was not Pakistan's war and that we were killing our own people for American dollars. When a young charismatic cleric by the name of Maulana Fazlullah sprang into prominence in Khyber Pakhtunkhwa's Swat valley, fomenting unrest following the Red Mosque affair, the government took the opportunity to terrify Pakistanis with the idea that the Taliban had their sights on Islamabad. Now many people – particularly our country's opinion-makers, who know nothing of rural Pakistan – do not understand the difference between Swat and the tribal areas. They think all Pashtuns are the same. But Swat is very different to the tribal areas – in terms of politics, history and geography. Where much of the tribal areas are made up of inhospitable moun-tain terrain, Swat is a green and fertile valley, once known as the Switzerland of the East. It was a princely state until 1969, run like a personal estate by the Wali of Swat with a com-bination of tribal customs and sharia law. It had a rich Buddhist history, one of the highest literacy rates in Pakistan and was relatively crime-free, safe enough to draw hippies in the 1970s looking for a chilled-out haven in which to smoke pot. Until 2007 it was still a popular ski resort and weekend getaway for the elite of Islamabad. Unlike in the tribal areas, where only forty-four federal laws apply, Swat, like the rest of the settled areas, is legally and politically run like the rest of Pakistan. And unlike the tribal areas, it shares no border with Afghanistan.

There had, though, since Zulfikar Ali Bhutto ousted the Wali in 1969 and incorporated Swat into the civil administration of Khyber Pakhtunkhwa, been discontent. Political interference and manipulation by various Pakistani governments along with the corruption of government officials had corroded traditional tribal democracy and over the years crime rates had risen. According to my cousin Jamshed Burki, who used to be commissioner of Malakand, the administrative division Swat comes under, when Pakistan's justice system was established in Swat the murder rate shot up from ten a year in 1974 to seven hundred a year in 1977. Consequently, resentment against the Pakistani government system of justice – which was seen as corrupt, expensive and inefficient – had been simmering, eventually feeding into a movement calling for sharia law. Known as Tehreek-e-Nafaz-e-Shariat-e-Mohammadi (Movement for the Enforcement of Islamic Law), this was founded by Maulana Fazlullah's father-in-law, Maulana Sufi Muhammad, an Afghan jihad veteran. When Muhammad was imprisoned in 2002, the more radical Fazlullah assumed leadership of the movement. Fazlullah earned the nickname 'Radio Mullah' after setting up a radio station to propagate his movement. He was almost like a televangelist, and drew a strong female following, who would donate their jewellery to his cause. Fired by the bloodshed of the Lal Masjid affair, he urged his followers to rebel against the government and its security forces. He appealed to the poorest strata of society, claiming Musharraf's government was a stooge of the US and out to destroy Islam. He also tapped into resentment against local landowners, some of whom had unfairly taken over common land when Swat joined Pakistan. Militants targeted certain big landowners and in some areas distributed the profits from their crops amongst landless peasants.

Worried by Fazlullah's growing band of followers and their lawlessness, Musharraf sent the army into Swat in the autumn of 2007 to crush the militants. But in early 2008 the PPP-led coalition took power and initiated peace talks, which took a long time. Sufi Muhammad was released from prison and brokered a deal that saw sharia law imposed on the Swat valley in return for the Taliban laying down their arms. Westernized Pakistanis saw the implementation of sharia as a backward step but all Sufi Muhammad was doing was tapping into a longstanding desire amongst ordinary Swatis for accessible justice. Sher Khan, a former union council *nazim* (local mayor) who had stood as a candidate for my party in the provincial assembly elections, was involved in these negotiations. He told me that as part of the accord about 1,500 militants surrendered themselves to the army, only to be brutally tortured in custody. This treatment only served to radicalize the young men, and most of them later became fanatics. Sher Khan, who had helped bring about this peace deal in good faith, was appalled. Once again, strong-arm tactics by the establishment backfired. When the army withdrew from Swat and released the detained insurgents, many of these men, hungry for revenge against the security forces, rushed into the power vacuum. According to Sher Khan, some of the greatest atrocities committed at this time were by those who had been brutalized while in army detention.

Fazlullah's forces had been further bolstered by a rag-tag collection of jihadi and sectarian groups, common criminals, sharia law supporters and angry peasants. Locals began to turn against the Taliban as they imposed their brutal rule with a campaign of violence, beheading anyone who opposed them or whom they suspected of being a government spy, kidnapping, burning down schools and attacking DVD shops and barbers. The Pakistani government was able to use this total breakdown of law and order to convince their public both that this was an extension of what was happening in the tribal areas and that the Taliban were set to march on the capital. Again the media were manipulated to rally support for army intervention. A journalist in Swat told me at the time that intelligence agencies had told him to put out more stories on Taliban atrocities. He also said the agencies were trying to sideline the Deobandis, the ideological brethren of the Taliban, stoking Barelvi concerns about Deobandi and Taliban desecration of Sufi shrines and tombs in order to rally opposition to the militants.

I am cynical about how the government handled the whole operation. Zardari dithered for two months before endorsing the terms of the February 2009 peace deal, waiting till April to sign the law introducing Islamic sharia law as demanded by the militants. While he dithered Swat further descended into chaos. Within a few weeks a couple of jeeploads of Taliban were spotted in the district south of Swat, Buner. This unleashed a wave of panic with newspaper headlines warning that the Taliban had advanced to within sixty miles of Islamabad. The army operation was timed to coincide with Zardari landing in Washington and it was no surprise that he was praised for the Swat operation and used that to pitch for more aid. 'We are fighting to save the world,' he told a meeting of the Friends of Pakistan in Japan a couple of weeks later, as if a few thousand Taliban in Pakistan were going to destroy the half-a-million-strong army and threaten global security. Yet what was going on in Swat was a shambolic and mainly criminal revolt that did not even have the popular support of the locals. The government should have implemented a focused commando operation to take out the movement's top leadership. Instead, the army's full-scale assault meant more than two million people were displaced, many innocent lives were lost and the local economy was devastated. Alarmed at the situation, I went to Swat just as people were streaming out of the area. Locals told me that they had been given an hour to leave before the military bombardment started. A young boy told me he had seen dead bodies – civilians killed in army bombing. There is no doubt people hated what the Taliban were doing but they were angry about the army's heavy-handedness. Despite the intervention, Fazlullah and his main accomplices got away, and are believed to have fled to Afghanistan. Anyone who opposed the government's strategy – including me – was branded a Taliban sympathizer. A friend of mine, Nadeem Iqbal, spent three months working in camps for people displaced by the fighting in Swat and after many conversations with the camp inhabitants and army officers he came to the same conclusions – the Swat operation was done because the government wanted more aid money from Washington for services rendered, and that a more focused commando operation would have done the trick. Nadeem said it was the only time he had wanted to give up on Pakistan and get a Canadian passport.

This American manipulation of Pakistani politics has only served to undermine its puppet rulers. When people see how dependent our already unpopular leaders are on Washington it erodes their authority even more. Pakistanis are understand-ably incensed that the government clearly allows American intelligence agents to operate unimpeded within their country, a fact revealed by the case of Raymond Davis, the CIA operative who shot two people dead in Lahore in January 2011. Another man died when a car from the American con-sulate knocked down a passing pedestrian in its rush to assist Davis. Defying Islamabad's demands for those in the car to be handed over, Washington has allowed them to flee the country. Davis was promptly arrested, though, and the Americans have tried to claim diplomatic blanket immunity from prosecution for him, saying he killed the men in self-defence during an attempted robbery. However, newspapers have reported that he shot them repeatedly in the back, undermining that story. American officials have admitted to the press that Davis was part of a covert, CIA-led intelligence team surveying militant groups. One of the dead men's wives, nineteen-year-old Shumaila Kanwal, committed suicide by swallowing rat poison in despair of ever getting justice for her husband. In a scene that was played over and over again on Pakistani news channels, she told reporters at her hospital bedside just before her death that she wanted 'blood for blood'. She told them she was committing suicide 'because I will not get justice'. The Davis case triggered demonstrations across the country, created a diplomatic firestorm and inflamed anti-American feelings more than ever.

Shumaila Kanwal's distraught words illustrate the kind of anger and despair that in the tribal areas leads people to blow themselves up to avenge the death of their relatives, whether from drone attacks or military operations. As David Kilcullen, a counterinsurgency expert and former adviser to General David Petraeus, and Andrew Exum, a fellow at think-tank the Center for a New American Security, wrote in the *New York Times*: every dead civilian killed in a drone strike 'represents an alienated family, a new desire for revenge, and more recruits for a militant movement that has grown exponentially even as drone strikes have increased'. Sure enough, as military operations by the Pakistani army and drone strikes have intensified, so have terrorist attacks. According to Farrukh Saleem at Pakistani think-tank the Centre for Research and Security Studies, there were only 189 terrorism-related deaths in 2003 but the toll peaked at 11,585 in 2009 – when army intervention was at its height. Civilians bore the brunt of this as the terrorists shifted their attention from security forces to increasingly soft targets, such as the campus of Islamabad's International Islamic University, and markets in Lahore and Peshawar. One glaring example of the way in which the government's policy simply escalated the violence was the 2006 airstrike on a madrassa said to harbour militants in Bajaur, the smallest of the FATA territories, near the Afghan border. At least eighty people died and news reports cited locals saying sixty-two of them were children under the age of eighteen. Militants vowed revenge and it was swiftly followed by a suicide bombing attack on a military garrison, killing forty-two army recruits. The man who carried out the assault was said to have been a relative of one of the children killed in the Bajaur madrassa. Still worse was the cack-handed cover-up of American involvement in the madrassa bombing. The Pakistani military claimed responsibility for it, but locals and opposition politicians said that the strike was conducted by an American drone aircraft. According to the *New York Times*, residents said Pakistani army helicopter gunships appeared firing rockets after the initial explosions. The Pakistani government denied the claim, although Christina Lamb of the *Sunday Times* later reported that a key aide to Musharraf had admitted that they had thought 'it would be less damaging if we said we did it rather than the US'.

Nor has US foreign policy or military strategy fared any better in Afghanistan. Hamid Karzai's regime is undermined by the weakness of Afghanistan's state institutions, allegations of vote rigging and its inability to control either rampant government corruption or the diabolical security situation. US and NATO forces are resented for their intrusiveness, for the bombing of fields, orchards and houses, but most of all for blunders that have led to civilian deaths. There is also immense suspicion about where most of the US$56 billion development budget approved by the US Congress for Afghanistan has gone. Only a fifth of this money was at the disposal of the Afghan government; the rest was to be used by the US State Department, the Department of Defense and USAID. This all of course plays into the hands of the Taliban, who can argue that their regime provided, if not freedom, then more security than Karzai's US-backed administration. They are further uprooting what state infrastructure exists by setting up their own shadow government in parts of the country. The United States and its allies have at times tried to justify the invasion of Afghanistan by claiming they wanted to protect Afghan women's rights, but the Afghan politician and women's rights activist Malalai Joya has highlighted the fact that many of the warlords returned to power with Karzai's government have just as unpleasant views on women as the Taliban. 'Dust has been thrown into the eyes of the world by your governments,' she told the *Independent*. 'You have not been told the truth. The situation now is as catastrophic as it was under the Taliban for women. Your governments have replaced the fundamentalist rule of the Taliban with another fundamentalist regime of warlords.' Joya herself has received intimidation and death threats from Afghan MPs after slamming the Afghan government for including notorious warlords in power.

The question I am surprised no one asks is about men who fought the Soviet invaders of their land, and in the process lost one million men, but won; why would they not fight the Americans? The US government might have convinced their own public they were the good guys while the Soviets were the bad guys, but the people of Afghanistan saw them both as invaders.

Bob Woodward has revealed how Obama – while debating whether to send more troops to Afghanistan or not after coming to power – always asked the right questions: what are we fighting for, what will we achieve and what constitutes victory? The generals resort to their usual policy of fear-mongering and claim that if they don't win in Afghanistan then they will have to fight Islamic militants on the streets of New York. Part of the distortion of the truth is that the US are not fighting freedom fighters but the 'Taliban ideology'. These words are very similar to those spoken by the men who pro-moted the Vietnam War, talking about the 'domino effect' – that if they didn't fight in Vietnam, other countries would fall to the communists till they were on America's doorstep; and later, when Vietnam fell to the communists, 3 million people had died – and there was no domino effect.

The parallels with Vietnam go deeper. The failure of the war in Afghanistan has led to Pakistan becoming a punchbag for the US, just as Cambodia became one over Vietnam. In the so-called 'safe haven' in North Waziristan, the Haqqani Taliban group – viewed by the US as one of its deadliest threats in the area – fields a maximum of 5,000 men, although the number is probably less than that. Is it plausible that the US, with all its military might, is losing in Afghanistan thanks to these 5,000? Senior US officials push the Pakistan army to do more, blaming Pakistan for their failures in Afghanistan on the Haqqani. It is very important Pakistan doesn't share Cambodia's fate. If the Pakistan army goes into North Waziristan, after the 5,000 militants, what is going to be the fate of the 350,000 inhabitants of the area? Will they become 'collateral damage'?

CIA director Leon Panetta, according to Bob Woodward, also piled the pressure on Obama, advising him that no democratic president can go against military advice. Sadly Obama – going against all his better instincts – heeds him rather than Colin Powell, who tries to tell him he doesn't always have to listen to the generals. What makes me feel sorry for Obama is that during this whole debate there was no credible government in Pakistan to advise him. A sovereign and credible Pakistani government could have helped him find an exit strategy for Afghanistan, could have pledged to prevent al-Qaeda fighters from using Pakistani soil to launch attacks on the West, could have facilitated talks, could have played a major role in bringing the various parties together. Pakistan, after Afghanistan, had the most to lose from a troop surge, yet when this vital debate was taking place, there was no input from the Pakistan government. Instead, all Zardari was interested in doing was giving Obama whatever advice would lead to Washington pumping more money into Pakistan to prop up his corrupt government. The supreme irony was that it was the US who was responsible for engineering the 2008 elections to get a corrupt and pliant government to do its bidding.

The current strategy can only increase radicalization – a dangerous prospect given that Pakistan is a country with a fast-growing population, a youth bulge and high rates of unemployment. Now there will be a generation born of anger, an army of young men who lost relatives to US drones or Pakistani military operations. And that radicalization will not just be limited to the poor and dispossessed. Even for the youth of the rich elite, Pakistan's abdication of responsibility for its own sovereignty is a searing humiliation. A CNN poll has revealed that 80 per cent of Pakistanis now view the United States as a bigger security threat to the country than India – no mean achievement by the US, bearing in mind Pakistan has fought three wars with India. Anger against America's political coercion and imperial designs blends with resentment against the breakdown of traditional societies by Western cultural forces into a combustible mix. For some Pakistanis, as with other Muslims, westernization is seen as a destructive force, provoking a retreat to the security and certainty of religious codes and traditional ways of life.

The tragic shooting of the governor of Punjab, Salman Taseer, in early 2011 showed only too clearly the growing polarization of Pakistani society. Taseer had attempted to defend a Christian woman sentenced to death under Pakistan's blasphemy law, and spoke out against it being used to persecute innocent people, both Muslims and minorities. As a result he was shot dead in broad daylight outside a fashionable café in Islamabad by one of his own guards. The 'war on terror' has divided the country into those who are pro-American and anti-Islam, and those who are anti-American and pro-Islam. Before 9/11 Taseer's remarks recommending a change to the blasphemy law in order to prevent its misuse might not even have got a mention in the newspapers. At the worst they might have roused a few statements by clerics wanting to mobilize support amongst their constituencies, but in the current polarized climate everyone and anyone is at risk if they happen to be on the wrong side of the divide. The Taliban labels anybody who opposes them as pro-American. Imams of mosques who have condemned suicide attacks as being anti-Islamic have been accused of being American collaborators and shot or blown up by suicide bombers. Members of the pro-American Awami National Party (ANP) that governs Khyber Pakhtunkhwa have been repeatedly targeted by the Taliban for the party's stance against the militants, who also see Christians, Shias, Ahmedis (regarded as 'non-Muslims' in Pakistan) and their places of worship as fair game. On the other side, those of us who have objected to the military operations and excessive collaboration with the United States are labelled Taliban sympathizers. This means that a meaningful debate on this whole issue of 'war on terror' will become more and more difficult. People are petrified of being caught on the wrong side of the argument.

The other thing Taseer's death has revealed is the erosion of the writ of the state. His murderer was lionized and showered with rose petals by lawyers when he appeared in court. No action was taken against religious leaders who in mosques, at rallies and on television arguably incited murder during the period of fevered national debate that led up to the shooting. Zardari, a close friend of Taseer's, did not even attend his funeral. Two months later, the minorities minister Shahbaz Bhatti was killed by a gunman outside his mother's house in Islamabad. As the state gets weaker and weaker, different power players are jostling to assert themselves, just as during the decline of the great Mughal Empire various warlords and governors started forming their own independent power bases. As the politicians barricade themselves in with ever greater security details, diverting scarce resources from the streets of Pakistan, daily murders in Karachi and Baluchistan go unchecked, a civil war rages along most of our western border and crime and corruption surge higher and higher. America frequently invokes fear of the state collapsing and Pakistan's nuclear weapons falling into the wrong hands, but its tactics are fuelling polarization, radicalization and chaos, which could lead to exactly the kind of destabilization that it most fears. The weaker the Pakistani state gets, the less it will be able to control extremism. When in 2010 news reports said that senior US commanders in Afghanistan were pushing to expand Special Operations ground raids into Pakistan's tribal areas to seek out Afghan Taliban, Anatol Lieven, professor in the War Studies Department of King's College London and a senior fellow of the New America Foundation in Washington, described it as 'a lunatic idea'. He wrote in an article widely reprinted in Pakistan that 'the one thing that would certainly lead to the collapse of the Pakistani state and an immense surge in extremist and terrorist strength would be if the Pakistani Army were to split and parts of it were to mutiny against the alliance with America'. He goes on to explain that various Pakistani army officers have warned him that 'the entry of US ground forces into Pakistan in pursuit of the Taliban and al-Qaeda is by far the most dangerous scenario for both Pakistan–US relations and the unity of the Pakistani Army. As one retired general explained, drone attacks, though ordinary officers and soldiers find them humiliating, are not a critical issue because the Pakistani military cannot do anything about them.' It's also worth bearing in mind that assassination attempts against Musharraf and an attack on the Pakistani army headquarters in Rawalpindi by militants were both inside jobs, while Taseer's murder by one of his own guards sparked fears about possible radicalization within the country's elite security forces.

The discovery of Osama bin Laden's hiding place on 2 May was humiliating for every Pakistani, but his death was devastating for the Pakistani armed forces. For the first time, people openly criticized the army in the media, asking repeatedly: how can we spend such a large part of our budget on the army, and yet it could not protect our sovereignty? How could the army not respond to helicopters flying about, to the sound of explosions and gunfire going on for nearly three-quarters of an hour, so close to their academy? No one knew the building under attack was Osama bin Laden's then – it could have been anyone's – so where was the army? Why was it not at least making the effort to protect its citizens, before the true identity of the inhabitant was revealed? There was a tremendous amount of anger, and my biggest worry remains that if things continue as they are we could face a rebellion within the army's ranks, the ultimate nightmare situation for Pakistan.

Aside from the tremendous losses to Pakistan and Afghanistan caused by Washington's callous and misguided policies, these cause huge detriment to America's own interests. This has been revealed again and again. Most infamously, Faisal Shahzad, the Pakistani-American sentenced for the botched Times Square bombing, cited US foreign policy as justification during his trial. 'I want to plead guilty, and I'm going to plead guilty 100 times over,' he said, 'because until the hour the US pulls its forces from Iraq and Afghanistan, and stops the drone strikes in Somalia and Yemen and in Pakistan, and stops the occupation of Muslim lands, and stops killing the Muslims, and stops reporting the Muslims to its government, we will be attacking the US, and I plead guilty to that.' When asked by the judge about the children he might have killed had his attack in New York been successful he pointed out that drones in Afghanistan and Iraq 'don't see children; they don't see anybody. They kill women, children. They kill everybody.' Personally, I think the radicalization of Muslims in the West as they watch the bloodshed and chaos spread by Washington's policies – not just in Pakistan and Afghanistan, but also in countries like Somalia and Yemen – is a far greater threat to Western security.

Most of the struggles against colonialism in the twentieth century were led by people who had studied in the West. Jinnah, Gandhi and Nehru all had the opportunity to see Western democratic societies in action and were inspired to campaign for the same rights for their countrymen. My own awareness of democracy, the rule of law and the welfare state was awakened when I first went to England to study. Muslims who have grown up and been educated in the West will have a greater awareness of the ways in which human rights laws are broken in the name of the 'war on terror' than many of those living in Muslim countries. They will be aware that no civilized law allows anyone to be judge, jury and executioner, as the CIA is when it fires on people with its drones, eliminating suspects along with their wives, children and neighbours. The Americans may believe that terror plots originate in Pakistan, but to blow up civilians in the United States and Europe terrorists need Western-based Muslims to carry out the attacks. Unfortunately, the next Faisal Shahzad may succeed.

Pakistan should have remained neutral. We could have offered to assist the Americans, but not let our army act as mercenaries. The carnage now going on is because the army is seen as agents of America, and they are being squeezed – by the anti-US forces who see them as puppets of the Americans on one side, and on the other by the Americans themselves – to carry out more operations against their own people. With jihad declared against it by the militants, there have been forty major attacks on army installations.

The first thing Washington has to accept is that it must withdraw from Afghanistan as soon as possible. With the death of Osama bin Laden, this is the perfect time for President Obama to announce victory, and move out, and give peace a chance. After all, it was only for Osama that the Americans first arrived in Afghanistan. This is the single most important step it can take in order to quell Muslim anger around the world, and give the Afghan people a chance of peace and self-government. This would prevent Pakistan from descending into more violence, but this has to be managed properly so as to prevent a bloodbath along the lines of the post-Soviet Afghan chaos. Obama's bid to turn around the war with 30,000 additional troops has failed. He allowed himself to be swayed by generals whose understanding of strategy is confined to the battlefields and who cannot fathom Afghanistan. The deadly combination of a war of resistance against foreign occupation and the religious injunction to protect one's freedom means the Americans will never win. There will never be a shortage of recruits and people willing to die for their country. This war is not about numerical or armament might. In the words of Pakistani journalist Mir Adnan Aziz, 'Afghanistan is a lost duel. History, geography and culture make the area a nightmare for any foreign presence attempting to impose its will on the nation.'

The urgent need to seek some kind of deal with the Taliban in Afghanistan was gaining currency in 2010 and early 2011. There were reports that the United States had begun direct, secret talks with senior Afghan Taliban leaders on finding a political settlement; US ally the UK also seems to have been pushing for a peaceful solution; and the head of its armed forces, General Sir David Richards, said a defeat of Islamist militancy 'in the sense of a clear-cut victory' is unnecessary and unachievable, and that it can only be contained. Meanwhile, a British parliamentary report warned in March 2011 that the window of opportunity for talks was closing. The Taliban, for all their faults, are an Afghan not an international group. Afghans have not risen up and joined the international jihad espoused by al-Qaeda. Afghans have not been found to be involved in terror attacks or plots in the United States or Europe. They are also unlikely to allow a new Taliban regime to operate as it did before or permit al-Qaeda to exert so much influence over their government again. This is backed up by a report by Kandahar-based researchers Alex Strick van Linschoten and Felix Kuehn saying Afghan Taliban leaders would be willing to make a break with al-Qaeda in order to end hostilities and could be persuaded to ensure Afghanistan was not used as a base for terrorism. The Taliban, therefore, need to be dealt with through an Afghan political system with peace talks and the establishment of a new government of consensus negotiated with the assistance of Iran, Pakistan and Saudi Arabia. They should also be given some kind of incentive to isolate al-Qaeda. At the moment, the US has a totally confused policy of a 'fight and talk' approach. They want to open dialogue, but keep bombing at the same time. Tragically, their approach is never going to work, when so many civilians are being treated as Taliban fighters by the Americans – 80 per cent of those taken as 'Taliban' are released within two weeks because they are civilians. And in July 2011 the UN has said there has been the largest number of civilian casualties since the surge.

Pakistan's position is made worse by its geographical situation: hemmed in from the south and east by an unfriendly India, bordering an Iran that fears being sandwiched between a pro-US Iraq and a pro-US Afghanistan, and not far from a Russia that doesn't want the Muslim republics to feed off the strife in Pakistan and Afghanistan. The US will always be worried about a hostile al-Qaeda. All the players have a stake there, and peace will only come when all the players are at the table. And as for what government there should be in Afghanistan? The people of Afghanistan will have to find a solution for themselves without outside interference.

Withdrawal from Afghanistan is essential for defeating the insurgency in Pakistan. As Graham Fuller, former CIA station chief in Kabul and author of *The Future of Political Islam* wrote in the *Huffington Post* in 2009: 'Only the withdrawal of American and NATO boots on the ground will begin to allow the process of near-frantic emotions to subside within Pakistan, and for the region to start to cool down. Pakistan is experienced in governance and is well able to deal with its own Islamists and tribalists under normal circumstances; until recently, Pakistani Islamists had one of the lowest rates of electoral success in the Muslim world. But U.S. policies have now driven local nationalism, xenophobia and Islamism to combined fever pitch. As Washington demands that Pakistan redeem failed American policies in Afghanistan, Islamabad can no longer manage its domestic crisis.' Having talked to people like General Aurakzai, Rustam Shah and Ayaz Wazir (two former Pakistani ambassadors from FATA), as well as former political agents for the tribal area, my personal estimate is that about 90 per cent of the militants in the tribal areas are neither religious extremists nor terrorists. They are simply our own tribal people fighting because of army interventions, drone attacks (and their 'collateral damage') and anger over the US occupation of Afghanistan. We only need to deal with the remaining 10 per cent. Some of these will be men who were part of the original jihadi organizations that once fought the Soviets and now consider themselves Taliban. Others will be members of al-Qaeda. Some will be hardcore ideologues who believe in an Islamic emirate and some will be people driven to extremism because of injustices like the Lal Masjid bloodbath. The solution does not lie in more military action, it lies in isolating that 10 per cent. But it can only happen if the United States withdraws from Afghanistan, or Pakistan pulls out of the 'war on terror' and the army withdraws from tribal areas. I have spoken to General Pasha, head of the ISI about this, and he too believes that if we disengage from the US war, start a dialogue with the tribes, and withdraw troops from the tribal areas, we could eliminate this 10 per cent in ninety days. The moment the US leaves Afghanistan, the anti-American feelings that feed into Islamic radicalism will dissipate. That will free Pakistan up to be able to deal with terrorism on its own terms and focus on bringing stakeholders together to agree on how to bring peace and reconciliation to the tribal areas. But only a credible Pakistani government that is not perceived to be a US stooge will be able to conduct a meaningful dialogue with insurgents and placate the tribes, who should be co-opted into helping the government tackle the real terrorists. As the situation changes in Afghanistan, we also have an opportunity now to decide what kind of country we want Pakistan to become.

Chapter Ten

Rediscovering Iqbal: Pakistan's Symbol and a Template for Our Future

ALLAMA IQBAL'S WORDS WERE A POWERFUL SOURCE OF guidance when Pakistan came into existence in 1947 and during its early years. Every morning Radio Pakistan broadcast his prayer for children that began: 'My wish comes to my lips as supplication – May my life be like a lighted candle, O God!' Iqbal's words left a permanent imprint on the minds of the children who heard it. However, over time, this prayer ceased to be broadcast, and today there are very few children who are familiar with it.

Though Iqbal lived in a historical context that was different from ours in several ways, what he said remains profoundly relevant to us and to our times. In fact, Iqbal's message is more relevant and important today than that of any other Muslim thinker of the past and present not only because he faced the challenges of both traditionalism and modernity fearlessly, but also – and more importantly – because he had a profound understanding of the integrated vision of the

319

Quran which he made the basis of his philosophy. This philosophy provides a comprehensive blueprint for how Muslims should live in accordance with the highest ideals and best practices of Islam. Its aim is to change ground realities in the light of the ethical principles of Islam. These realities change with time but the framework remains constant and continues to be a central point of reference and a guidepost for future generations.

The place that Iqbal occupies in the hearts and minds of Pakistanis is unparalleled, as is his poetry, even though few people appreciate the range and depth of his knowledge and creativity, or his philosophical system. Such are the power and charisma of his imagination and his pen that he is loved by millions who might know only a few of his verses but are inspired and moved by them. Without doubt, Iqbal is the most quoted figure in Pakistan, and his popular verses and favourite symbols, such as that of the shaheen, are known even to semi-literate Pakistanis. However, his philosophy, articulated through both poetry and prose, which should be taught in every educational institution in Pakistan, has been virtually eliminated from the curriculum, and only a small number of students in specialized disciplines have the opportunity to study it.

While some famous verses from Iqbal's poems are often cited in isolation, the core message of his poetry, reflecting his revolutionary spirit, his intrepid imagination and his passionate commitment to justice and the dignity of selfhood, has been excluded from public discourse.

Iqbal constantly referred to the Quranic verse, 'Verily God

will not change the condition of a people till they change what is in themselves' (Quran 13: 12). He was fully aware of the despair and despondency of Muslims who felt powerless to change their adverse circumstances and turned to prayer for an improvement in their lives. Iqbal had written much about the value of prayer but he believed that the way to change one's destiny was through the development of khudi. Iqbal's philosophy, rich as it is in ideas and concepts, is fundamentally action-oriented and its goal was personal and social transformation inspired by the Quranic vision embodied in the proclamation, 'Toward God is your limit' (Quran 53: 42).

Today when Pakistani youth are living in a society in which there is a gaping ethical vacuum, they are in critical need of a deep and comprehensive education based upon Iqbal's multi-faceted philosophy. Iqbal's work can be a source of profound guidance to help young Pakistanis as they seek to understand the nature of their own identity and their own religion. His powerful words challenge them to become a shaheen, which hunts for its food, rather than a vulture, which preys on the dead:

> The flight of both birds is in the same atmosphere
> But the world of the vulture is different from the world of the shaheen

To comprehend why Iqbal has suffered such amazing neglect by the country that at the same time hails him as its 'spiritual' founder, one has to understand the moral, intellectual, social and political degeneration that has sadly characterized most of Pakistan's history. Largely dominated by feudal and other powerful persons and groups with vested interests, Pakistani society has had very limited opportunity to think or act freely. Subjected to long periods of authoritarian rule, its spirit has languished and has lost the will to resist coercion and suppression.

Iqbal, the undaunted thinker who urged the oppressed masses to revolt against all forms of totalitarianism – religious, political, cultural, intellectual, economic or any other – was the vital force that was needed to free the Indian Muslims from their internal shackles and external bondage. But his words, his voice, his message, constituted a grave threat to those power-wielders in Pakistan who wanted to keep the people subservient, so that they would not challenge them or claim their own rights. To ensure the fulfilment of their purposes they had to silence Iqbal's anti-authoritarian voice as much as possible. The relegation of Iqbal's vision and message to obscurity was, therefore, not by accident but by design.

Orphaned by its two founding fathers – Iqbal and Jinnah – at such an early age, and neglected or plundered by successive leaders, Pakistan must turn to Iqbal's writings to reconstruct its intellectual and ethical foundation, such as his advice to the youth about the qualities needed to become a leader:

> Read anew the lesson of Truthfulness, Justice, and Bravery –
> To you will be given the task of leading the world

I quote this verse to the youth of Tehreek-e-Insaf, because truth, bravery and justice are among the most highly valued attributes of a human being.

We need to understand Iqbal's commitment to social justice

and the pain he felt when he looked at the plight of the world's indigent workers. His memorable verse addressed to God, in which he points out the discrepancy between the justice of God and the unjust plight of those who laboured hard for a meagre living, is meant in fact to jolt the conscience of those rich people who exploit the ones who labour for them:

> You are Almighty and Just, but in your world,
> Intensely bitter is the life of the poor labourers

It is difficult to find a poet or thinker of Iqbal's calibre who has championed the cause of justice for the oppressed and wronged people of the world as passionately and consistently as he did. If we follow Iqbal's teaching, we can reverse the growing gap between the westernized rich and traditional poor that helps fuel fundamentalism.

The best weapon against fundamentalism is enlightened Islam. Fanatics on both sides of the argument need to be told about Islamic history, how other religions and other points of view were tolerated by Islam in the days when Europe was ruled by bigotry and ignorance. During what was known as the Golden Age of Islam, from around the mid-eighth to the mid-thirteenth century, the Muslim world, which stretched from Iberia and North Africa across to south-west and central Asia, was known for its spirit of intellectual discovery and religious tolerance. Islam never knew the savagery of the Inquisition. The set of legal principles stated or implied in the Quran has a great capacity for expansion and development, as frequently pointed out by Iqbal.

As early as the ninth century AD, Muslim scholars were debating the rights of the child. The sophistication of this debate was such that a scholar, before putting forth his point of view, would start by saying, 'It is possible that I may be wrong.' This spirit of openness was to be expected since freedom of thought is guaranteed by Islam. The Prophet's (PBUH) conflict with the Meccans was over the right to express his opinion. When the state of Medina was formed, freedom of speech was considered every citizen's right. The Prophet (PBUH) once said that a difference of opinion in his community was a sign of Allah's grace. It was this freedom of thought and the spirit of inquiry which created the intellectual atmosphere that led to the blossoming of the Muslim civilization. For hundreds of years all top scientists were Muslims, dominating the fields of logic, metaphysics, chemistry, algebra, astronomy and medicine. Until the advent of Islam, scientific knowledge amongst the Arabs had been stagnant for centuries. By the eighth century medical and philosophical texts were translated into Arabic, allowing the Arabs to build on the wisdom of the past and make vast leaps forward in science. Islamic scholars had a profound effect on European thought centuries later. By the tenth century everything worth translating from Ancient Greek works was available in Arabic. It was also during this period of cultural flowering that Muslim merchants developed modern commercial instruments such as cheques, letters of credit and joint stock companies.

Ibn Sina (980–1027), Ibn Rashid (1126–98) and Al Ghazali (died 1111) were amongst the Islamic philosophers who had a huge impact on European thought. Roger Bacon, one of the greatest names in Western science, considered Ibn Sina 'the prince and leader of philosophy'. Bacon learned from Arab thinkers about experimental science and Aristotelian philosophy. He was also a great transmitter of Arab knowledge into the mainstream of European thought. By the end of the eleventh century, Latin translations of Arabic works on science began to filter into Europe mainly from Muslim Spain, Iraq and Sicily. Among the centres of European learning that helped diffuse Islamic knowledge throughout the European world was the Arabist school at Montpellier in the south of France. From Montpellier scholars spread in all directions across Europe. The philosopher Al Ghazali's work had great influence on both Islamic and European scholars. His development of Greek philosophies, especially Aristotle's, influenced European philosophers like Thomas Aquinas and St Francis of Assisi. In turn it was the work of Aquinas that helped spark off the spirit of inquiry in Europe that would later lead to the Reformation.

According to the historian W. Montgomery Watt:

When one becomes aware of the full extent of Arab experimenting, Arab thinking and Arab writing, one sees that without the Arabs, European science and philosophy would not have developed when they did. The Arabs were no mere transmitters of Greek thought, but genuine bearers, who both kept alive the disciplines they had been taught and extended their range. When about the year 1100 Europeans became seriously interested in the science and philosophy of their Saracen enemies, these disciplines were at their zenith; and the Europeans had to learn all they could from the Arabs before they themselves could make further advances.

The quest for knowledge was reflected in the libraries that existed in the Islamic cities of Baghdad, Damascus and Cordoba. In 1171 when the legendary warrior Salahuddin entered Baghdad, the public library had 150,000 volumes. In Cordoba, Al Hakim's library had between 400,000 and 600,000 volumes. At this period in history, the universities in Europe had hardly any access to books. In his book *The Rise of Humanism in Classical Islam and the Christian West*, the Arabist and Islamicist George Makdisi traces the origins of humanism, the modern system of knowledge imparted in Western universities, to the early Islamic era. He writes about how from the eighth century onwards there was an environment of learning in Arab colleges, madrassas and the courts of Iraq, Sicily, Egypt and Andalusia, where disputation, dissent and argument were the order of the day. By the end of the eleventh century most Muslim cities had universities.

The decay and decline in Islamic intellectual thought, according to Iqbal, set in five hundred years ago when the doors to *ijtihad*, a scholarly debate on our religion and its traditions, were closed. The Quranic principles – which for Muslims are eternal principles – needed constantly to be reinterpreted in light of new knowledge. In his Lectures on the Reconstruction of Religious Thought in Islam, Iqbal cites three reasons for this stagnation. First, around the tenth century, there was controversy between two schools of thought – one rationalist and one conservative – about issues such as the eternity of the Quran. The ruling Islamic dynasty of the time, the Abbasids, threw their weight behind the conservatives, fearing that unrestrained adherence to a particular type of rationalism could endanger the stability of Islam as a social polity.

The second reason was the rise of ascetic Sufism, which grew partly in reaction to the increasing conservatism of the Islamic establishment. The Sufis, the mystics of Sunni Islam, wanted to focus more on inner spirituality, rather than a rigidly guarded set of rules. But according to Iqbal, their concentration on otherworldliness ignored Islam's role as a means of organizing society and politics. He complained that ascetic Sufism ended up attracting and finally absorbing the best minds in Islam. The Muslim state was thus left generally in the hands of intellectual mediocrities, and of the unthinking masses of Islam, who found their security only in blindly following the 'schools' of the great Islamic jurists such as Abu Hanifa and Malik Abn Anas. Iqbal – pointing to the Quran's emphasis on 'deed' – believed it was contrary to the true spirit of Islam to turn away from the real world, as some Sufis did. He felt that becoming a hermit or ascetic meant avoiding the joy and struggle of real life. To those who taught Islam he said:

> To teach religion in the world – if this be your aim,
> Do not teach your nation that it should withdraw from the
>   world

The third and probably most decisive factor was the Mongols' destruction in 1258 of Baghdad – the centre of Muslim intellectual life. Had the Mongol hordes not taken over swathes of the Muslim world, our history might have been very different. This legendary tribe from Mongolia laid waste to cities and decimated populations across Central Asia,

South Asia and the Middle East. Their merciless sacking of Baghdad, which had at one point been the centre of wealth, commerce and learning of the Islamic world, has historically been seen as the death blow for the Golden Age of Islam. With the destruction of its famous libraries, centuries of learning were lost, and this huge cultural trauma inevitably led to greater conservatism as Muslims feared the eradication of their civilization. Although the Mongols had by the early fourteenth century converted to Islam, their autocratic rule clamped down on the capacity of the *ulema* (Muslim legal scholars) for independent judgement. The gates to ijtihad were declared closed. Unity became key, dissension discouraged and foreigners became suspect.

In the eighteenth and nineteenth century when Indian Muslims, like us, were confronted with serious external and internal impediments, the rallying cry of the modernist reformers, from Sayyid Ahmad Khan to Iqbal, was 'Back to the Quran, Forward with Ijtihad'. 'Back to the Quran' meant the rediscovery of the fundamental teachings and principles of the Quran, and 'Forward with Ijtihad' meant the mental effort made to form an independent judgement on a legal point so that normative Islamic principles could be applied in modern times. Iqbal was acutely conscious of the stagnation and decadence that had sapped the creative energy of Muslim societies. Therefore, while strongly advocating a return to the Quran, which he regarded as fundamental to Islam, Iqbal also sought to re-infuse the dynamism of original Islam through ijtihad, which he regarded as 'The Principle of Movement in the Structure of Islam'.

According to Iqbal, such was the fear about the future of Islam that the 'conservative thinkers of Islam focused on preserving a uniform social life for the people by a jealous exclusion of all innovation in the laws of Sharia as expounded by the early doctors of Islam'. He believed that the 'ultimate fate of a people does not depend so much on organization as on the worth and power of individual men. In an over-organized society the individual is altogether crushed out of existence'. Iqbal felt that a man lost his soul under the weight of such conformism and that 'a false reverence for past history and its artificial resurrection' was no remedy for a people's decay. He maintained that the only power that counteracts the forces of decay was freedom of thought, the 'inner impulse' of Islam, and that 'the only alternative given to us is to tear off from Islam the hard crust that has immobilized an essentially dynamic outlook on life and to re-discover the original verities of freedom, equality and solidarity with a view to rebuild our moral, social and political ideals out of their original simplicity and universality'.

In the context of ijtihad, Iqbal pointed out in his sixth lecture – of his outstanding Lectures on the Reconstruction of Religious Thought in Islam – that in the modern period things had changed 'and the world of Islam is today confronted and affected by new forces set free by the extraordinary development of human thought in all its directions'. He went on to make a statement that has an extraordinary significance and relevance for us: 'The claim of the present generation of Muslim liberals to re-interpret the foundational legal principles, in the light of their own experience and altered conditions of modern life is, in my opinion, perfectly justified.

The teaching of the Quran that life is a process of progressive creation necessitates that each generation, guided but un-hampered by the work of its predecessors, should be permitted to solve its own problems.'

Iqbal once wrote that 'all search for knowledge is essentially a form of prayer'. Far from dismissing Western scientific advances, he believed we should study them and incorporate their positive content in our paradigm for a new country that would be informed by Islamic ideals as well as modern know-ledge. Instead, we allowed Pakistan to stagnate, virtually since its inception. The westernized elite who took over from the departing British colonial rulers had little interest in seeking this fusion of Islamic ideals and scientific progress. Rather they adopted a system that allowed them to perpetuate them-selves in power, never allowing true democracy to flourish. Our reactionary mullahs promoted a medieval attitude to reli-gion that grew ever more distorted as Islam was hijacked as a political tool.

Iqbal had stressed the need to use 'ijtihad with a view to rebuild the law of Sharia in the light of modern thought and experience'. He had pointed out that just as the European Renaissance and Reformation were inspired by the acquisition of knowledge from the Muslim universities of Spain and the Middle East during the Crusades, contemporary Muslims should use Western knowledge in their reconstruction of their own religious thought.

Like Iqbal, the nineteenth-century Egyptian scholar Muhammad Abduh also identified 'excessive conformism' (which sadly exists in the majority of the Muslim world today) as one of the causes of the decline of the Muslims. He felt that excessive adherence to the outward aspects of law led 'to a habit of blind imitation (*taqlid*), which was far from the freedom of true Islam'. And he linked the spread of taqlid to the rise of Turkish power. The Turks 'encouraged a slavish acceptance of authority, and discouraged the free exercise of reason among those they ruled. Knowledge was their enemy for it would teach their subjects how bad the rulers' conduct was, so they introduced their supporters into the ranks of the Ulema, to teach the faithful a dull stagnation in matters of belief and the acceptance of political autocracy.' It was a succession of Turkish invaders from the north-west – the Ghaznavids, the Ghorids, the Timurids and then the Mughals – who consolidated Islam in South Asia from the mid-tenth century on.

After the Turks came the British, whose rule also con-tributed to the spread of fundamentalism, stoking fears that Western culture was in danger of overwhelming the Islamic way of life, just as a thousand years ago the Europeans were similarly threatened by the rise of Islam. Fundamentalism at its outset was a reaction to colonialism, particularly among the Muslims for whom religion and culture are intertwined. Muslim reaction to the competition posed by Western power – often seen as synonymous with the forces of modernity – has usually followed two patterns. One school of thought decides the Islamic world must beat the West at its own game, using Western tools to solve Eastern problems and confining Islam to the private sphere. Hence the Arab world's various stabs at nationalism and socialism in the twentieth century in reaction to the spread of nineteenth-century European colonialism. The other school recoils, calling for a retreat to time-honoured traditions, a return to the simplicities of the original Muslim lifestyle in the desert and an older, 'purer' form of Islam stripped of the various cultural influences it has acquired in its dissemination.

In British India these two competing responses emerged after the 1857 Uprising against British rule and the humiliation of the last Mughal emperor, whom they deposed and exiled to Burma. William Dalrymple's *The Last Mughal* ends with the foundation of two very different educational establishments. One is Aligarh Mohamedan Anglo-Oriental College, a bid by the Anglophile Sir Sayyid Ahmad Khan to revive the fortunes of Muslim Indians through Western-style education. The other is a madrassa in Deoband that went on to propagate a narrow version of Islam that rejects all forms of westernization and still to this day competes in South Asia with the Barelvi movement, whose teachings are more in line with Sufi Islam. Dalrymple points out that the Taliban emerged out of Deobandi madrassas in Pakistan and Afghanistan: 'As we have seen in our own time, nothing threatens the liberal and moderate aspect of Islam so much as aggressive Western intrusion and interference in the East, just as nothing so dramatically radicalizes the ordinary Muslim and feeds the power of the extremists: the histories of Islamic fundamentalism and Western imperialism have, after all, often been closely, and dangerously intertwined.'

Today, we need to reclaim the vision and wisdom of the modernist reformers who paved the way for the creation of Pakistan. We need to do this because we badly need a cultural, intellectual and moral renaissance in Pakistan so that we are able to create societies and communities that are educated and enlightened, just and compassionate, forward-looking and life-affirming. We need to utilize our rational faculties and engage in scholarly discussion and reflection to find a solution to contemporary issues such as the blending of the positive aspects of Western culture with Islam. The new renaissance must also offer an alternative to the Western materialism and consumerism that has been totally imbibed by our ruling classes and which our country cannot afford.

Iqbal and other modernist reformist thinkers had been deeply concerned about the reluctance of many Muslims to respond positively to Western culture, in particular the rigidity of the mullahs whose mindset had been fossilized in medieval times. The combination of ruling oligarchies and a rigid religious mindset had stopped the forward movement of rational, academic and scientific interaction with the changing world, which would have led to a dynamic Islamic culture. Unfortunately, this is why the concept of ijtihad is so absent, not just in Pakistan, but in the Muslim world at large. Democracy and freedom of speech have been stifled for decades. Moreover education, research and the quest for knowledge are simply not priorities. That is why the greatest hope for a true Islamic renaissance lies with Islamic scholars in the Western countries who are neither afraid of oppressive Muslim regimes nor of the religious bigots who claim a monopoly on Islam. While Western countries forge ahead in every field of knowledge, the Muslim world seems to have given up and relies on being spoon-fed whatever knowledge is passed on by the West.

Iqbal called for Muslims to keep their minds open to reinterpretation of the Quran and Islamic law so that they remained relevant in a fast-changing world. He was also strong in his condemnation of the 'myth-making mullahs' who were not equipped to answer the questions of the modern Muslims on contemporary issues. He was apprehensive of their bigotry and intolerance against science, arts and original thought and wanted to set up a university for ulema and religious scholars to equip them with the modern tools of knowledge. Iqbal believed that rather than spurning the discoveries of the modern world as 'un-Islamic', the Muslim world should use the technological and scientific discoveries of the West without subordinating itself to Western values and culture. In one of his verses he also urged Indian Muslims not to imitate the West but to be creative while using their own resources:

> Do not be beholden to Western glass-makers –
> With the earth of India, make a goblet and cup

To revisit what is of enduring value in Iqbal's thinking, we need fresh and original minds capable of combining the aspects of Western democracy that suit us with our indigenous system of local governance. For hundreds of years villages in the Indian subcontinent were self-contained, running their own schools and councils, their health centre and their system of justice, a system known as *panchayat*. To a certain extent this still exists in Pakistan in the tribal areas' jirga system. We need to revive *panchayat* and jirga systems to liberate our rural areas from the oppressive feudal culture, and empower people at the grass roots.

Surely there is much to learn from Western culture, most of all, its strong institutions, its constant quest for knowledge and the fierce protection accorded to freedom of expression. This has in turn led to creativity and dynamism. I also feel we can learn from the way democracy has given freedom to most of the Western world in sharp contrast to the sham democracies we have experienced in Pakistan and other parts of the Muslim world. People are fully aware of their rights and there is public outcry as soon as any one of them is violated. At times, however, the right of an individual can take precedence over the larger interest of the community, unlike in Eastern societies where the community's interest is paramount. However, the foundations of a just and equitable Islamic society are only to be found in the Quran.

Sadly, more than sixty years after its birth, neither Iqbal nor Jinnah would recognize the country Pakistan has become. Economically ruined by a ruling elite hungry for money and power, it has become the only nuclear-armed Islamic country, yet cannot protect its people from near daily bombings and is one of only four countries in the world that have never beaten polio. A succession of military rulers and corrupt civilian governments has been unable to deliver even the most basic services like healthcare and education to the ordinary people in whose name the country was created. Although never quite a failed state, Pakistan has become a failing state.

The Quran asks Muslims to follow the 'Middle Way', the narrow path that lies between all possible extremes. Only an informed public is capable of making informed choices, and an informed public needs an informed ulema. In the 1960s a brilliant Pakistani scholar, Dr Fazlur Rahman, who taught in the US at the University of Chicago, was invited by President Ayub Khan to set up the Central Institute of Islamic Research. Dr Rahman aimed to recruit the best minds in the country and get them to undertake a study of the Quran in its historical context so that certain verses could not be misused. He felt people were being misled by the preachers who wanted a selective Islam to suit their own interests and quoted isolated verses of the Quran out of context. Sadly, his views clashed with those of the religious traditionalists and not only was he hounded out of Pakistan but was one of the causes for the downfall of Ayub Khan.

The main difference Islamic sharia has from Western secular society is in the realm of public morality. This protects our family system, one of Pakistan's greatest strengths. Infidelity is strongly condemned and considered one of the greatest sins, as it is in all great religions. People who believe in God know that while they can deceive their spouse, they cannot deceive the Almighty. An Islamic society tries to protect the sanctity of marriage by creating an environment that affords the least temptation for people to commit infidelity. Secondly, it tries to protect impressionable young people from public immorality, the same concept behind the 'adults only' film classification. Furthermore, Islam puts huge emphasis on responsibility to the family. According to the Prophet (PBUH): 'The best of you is he who is best to his family, and I am the best among you towards my family.' Today millions of Pakistani men and women are toiling away at great personal cost to simply feed their family. This is what binds our society. Despite the grinding poverty and injustice that beset many Pakistanis, it is the structure of the family that provides the net that keeps the social fabric intact. I know of so many people whose extended family members are all pooling resources to feed other relatives. With absolutely no social security net whatsoever, were it not for our powerful family system, the country would have descended into bloodshed long ago.

So apart from these vital provisions aimed at protecting the family, a true Islamic society would be no different from the democratic welfare states of Europe. Human rights are, after all, at the centre of the Quran. The right to life, justice, respect, freedom of speech and movement, privacy, protection from slander and ridicule, a secure place of residence and a means of living are all enshrined in the Quran. Islam gives all the freedom of a secular society – yet an Islamic state cannot be secular. To understand secularism as it exists in the West today, it is important to remember the evolution of Christianity within the Roman Empire. When the Roman Empire became Christian, the State and Church had their distinct boundaries. Over the centuries many other influences have shaped modern-day secularism. But the separation of Church and State could not happen in Islam as it has no concept of a Church.

As Iqbal stated: 'Islam was from the very beginning a civil society having received from the Quran a set of simple legal principles, which like the twelve tables of the Romans, carried, as experience subsequently proved, great potentialities of expansion and development by interpretation.' Elaborating his point, Iqbal said, 'This dualism (separation of State and Church) does not exist in Islam.' He went on to warn that when a state is governed without the moral values that are rooted in religion then naked materialism is likely to replace it – exactly the observation made by Mohandas Gandhi when he remarked, 'Those who say religion has nothing to do with politics do not know what religion is.' The two greatest institutional tyrannies of all times, the Nazi Reich and the Soviet Union, were Godless constructs.

Islamic culture is rooted in spirituality, while capitalist culture is rooted in materialism. This is not to say that spirituality in Islam is to the exclusion of wealth accumulation. On the contrary, it is even encouraged, but it is not an end in itself as it is in capitalism. For example, it would be necessary for a humane and truly Islamic society to sacrifice economic growth in order to protect the environment. The welfare of both the current and future generations would take precedence over greater material wealth. True spirituality will always support any movement that is struggling to save our environment from human greed. One of the names of the Quran is *Al Furqan* (the Criterion) precisely because it was meant to enable humanity to make this distinction.

The number of religious fanatics is growing by the day thanks to the 'war on terror'. As we saw with the insurgency in Swat, the dispossessed with no stake in the system can become vulnerable to crime and militant Islam. It is not hard to see why the idealistic and romantic are driven to take up arms. There are, of course, religious zealots who through sheer ignorance have decided to enforce their uninformed version of Islam through the barrel of the gun. They have done tremendous damage to Islam, failing to understand that the religion is a battle for conquering hearts and minds. There are others who have killed fellow Muslims in the name of their sect. These fundamentalists are not only anti-West but also virulently against the westernized Pakistani elite, whom they contemptuously see as toadies to the West. While the masses in Pakistan are impressed by the tremendous technological progress of the Western world, their understanding of the Western moral value system mainly comes from watching television and they do not respect what they see. Therefore they are deeply suspicious of any attempt towards western- ization – particularly women's liberation. They don't regard this as women having the right to fulfil their potential, but rather as women having the right to be sexually permissive. Therefore westernized Pakistanis are considered to have loose morals too. One of the many derogatory things ordinary people say about westernized couples is that 'he does not get angry and she has no shame'. It is because of this attitude that sometimes modernization is resisted because it is perceived to be westernization. People are also therefore wary of foreign NGOs dealing with women.

The gulf between the different strata of Pakistani society is so great now that those at the other end of the extreme are called the 'liberal fanatics'. To liberal fanatics modernization means westernization and Islam can only impede Pakistan's progress. Lacking a proper understanding of Islam they see the religion through Western eyes and are convinced that it is a retrogressive, primitive creed of ancient desert folk. Sadly, they are not equipped to hold any dialogue with the religious fanatics because they are not armed with sufficient knowledge of Islam. For them every solution to Pakistan's problems is imported. Hence liberal fanatics have variously advocated

Marxism, a radical version of women's liberation, market economics and other Western beliefs. These people only have to study the colonial history of the past two centuries to realize that wherever an alien culture was imposed on an indigenous people it caused mass upheaval, disruption and destruction to their way of life. From the Aborigines of Australia to the Indians of the Americas and most of Africa, the local people fell between two stools in the name of modernization.

The societies that have been success stories, such as Japan and China, have all used Western knowledge but developed it in the context of their own culture and environment. Pakistani liberal fanatics preach secularism, yet they don't fully understand the evolution of secularism in Europe. Martin Luther's movement was aimed at freeing religion from the stranglehold of the Catholic Church, not at abolishing religion altogether. Unfortunately our liberal fanatics are bent upon imposing Western secular values on a country where the vast majority's entire way of life is influenced by religion. The liberal fanatics have only one solution, Hitler's final solution; they want the Pakistani army to exterminate the religious fundamentalists. They only have to look at the history of Iran, Algeria and Egypt to know that whenever fundamentalism is suppressed it gets violent. These two sections of Pakistani society have become further polarized with the 'war on terror' and each tends to dehumanize the other.

If our westernized class started to study Islam, not only would it be able to project the dynamic spirit of Islam but also help our society fight sectarianism and extremism. They would be able to help the Western world by articulating

Islamic concepts correctly. How can the group that is in the best position to project Islam do so when it sees Islam through Western eyes? The most damaging aspect of the gulf between the two sections of our society is that it has stopped the evolution of both religion and culture in Pakistan. The elite that consumes most of the country's educational resources is incapable of providing the intellectual leadership needed to move forward either the religion or the culture. Western education simply does not equip them to do so.

There is no confusion about the role of Islam in Pakistan among ordinary people who are comfortable with their Islamic heritage and live by their faith. Only in the minds of the westernized English-speaking elite, the inheritors of British colonial rule, is there a confusion of identity. The secularists in Pakistan, with their scant knowledge of Islam, believe that an Islamic state persecutes religious minorities. They quote the lines on freedom of worship from Jinnah's famous speech to the Constituent Assembly in 1947 to justify their claim that Pakistan was meant to be a secular state that gave equal rights to the minorities. Jinnah, however, was simply highlighting the tolerance that exists in Islam towards non-Muslims when he said: 'You are free; you are free to go to your temples, you are free to go to your mosques or to any other place of worship in this state of Pakistan. You may belong to any religion, or caste or creed – that has nothing to do with the business of the State.'

While Islam and the Two-Nation Theory – the ideology on which the split between Pakistan and India was based – remain the bedrock of Pakistan's foundations, it is clear that religious dogma should not be used to spread prejudice, intolerance and sectarianism. Unfortunately, though, one of the worst aspects of Muslim religious bigots is that they preach hatred towards minorities or other Islamic sects, taking Quranic verses out of context to justify their actions. They ignore – or are ignorant of the fact – that the Prophet's (PBUH) life has many examples of tolerance towards other religious groups. There were incidences of both Jewish and Christian delegations being allowed to pray in his mosque.

The Prophet's (PBUH) last sermon encapsulates his vision of universal human rights.

> All of you come from Adam, and Adam is of dust. Indeed, the Arab is not superior to the non-Arab, and the non-Arab is not superior to the Arab. Nor is the fair-skinned superior to the dark-skinned nor the dark-skinned superior to the fair-skinned; superiority comes from piety and the noblest among you is the most pious . . . Know that all Muslims are brothers unto one another. You are one brotherhood . . . And your slaves! See that you feed them with such food as you eat yourselves and clothe them with the stuff that you wear. If they commit a fault which you are not inclined to forgive, then part with them, for they are the servants of the Lord and are not to be harshly treated.

It is evident that discrimination on the grounds of religion, race or class is prohibited by the Quran, which also stresses, 'There is no compulsion in religion' (Quran 2: 256).

In fact, Islam goes further than many religions, actually acknowledging the legitimacy of other faiths. As the religious scholar Karen Armstrong has pointed out, the Quran is 'almost unique in its positive view of other peoples, other religious traditions. There is nothing like Quranic pluralism in either the Torah or the Gospel . . . The Quran declares that every people on the face of the earth has received a divine revelation.' She has slammed the West's 'medieval conviction' about the inherent intolerance of Islam, arguing that extremism today stems from 'intractable political problems – oil, Palestine, the occupation of Muslim lands, the prevalence of authoritarian regimes in the Middle East, and the West's perceived "double standards" – and not to an ingrained religious imperative'.

Through hundreds of years of Islamic history, non-Muslims played a significant role in Muslim communities: the Rajputs in Mughal India, Christians and Jews in Muslim Spain and the Greek Orthodox and Jews in the Ottoman Empire. The tolerance shown to non-Muslims was unknown to religious minorities in the Europe of the Middle Ages. Yet in the West, Islam is perceived as a religion that encourages aggression towards others. Even if some try to use Islam to justify violence, the Quran and the *hadith*, or sayings, of the Prophet (PBUH) do not sanction this behaviour. The Quran – in no uncertain terms – prohibits the desecration of houses of worship, suicide and murder. According to journalist and historian Paul Johnson, 150 million people were killed by state violence in the twentieth century. Muslim countries had an insignificant share in this slaughter, never witnessed before in the history of humanity. The two greatest butchers of the twentieth century were born Christians; Hitler was born and brought up a Roman Catholic and Stalin was once a Russian Orthodox apprentice monk. It is as ridiculous to blame

Christianity for their deeds as it is to blame Islam for any inhuman behaviour by a Muslim.

Jinnah's speech to the country's economists at the State Bank on 1 July 1948 underlined the fact that Islamic principles today are as applicable to life as they were 1,300 years ago. He said: 'Islam and its idealism have taught democracy, Islam has taught equality, justice and fair play to everybody. What reason is there for anyone to fear democracy, equality, freedom on the highest standard of integrity and on the basis of fair play and justice for everybody?' This would be in line with Iqbal's 'spiritual democracy' where people would be free from oppression and where no policies could be made that did not make people the main focus. This is what is meant when Allah says in the Quran to hold on to the 'rope of the people'. I am convinced that Pakistan has lost its way because there has been no serious attempt to translate this vision into practice.

The Quran lays great emphasis on both justice and education, yet in both these areas the Islamic Republic of Pakistan has sorely failed. Our failure in each of these areas has fed into the other. Our education system breeds injustice. Our unjust society neglects education for the masses. At the core of an Islamic state is the principle of justice. That is why I named my party *Tehreek-e-Insaf*, Movement for Justice. The Quran says, 'O ye who believe, stand out firmly for justice, as witnesses to God, even as against yourselves or your parents, or your kin and whether it be against rich or poor' (Quran 2: 135). Being fair and just was considered one of the greatest virtues in the religion. Every human being was supposed to be equal in front of the law. This was a revolutionary concept in the Prophet's (PBUH) day because the administration of laws without discrimination on grounds of race, colour and language was not known before the advent of Islam.

Initially envisaged by Iqbal and Jinnah as a democratic country in which people – regardless of race, tribe, religion or sect – would live in peace and harmony free from exploitation and discrimination, Pakistan is now a deeply divided nation. The concentration of power at the centre has negated the spirit of federalism with Pashtuns, Baluchis, Sindhis, Kashmiris and Mohajirs resentful of Punjabi hegemony. A sense of deprivation and marginalization right from the country's beginning led to the loss of East Pakistan and prevented the formation of a national identity strong enough to bind our new nation together. Meanwhile, the elite has looted the country's riches and squandered its resources and the poor have lived in deprivation and hardship. The majority of the country is deprived of access to education, healthcare and a free and efficient judicial system.

Two of the most corrupt government departments are the police and lower judiciary. The tile case against Jemima was an example of how our judiciary is unable to protect citizens from state tyranny. And as my time in detention taught me, most of the inmates of our dirty, overcrowded, underfunded jails are poor people who did not have the means to buy themselves a fair trial (yet there was no concept of detention in the Islamic justice system except in rare cases). The rich can buy themselves out of any legal trouble. In the rural areas poor people are harassed in every way. Therefore the poor vote not for the man who is clean and honest, but for the one who can protect them from the powerful. The party in power has the entire state machinery at its disposal to try and eliminate the opposition. Hence without an independent judiciary we will never have real democracy. The great ideal where safeguards in the law were meant to protect the innocent has been perverted in Pakistan to protect powerful criminals. Whenever there is talk of reform, we are told that the government has no money either to give adequate salaries or modernize the two departments. We do not have the resources to pay the judges adequately or build more courts to cater for our expanding population. I feel that, in rural areas at least, one thing that would help would be a return of the village councils (panchayats and jirgas) that dispensed justice so successfully to the people of the subcontinent for centuries. Let the village elders (selected through village consensus) adjudicate petty crime and land disputes and award punishments in the traditional way, with the victim compensated, rather than the culprit jailed.

Pakistan's feudal system has cursed us with a grossly unfair social system in parts of the country. There are horrendous stories of exploitation, especially of women. In the feudal areas the powerful treat the women from poor families as their property and their menfolk are too powerless to do anything about it. During the 2010 floods there were reports that big landlords in south Punjab and Sindh diverted the flood waters and breached embankments in order to save their own land, immune to the damage and suffering this caused many ordinary people. The attitude of the feudal and other powerful groups that they are above the law fuels corruption. This is one of the reasons Pakistan has such an enormous rich–poor divide.

While our elite have private jets, security cavalcades and

numerous apartments and mansions in swanky locations around the globe, more than half the country suffers from what the UNDP (United Nations Development Programme) calls 'multi-dimensional deprivation' – lack of access to proper education, health facilities and a decent standard of living. Instead of following the example of the Holy Prophet (PBUH) and his initial successors, all of whom lived with simplicity, Pakistani politicians have always wanted to set themselves up like Mughal emperors. In contrast, in the UK the tone is set by the simplicity of the prime minister's Downing Street residence. Why should Pakistan's politicians be allowed to stash so many of their assets abroad? Especially when they have no known source of income outside the country. What kind of leader needs an insurance policy like that? I am the only political leader to have all my assets declared in my own name, and all of them in Pakistan; and most of my earnings came from playing professional cricket abroad. People will pay taxes if they felt their hard-earned money was not being wasted on the shamelessly luxurious lifestyles of our rulers or siphoned off out of the country. Crooks like this across developing countries loot and plunder while in power and prepare for their retirement in Western cities and resorts with bulging Swiss bank accounts. There should no bank-secrecy laws for those third-world politicians, bureaucrats and generals who are prosecuted on corruption charges. And they should be immediately extradited to the country they have plundered. This would be the greatest gift of the West to the developing world; this would help the impoverished masses much more than either aid or loans.

Our economy is filled with injustices too. First, our ruling elite has been totally inhuman and immoral in colluding with the IMF, crushing the poor to service our debts. In each budget the voiceless majority is burdened with indirect taxes, which hit the poor disproportionately. Of course it would be far too much to ask the rich to pay direct taxes so instead we penalize the poor. When there is no reaction from them, emboldened, the government increases their load each year. The people were neither consulted when the loans were taken nor do they know how the loans were spent. There has never been an audit of where the loans disappeared to. Between 2008 and 2011 our debt has doubled from 5 trillion rupees to 10 trillion (from US$59 billion to US$120 billion). About 65 per cent of all tax collected goes into debt repayment. Pakistan spends more than 60 per cent of its national budget each year on defence and servicing its debt while 1.5 per cent goes on education, and only 0.5 per cent on health. In addition, the country has lost about 256 billion rupees in loans to the rich and powerful that have been written off. Meanwhile, crippling inflation – aggravated by Islamabad's habit of borrowing from its own State Bank – and rising utility and fuel bills have meant that the salaried class cannot survive without taking bribes. As corruption in the bureaucracy rises, the life of the citizens becomes more and more unbearable. And policy implementation by the government becomes yet more difficult with such a corrupt civil service.

This is not just about economics, but about the nation's self-esteem. How can Pakistanis ever be encouraged to achieve their potential while we remain a cowed nation that cannot operate without international aid? In cricket I discovered a team that has self-esteem and belief in itself will play way beyond its capabilities and can even thrash a more talented team. The tragedy of Pakistan is that we have become accustomed to these crutches from the US and multilateral and bilateral lenders. Not only has it destroyed our self-belief but we have never learned to live within our means and our corrupt and incompetent ruling elite are bailed out time and time again. Pakistan's $167 billion economy was hit badly by the 2010 floods, the worst in its history. The Asian Development Bank and World Bank put the damage at about $10 billion. As usual, rather than relying on the skills and resilience of its own people, the government – as it did after the 2005 earthquake – immediately turned to the rest of the world with its begging bowl. The fact that the international community was reluctant to donate to flood relief in 2010 but that somehow the country has soldiered on demonstrates that Pakistan's recovery was in the end mainly due to the hard work, perseverance and generosity of the Pakistani people. For example, in 2010 I headed a campaign to raise funds for the flood victims, and in one month collected 2 billion rupees. Everyone I knew contributed for the flood victims, such was the spirit amongst the people.

By restoring the trust of the people in public institutions, we can harness their potential and mobilize them for a better tomorrow. In the meantime, our rich agricultural land, our enormous mineral wealth (consisting of billions of dollars of copper and gold reserves, ten different types of marble, highest-quality granite, and emerald deposits in Swat), new-found gas reserves in Kohat, our six million overseas community (whose annual income is equal to that of 180 million Pakistanis, a huge resource for investment if we tapped into it) and our huge youthful population go to waste. One of the often mentioned ironies of Pakistan is that it was founded as a homeland for the subcontinent's Muslims, yet every year thousands of Pakistanis go abroad in a bid to build a better life. The greatest asset of a nation is its people but here the rich get US green cards or Canadian passports and the poor go to the Gulf to toil on construction sites. Every year my cancer hospital loses about a third of its nurses to the Gulf countries. We cannot hope to compete with the salaries they are offered there.

Yet how can we harness our country's potential when we have one of the worst education systems in the world? The sad thing is the British, when they departed, had left behind quality universities; when I was growing up, students from the Middle East, and much further afield, used to come and study at our universities. Princes from Malaysia would come and study alongside us at Aitchison College. Unfortunately, successive governments have allowed our education system to decline. Many analysts point to the potentially destabilizing factor of millions of young, uneducated, unemployable people in a country of ever-decreasing resources. Half of Pakistan is under twenty and two-thirds of its population is below the age of thirty. The population has trebled in less than half a century. It is forecast to grow by around 85 million in twenty years, which – as a report on the youth of Pakistan commissioned by the British Council points out – is roughly the equivalent of five cities the size of Karachi. We have a small window of time to turn what could be Pakistan's downfall into its redemption. An army of disenfranchised and angry people competing for dwindling resources could instead be an energetic labour force and a strong domestic market of potential consumers. But Pakistan has spent less of its resources on its education than many poorer countries. Only half of its children go to primary school while a quarter attend secondary school, and a mere 5 per cent receive higher education.

Not only has Pakistan consistently failed to invest enough money in education, but it failed right at the outset by not integrating the education system after independence. There are effectively three types of education in our country – private English-medium, Urdu-medium schools and madrassas. Each of these operates in entirely different ways and produces an entirely different student. While the top-level English-medium schools are maintaining their standards by linking their syllabus to English or American curricula, the Urdu-medium schooling system has collapsed after decades of being starved of government attention and funds. No longer can the Urdu schools produce students that can compete with those from the English ones. (Our best intellectuals until the seventies came from the government schools.) Then there are the madrassas; some of these, it has to be said, do provide a quality education and get excellent results, drawing children from the middle classes whose parents want their children to have a solid religious base. However, they mainly produce students trained to work in madrassas or mosques but ignorant of the modern world, sidelined from the mainstream economy and susceptible to the kind of ideology that promotes sectarianism. Poor parents often send their children to madrassas because not only is the education free, but often board and lodging are provided.

With the collapse of the state education system, private schools have become a booming business. All the country's rich and powerful send their children to private English-medium schools, but even in rural areas, poor families are dedicating a large portion of their income to educating their children. This demonstrates that many parents – whatever their economic background – fully understand the importance of education. Despite various reports and white papers over the years which have recommended implementing one school system throughout the country, this was never allowed to happen, partly because the elite wanted to maintain the privileged position in society that this unfair system gave them. The nationalization of the education sector in the 1970s is also partly to blame for the dire situation. Even Prime Minister Yousaf Raza Gilani has admitted that the state seizure of Pakistan's schools by Zulfikar Ali Bhutto's PPP government in 1972 was wrong. Making teachers public servants allowed politics – and the corruption that inevitably seems to go with it in Pakistan – to seep into the teaching profession. Teachers no longer needed to be loyal to a school because the school itself no longer had the power to fire and hire staff. Teachers with political connections could get themselves transferred to a better posting if they wanted to. Placing teachers became a system of patronage with politicians rewarding supporters with teaching jobs regardless of their qualifications.

All over Pakistan there is the phenomenon of 'ghost schools' where teachers collect their wages but fail to turn up. Sabiha Mansoor, dean of Pakistan's Beaconhouse National University and a former fellow at the Woodrow Wilson

International Center for Scholars in Washington, DC, has written about how it all went wrong: 'Bhutto's nationalization of schools created a bureaucratic behemoth. The lumbering giant grew larger and presented more opportunities for corruption in the decades that followed. Today, Pakistan has one of the highest public sector nonteaching-to-teaching staff ratios in the world. State control also meant that the character of schools would change with the character of the regime in power.'

This educational crisis is one of the reasons I founded Namal University in Mianwali. It is Pakistan's only private-sector university in a rural area. I first had the idea for it because I was dismayed at the effects of unemployment in my constituency. Some villages had a real problem because jobless young men had turned to drugs and crime. So I decided I would set up a technical college. About the same time the UK's University of Bradford offered me the position of chancellor so I thought this was a great opportunity to leverage that and collaborate with them on a Pakistani university. When I met the locals to discuss the idea they were so generous in offering their land that my plans expanded. Why just have one small college? I wanted a green and self-sustainable knowledge city, a series of academic institutions, an Oxford of Pakistan. The first construction phase is complete and the first batch of students started in 2007 and will be graduating with a University of Bradford degree in 2012. There is such a skills shortage in the area they will be immediately employable. Eventually, at this beautiful site next to Namal Lake I envisage a technology park and commercial areas. In the mountains behind the college there is a resort built by the

British where I would love to build a summer retreat for the students. The only people to have opposed the project were the local politicians who tried to create as many hurdles as possible. As soon as I presented the plan, the government started building a college 10 kilometres away. Despite spending three times more on it than I have on Namal University, it is still a shell.

The political elite have no interest in providing education for the masses or changing the status quo. Yet this three-tier system has had far-reaching repercussions for our society, widening the gap between the small but affluent westernized elite and the masses, and feeding fundamentalism. If anyone read the English newspapers and compared the contents with those of the mass Urdu newspapers, it would seem that they belonged to two different countries. Every day there is some article in an English paper ridiculing or criticizing some local custom, yet it makes no difference to the masses because only a small percentage of the population reads them. Most of the students from the top English-medium schools become aliens in their own country and struggle to communicate with the Pakistani masses. When we hired graduates from the top business college in Lahore for the cancer hospital's marketing department, I found they had problems dealing with our main donors, the trading community in Lahore. While the traders could barely speak Urdu, their native tongue being Punjabi, our marketing team would converse with them in broken Urdu with plenty of English words thrown in. It really was a pathetic sight because our top business school had prepared these graduates for jobs either in multinationals or abroad. On the other hand, students coming out of Urdu-medium schools and madrassas have little understanding of Western culture and resent the elite. Some have been educated to condemn everything Western as un-Islamic.

As much of the Middle East struggles to find its way in the next chapter of decolonialization, breaking free from the dictators that have held power since independence, Pakistan too stands poised for change. Like the Middle East, it lies between the status quo – a small elite hogging the resources – and the anti-status quo, a younger generation that desires a participatory democracy. In many ways, Pakistan has many advantages. While it has suffered more than three decades of dictatorship, it also has experience dealing with the growing pains of a newly democratic nation. It has political parties with decades of experience, a largely free media and the space for dissent that was long denied many other Muslim countries. The people's creativity and initiative have not been suppressed by a police state or the personality cult of any omnipotent dictator. There is still a healthy irreverence towards the powerful. However, Pakistan does have to make sense of the many and sometimes conflicting ideologies that have been thrown at it. It does have to make peace with the complexities of its ethnic mix and the tensions inherent in its geographical and cultural location at the crossroads between South and Central Asia and the Middle East. That location should of course be an economic advantage, rather than a source of never-ending geopolitical troubles. I can see that young people are civic-minded, if deeply disillusioned with Pakistani politics and national institutions like the police. The participation of thousands of young people in the lawyers' movement that restored the chief justice of Pakistan in the face of formidable opposition in 2010 preceded the rights movement in the Middle East. Though the anti-status-quo wave known as the lawyers' movement for genuine democracy was hijacked, it remains simmering beneath the surface; I am convinced the moment the next elections are announced, a 'soft revolution' will explode on our political horizon and sweep away the corrupt status quo from Pakistan once and for all.

Epilogue

Ay ta'ir-e-lahooti uss rizq say maut achhi,
Jis rizq say aati ho parwaaz main kotaahi
O heavenly bird, death is better than those means of livelihood,
Which make you sluggish in your soaring flight

Allama Muhammad Iqbal

O N 2 MAY, TRAVELLING TO SUKKUR FROM KARACHI EARLY IN the morning, I heard the news: US navy commandos had killed Osama bin Laden in a helicopter raid in Abbottabad. It was bad enough that the world's most wanted man was not found in some cave but in a city only 50 kilometres from Islamabad, and a mile from Pakistan's Military Academy. What made it worse was that the news was broken to us Pakistanis, and the rest of the world, by President Obama.

It was several hours later when a statement came from our government congratulating the US and taking credit for providing the US with all the information about Osama's location. This begged the obvious question for all Pakistanis: if we knew about his whereabouts, then why did we not capture him ourselves? The media in India and the rest of the world went wild, blaming Pakistan's ISI (in other words, the army) for having kept Osama in a safe house for the past six years. The foreign media managed to find me in Sindh; I had no clue what to say, hoping that the civilian and the military leadership would provide us with answers. But rather than provide any answers, our leaders added to our embarrassment by constantly changing their statements.

Three days later, the army chief denied all knowledge of the operation and announced that any such violation of our sovereignty would not be tolerated again. A week later the PM only added to the confusion when he finally gave a statement, suggesting 'a matching response' to any attack against 'Pakistan's strategic assets'. For Pakistanis, especially those living abroad, this was one of the most humiliating and painful times. The CIA chief Panetta further rubbed salt in our wounds by bluntly saying that the Pakistan government was either incompetent or complicit.

Ours is a country that has fought the US's war for the last eight years when we had nothing to do with 9/11. Pakistan has over 34,000 people dead (including 6,000 soldiers), has lost $68 billion (while the total aid coming into the country amounted to $20 billion) and has over half a million people from our tribal areas internally displaced, and with 50 per cent facing unprecedented poverty (while 140,000 Pakistani soldiers were deployed all along our border). It is probably the only time in history that a country has kept getting bombed, through drone attacks, by its ally. A US soldier in Afghanistan costs the US $1 million per year whilst a Pakistani soldier costs a mere $900 to the US. Yet here we were, embarrassed and humiliated.

Now there was a sense of foreboding that the US would

push its puppet government in Islamabad to 'do more', i.e. conduct more operations in our tribal areas, and specifically in North Waziristan. All Pakistanis knew that the backlash from these operations would be felt in our urban centres with more suicide attacks; al-Qaeda and the Taliban had already announced that they would attack our government and army to avenge Osama because they had collaborated in his killing.

And sure enough, the month of May saw a series of suicide attacks against the Pakistan security forces, the worst being on the naval headquarters in Karachi and on an army camp in Khyber Pakhtunkhwa, where a hundred soldiers died. We are in a nutcracker situation, with extremists attacking us from within while the US puts pressure on the army to conduct more operations. Worse – if any international terrorism takes place, especially in the US, Pakistan could be in real danger of being bombed.

I feel that 2 May could be a historical crossroads for Pakistan. Everyone is beginning to think that unless we change the way our country has been run so far – we are doomed.

The ruling elite has been completely exposed. General Ziauddin Butt, who served as the head of the ISI under Musharraf, stated on 30 May that General Musharraf had kept Osama in the safe house in Abbottabad to milk the US for dollars. Even if this is a false allegation, one thing is for certain: our ruling elite took us into this war with a web of lies and deceit for only one reason – US dollars. And whilst this 'aid' has brought the country to its knees, the ruling elite has never had it so good. Neither the people of Pakistan, nor the rest of the world, trusts this elite any more. The US openly accuses Pakistan of playing a 'double game'.

The greatest danger we face today is that if we keep pursuing the current strategy of taking aid from the US and bombing our own people, we could be pushing our army towards rebellion. After 2 May the army faced unprecedented criticism from within the country as well as from the West. Polls show that 80 per cent of Pakistan's people consider the US to be an enemy (because they believe that the US is not fighting a war against terror but against Islam). The same spread of opinion must exist within the Pakistan armed forces – the fact that only a few instances of terrorism have come from within the army so far is due to the excellent discipline that exists in the institution.

There is a feeling of humiliation within the army, similar to that felt after the surrender of 90,000 soldiers in East Pakistan in 1971. The policy of making our army kill its own people while the ruling elite rake in dollars is no longer feasible. It is only a matter of time before serious unrest within the army could throw the country into total chaos. The regular revelations in the WikiLeaks cables, showing the ruling elite to be two-faced and totally subservient to the US embassy in Islamabad, have further accelerated the movement for change.

A country that begs and borrows for its survival had to face such humiliation sooner or later. The way forward has to be for this puppet government to resign, as it has failed on every front. Then, under the auspices of the Supreme Court, free and fair elections should be held. Only free and fair elections will bring in a credible sovereign government that represents the aspirations of the people of Pakistan.

Pakistan should disengage from this insane and immoral war. It should immediately open a dialogue with the various militant groups, as the US has done in Afghanistan, and set a timetable for the withdrawal of our troops from the tribal areas. A credible Pakistan government can play a role in helping the US make an exit from Afghanistan. The key to winning against terrorism is winning the hearts and minds of the people; if the community from which the terrorist is operating considers the militants terrorists, the war is going to be won. If they consider them freedom fighters, history tells us it cannot be won.

This new government should immediately thank the US for all the aid given so far and say, 'No more.' It should also say goodbye to the IMF once and for all, as the IMF's conditionality enriches the rich and impoverishes the poor. Without foreign aid, the government will be forced to balance its revenues and expenditure, which would lead to the long overdue reforms that our country so desperately needs to survive. The government will have to lead by example; the prime minister, the cabinet and the entire parliament should declare their incomes and assets, and bring – for the first time – the rich and powerful under the tax net. (It is worth noting that, before the French Revolution, the French nobility was exempt from taxes.) A massive austerity campaign would build the taxpayers' confidence by reassuring them that the government cares about their taxes and is accountable to them. Pakistan is a country which, per capita, gives the highest amount in charity (I am one of the biggest collectors of donations) and paradoxically pays the least amount in taxes. Our tax revenue is 9 per cent of our GDP, amongst the lowest in the world. The reason is that not only do the ruling elite not pay taxes, but a large part of the people's taxes disappears through corruption, while the people see no returns for this taxation. Hard work and honesty need to be rewarded rather than penalized.

We need surgical reforms in our governance system to tackle corruption, improve the police and lower judiciary, develop an effective local government system and create an environment which would invite investment from overseas Pakistanis – our biggest asset. We face an emergency in our education system; not only must it be radically reformed but funding must be increased threefold.

We need to have a new relationship with our tribal areas, where the lives of six million proud and honourable people have been devastated. There will have to be a South African-style 'truth and reconciliation' process, involving not only people from within our tribal areas who had taken up arms against our army, but also the old militant groups created during the days when our ruling elite were making dollars from the US-sponsored jihad. All militant groups within the country, including the private guards of politicians, should be disbanded, and the country de-weaponized.

Our foreign policy has to be sovereign and needs to be reviewed with all our neighbours – especially India. All our disputes with India should be settled through political dialogue, and the activities of the intelligence agencies – of both countries – must be curtailed. Only a credible and sovereign government can guarantee the US that there will be no terrorism in the future from Pakistan's soil. The US should be made to understand that it is in their interests to back a sovereign democratic government in Pakistan. The policy of planting pliant puppets has failed in Pakistan, just as it is failing across the entire Middle East, as shown by the 'Arab Spring'. To persist with this policy will only increase anti-Americanism, which would help the terrorists. Had Obama stood with Hosni

Mubarak, the Egyptians in the street would now be chanting anti-American slogans (as happened when the US-backed the Shah of Iran and opposed a popular democratic movement).

The threat to the universe is not from Islam or any great religion but from naked materialism. In the name of protecting 'our interests', the powerful have always plundered the resources of the weak. The hope of saving our planet lies in collaboration, rather than competition, amongst all the great religions of the world – along with the environmental movements that are fighting against limitless consumption and environmental degradation. Islam urges its followers to take care of the environment, 'to step lightly on this earth'. As Prophet Muhammad (PBUH) said: 'Live in the world as if you are living for a thousand years, and live for the next world as if you will die tomorrow.'

Finally, only a credible government can save and strengthen the Pakistan army by making sure that it remains within its constitutional role. According to WikiLeaks, our former finance minister, Shaukat Tarin, asked the US ambassador Anne Patterson how much aid was being given to the Pakistan army. Never again should such a situation be allowed to arise. Neither should our army chief ever be allowed to talk directly to the US or any other government. The example for Pakistan is that of Turkey, where the Army – which kept destabilizing democratic governments – had a constitutional role to uphold its secular ideology. It took a credible leader, of the stature of Erdogan, whose dynamic leadership and great moral authority has put the army in its rightful place, and taken Turkey towards a genuine democracy. The reason Erdogan could do this was because of his brilliant performance in tripling

Turkey's per capita income to $10,000 a year and registering the second-highest growth rate after China.

We have no other choice: in order to survive, we have to make Pakistan a genuine democracy as envisaged by our great leader Muhammad Ali Jinnah.

Some seven years ago, when my party was down in the dumps, and had hit rock bottom, my old and most loyal friend Goldie (Omar Farooq) and I called on Mian Bashir, who was not feeling well. The party was going through its most difficult phase; we were barely able to keep our heads above water and fighting for our survival. Uncharacteristically, Goldie was beginning to lose hope, and he asked Mian Bashir: 'When will our party come into power?' Mian Bashir closed his eyes and meditated for about five minutes, then opened them and looked at me as he said, when I was ready to take on the responsibility. When he said that, it occurred to me that I wasn't ready. Fifteen years after forming the party, I feel that my party and I are not only ready, but that mine is the only party that can get Pakistan out of its current desperate crisis. After fourteen years of the most difficult struggle in my life, my party is finally taking off, spreading like wildfire across the country, so that today it is the first choice of 70 per cent of Pakistanis under the age of thirty. This is backed up in two recent polls. YouGov recorded 61 per cent of respondents favouring my party and another poll, conducted by the US Pew Research Centre, had my party rated by 68 per cent as 'favourable', an increase of over 16 per cent since last year. For the first time, I feel Tehreek-e-Insaf is the idea whose time has come.

Islamabad, June 2011

Acknowledgements

I owe a debt of gratitude to an exceptional scholar and friend, Dr Riffat Hassan. This book would not have been possible without the assistance of Saifullah Niazi.

One book in particular was very useful to me in my researches: M. J. Akbar *Tinderbox*: *The Past and Future of Pakistan* (HarperCollins, New Delhi, 2011).

Picture Acknowledgements

All photos not credited below have been kindly supplied by the author and his family.

Every effort has been made to trace copyright holders; those who have not been credited are invited to get in touch with the publishers.

Photos listed clockwise from top left.

First section

2–3   Portrait of Muhmmad Iqbal: © INTERFOTO/Alamy; second Indo-Pakistani War, 7 September 1965: Gamma-Keystone via Getty Images; Ayub Khan: Popperfoto/Getty Images; Yahya Khan: Topham Picturepoint/TopFoto.co.uk; Zia Ul-Haq: AP/Press Association Images; Zulfikar Ali Bhutto: AFP/Getty Images; Muslim refugees flee India, 15 October 1947: AFP/Getty Images; partition conference, New Delhi, 3 June 1947: Gamma-Keystone via Getty Images.

4–5   View of Hunza Valley: © Sarah Murray; refugee camp, Nasar Bagh, June 1983: AP/Press Association Image; IK feasting with Afridis at a village in the Khyber Pass: from *Warrior Race* by Imran Khan, photo by Pervez A. Khan.

6–7   IK bowling during first Test Match against England, Birmingham, July 1982: Getty Images; IK bowling for the Rest of the World XI against the MCC at Lords, August 1987: Getty Images; last man Illingworth is out, IK (centre) and Moin Khan (kneeling) celebrate, World Cup final, Melbourne, March 1992: © Patrick Eagar; IK and team-mates celebrate World Cup win, Melbourne, March 1992: AP Photo/Steve Holland; IK lifts World Cup, Melbourne, March 1992: Getty Images; IK and Queen Elizabeth, Lords, 14 May 1971: Press Association Images/ S&G and Barratts/EMPICS Sport.

8   Mian Nawaz Sharif, 1 October 1990: Time & Life Pictures/Getty Images; Benazir Bhutto casts her vote, 16 November 1988: Zahid Hussein/AP/Press Association Images; Pervez Musharraf and IK, 19 February 2002: Reuters.

Second section

1   IK, Badshahi mosque, 2003: Stuart Freedman/PANOS; IK at prayer, 2003: Stuart Freedman/PANOS; IK, election campaign, 1 September 1996: © Patrick Durand/Sygma/Corbis; IK, election rally, Lahore, 29 January 1997: Khalid Chaudary/AP/Press Association Images.

2–3   IK, election rally, Karachi, 11 August 2002: Saeed Khan/Rex Features; protest march, Karachi, 3 May 2009: © Rehan Khan/Corbis; IK at protest rally, Lahore, 24 February 2008: AFP/Getty Images; IK, Downing Street, London, 28 January 2008: Getty Images; IK and Nawaz Sharif at a news conference, London, 9 June 2008: Lefteris Pitarakis/AP/Press Association Images; Jemima Khan, Qasim Khan, Annabel Goldsmith, London 18 November 2007:Eddie Mulholland/Rex Features; IK and students, Lahore, 14 November 2007: Reuters.

4–5   All photos courtesy Shaukat Khanum Memorial Cancer Hospital & Research Centre.

6–7   IK and Jemima Khan, Richmond Registry Office, 20 June 1995: AFP/Getty Images; Jemima Khan and IK's family, Lahore, 1995: Rex Features; IK and Jemima Khan, High Court, London, 18 July 1996: AFP/Getty Images; Jemima Khan and IK at the Sportsman of the Millennium award ceremony, Lahore, 29 April, 2000: K. M. Chaudary/AP/Press Association Images; IK , Shane Warne and Zac Goldsmith, charity cricket match, Ham Common, 14 July 2007: Getty Images; IK with Qasim and Suleiman, one-day cricket match between Pakistan and England, Rawalpindi, 19 December 2005: Getty Images; Jemima Khan holds Suleiman, 21 November 1996: Reuters/Kieran Doherty.

8   IK waves to supporters, Lahore, 26 November 2010: AFP/Getty Images; IK at anti-drone rally, Karachi, 21 May 2011: EPA/Rehan Khan; IK at a rally, Faisalabad, 24 July 2011: photo Abdul Majid, Faisalabad; IK addresses Faisalabad District Bar: 25 July 2011: photo Abdul Majid, Faisalabad.

Index